Celebrity, Aspiration and Contemporary Youth

ALSO AVAILABLE FROM BLOOMSBURY

Agency and Participation in Childhood and Youth, edited by Caroline
Sarojini Hart, Mario Biggeri and Bernhard Babic

Agency, Structure and the NEET Policy Problem, Leslie Bell
and Ian Thurlby-Campbell

The Identities and Practices of High Achieving Pupils, Becky Francis,
Christine Skelton and Barbara Read

Celebrity, Aspiration and Contemporary Youth

Education and Inequality in an Era of Austerity

Heather Mendick, Kim Allen, Laura Harvey and Aisha Ahmad

Bloomsbury Academic
An imprint of Bloomsbury Publishing Plc

B L O O M S B U R Y
LONDON · OXFORD · NEW YORK · NEW DELHI · SYDNEY

Bloomsbury Academic

An imprint of Bloomsbury Publishing Plc

50 Bedford Square	1385 Broadway
London	New York
WC1B 3DP	NY 10018
UK	USA

www.bloomsbury.com

BLOOMSBURY and the Diana logo are trademarks of Bloomsbury Publishing Plc

First published 2018

British Library Cataloguing-in-Publication Data
A catalogue record for this book is available from the British Library.

ISBN: HB: 978-1-4742-9420-1
PB: 978-1-4742-9424-9
ePDF: 978-1-4742-9421-8
ePub: 978-1-4742-9422-5

Library of Congress Cataloging-in-Publication Data
A catalog record for this book is available from the Library of Congress.

Cover image © Charles Gullung / Image Source / Alamy Stock Photo

Typeset by Newgen KnowledgeWorks Pvt. Ltd., Chennai, India
Printed and bound in Great Britain

CONTENTS

ILLUSTRATIONS

Figures

Table

ACKNOWLEDGEMENTS

The research and writing for this project has been a collaborative effort: from designing the research questions to feeling our way through data and finally to the process of writing. This commitment to collaboration is part of a feminist politics and ethics that challenges individualistic notions of authorship and recognizes the fruitful messiness of academic work. This collaboration extends beyond the four of us who worked on the project and have authored this book, and includes many others who supported the project along the way. In July 2014, as we approached the formal end of our funded work on the project, we posted thanks online to some of these people. We have updated these acknowledgements below.

Writing the bid that funded this research took ages. It grew out of a short and rejected proposal to the British Academy, and along the way we got much perceptive advice. Charmian Kenner got us to stop trying to do everything; Louise Archer convinced us to move from learner identities to aspirations and from three schools to six; Rachel Brooks pointed out that we had missed a whole section of the form; and Laurie Cohen helped us to make the key points come over even to a speed-reading reviewer. Finally, Hugh Cunning in the Brunel Research Support and Development Office worked with Heather as she stumbled through the financial details and internal processes at her then-new workplace. We also thank Yvette Taylor and Rachel Brooks for encouraging us to respond to the one negative review we got and to defend the project. And of course, we were and are delighted that the Economic and Social Research Council (ESRC) funded and supported this work.

Once the project kicked off it took a long time to find our schools. We owe a debt to Harry Torrance and Tony Brown at Manchester Metropolitan University, the Brunel Education Partnership Development Unit and Pete Fraser, who shared their contacts with schools in Manchester and London. Although they have to remain anonymous, we are grateful to the six schools that finally welcomed us through their doors and to the busy teachers who made the research possible. We would like to extend a special thanks to all of the young people who shared their views so generously. We hope that we have done justice to their words.

We had much help along the way, including two project administrators, Salihu Dasuki and Bazgha Sultana, and Gary Dear, who handled most of the finances at Brunel. Our amazing advisory group were Becky Francis, Imogen Tyler, Katy Jones, Laurie Cohen, Pat Morton, Pete Fraser, Ros Gill and Rosalyn George. They read draft papers, provided contacts, chaired sessions at our events and much more. It is very sad that Katy is no longer with us.

Heather would particularly like to thank Anne Chappell, Ali Silby, Ayo Mansaray, Barbara Hosier, Geeta Ludhra, Gwen Ineson, Mick Allen, Rob Toplis and Sarmin Hossain for solidarity during a difficult time at work; Dieuwertje Dyi Huijg, her virtual office mate after she went freelance; and her comrades in Momentum Hackney. Kim would like to thank a number of colleagues and friends for their support, kindness, humour and conversations along the way: Jessie Abrahams, Janet Batsleer, Laura Clancy, Tori Cann, Bridget Conor, Sara De Benedictis, Kirsty Finn, Sumi Holllingworth, Nicola Ingram, Tracey Jensen, Kirsty Morrin, Tracy Shildrick, Helene Snee, Katy Vigurs and Annabel Wilson. As well those named above, Laura would like to thank Ros Gill, Meg John Barker, Jessica Ringrose, Tansy Hoskins, Kiran Dhami, Fay Burchell and Ema Webb for solidarity, guidance and kindness. Laura and Aisha would like to thank Heather and Kim for their feminist ethic of genuine capacity building and support during their time as researchers on the project and since. In addition to the above, Aisha thanks Samana Fazel for her continued support and their animated discussions.

Some of the material and ideas discussed in this book draw on the following published open access journal articles: Allen et al. (2015b), Harvey et al. (2015) and Mendick et al. (2015, 2016). We are grateful for the feedback from the reviewers of these journals and for the many stimulating conversations we have had at conferences and seminars. This includes those who attended our End of Award Event, particularly our speakers Anita Biressi, Bim Adewunmi, Bryony Kimmings, Camilla Stanger, Geeta Ludhra, Justin Hancock and Rob MacDonald. Thanks also to Leon Lewis and Ms Cupcake for providing the food, and to Katy Vigurs for designing a celebrity-themed quiz and even supplying prizes.

The design of our websites is down to Marcus Miller at BowlerHat. Cat Drew created bespoke illustrations for our myth-busting site. We got ideas on how to link our research to practice from Anthony Barnes, Hamdi Addow, Jenny Grahame, Jill Collins, Jon Rainford and Tania de St Croix. Social media has been a big part of the project in ways we never envisaged. We saw the project's social media presence as an experiment and never envisaged how enjoyable and productive engaging with people online would be. The website, Twitter and Facebook have provided us with ways not only to communicate our research to a wider audience, but also to test out ideas and engage in conversations as we tried to make sense of our data. These online spaces led us to many new interactions and connections. Thanks also to everyone who contributed guest posts to the CelebYouth website.

Finally, we thank Bloomsbury Academic, particularly Maria Giovanna Brauzzi, Mark Richardson and Rachel Shillington, for their support. We are particularly happy that, unlike many academic publishers, they agreed to bring this book out in paperback from the start.

1

Introduction

*The mission for this government is to build an aspiration nation. ...
It's what's always made our hearts beat faster – aspiration; people
rising from the bottom to the top. . . . Line one, rule one of being a
Conservative is that it's not where you've come from that counts,
it's where you're going. . . . We just get behind people who want to
get on in life. The doers. The risk-takers. The young people who
dream of their first pay-cheque, their first car, their first home – and
are ready and willing to work hard to get those things. . . . We are
the party of the want to be better-off, those who strive to make a
better life for themselves and their families.*

(CAMERON 2012)

*'Cruel optimism' names a relation of attachment to
compromised conditions of possibility whose realization is
discovered either to be impossible, sheer fantasy, or too possible,
and toxic. What's cruel about these attachments, and not
merely inconvenient or tragic, is that the subjects who have
x in their lives might not well endure the loss of their object/
scene of desire, even though its presence threatens their well-
being, because whatever the content of the attachment is, the
continuity of its form provides something of the continuity of
the subject's sense of what it means to keep on living on and to
look forward to being in the world. . . . Cruel optimism is the
condition of maintaining an attachment to a problematic object
in advance of its loss.*

(BERLANT 2011: 21)

Since the financial crash of 2007–08 and the subsequent implementation of a programme of 'austerity', the United Kingdom has been characterized by political, social and economic turbulence. This turbulence has been felt on a global as well as national scale. It is manifest in protests, political coups and changing governments, volatile economies, levels of income inequality not seen for decades, and, most recently, Brexit and Donald Trump's election as US president. Young people have been particularly vulnerable to these transformations and the uncertainty they have unleashed. Rising youth unemployment, falling wages, a growing housing crisis and cuts to education have led many commentators to proclaim bleakly that this is a 'lost generation' who, facing significant hurdles in their transitions to adulthood, are losing hope in the future. Across the West, it is becoming apparent that this generation will fare worse than their parents. Despite this narrative of generational decline, some things are remarkably enduring. One of these is the dominant place of aspiration within national political agendas and wider social imaginaries. As exemplified in the words of the former UK Prime Minister David Cameron above, aspiration is a key preoccupation of government, figuring as an engine of economic competitiveness and social mobility. Helping people 'rise to the top', and reap the financial and social rewards that result from this, is central to the vision of Britain as a meritocracy.

In this book, we interrogate how aspiration continues to hold a prominent place, despite global transformations undermining the meritocratic promise of a society in which people of all backgrounds achieve based on their talents and efforts. Specifically, we consider how this focus on aspiration is lived by young people, and use celebrity to do this. We draw on data collected for the research project 'The role of celebrity in young people's classed and gendered aspirations' (www.celebyouth.org). Funded by the UK's Economic and Social Research Council and conducted between 2012 and 2014, the study included group and individual interviews involving 148 young people (aged 14–18) about their engagement with celebrity and their aspirations. We provide more detail on the participants and methods at the end of this chapter.

In this book, we define the current moment in which young people are forming and attempting to realize their aspirations as 'austere meritocracy'. As we will explain, this concept encapsulates the pivotal tension between the incitement of young people to aspire and invest in the idea of meritocracy and the dramatic erosion of opportunities for upward social mobility. This is an instance of what Lauren Berlant, in the quotation above, identifies as cruel optimism; young people must remain attached to aspiration, success and happiness in advance of their loss. They must continue to invest in the idea of the 'good life' and the American Dream at the very time that opportunities for 'upward mobility, job security, political and social equality and lively, durable intimacy' are dissipating (Berlant 2011: 3). This introductory chapter maps out the concept of austere meritocracy, and sets the scene for the chapters that follow.

Aspiration, education and meritocracy

In this book we are interested in tracking discourses – the patterns of meanings through which we understand the world – and their impact on young people's lives. Discourses are historically and culturally specific collections of meanings that make some ways of thinking possible and others impossible (Foucault 1976). Discourses can be used to position ourselves and to judge others and their hopes and dreams. The ways that people, issues, relations and events are spoken about creates them as forms of knowledge and sets the terms of reference for thinking about them. While there are always multiple competing discourses, some come to dominate and take on the status of 'truth'. These powerful fictions constitute our social reality, shaping our actions. Two of the key collections of discourses that we are concerned with in this book are those of aspiration and meritocracy.

Aspiration has been a central motif of successive UK governments, figuring in commitments to a meritocratic ideal. Originally coined by the sociologist Alan Fox and made famous by Michael Young's 1958 fiction *The Rise of the Meritocracy*, meritocracy has been adopted by parties across the political spectrum (Littler 2013). In Young's satire a meritocratic society has replaced the old aristocratic order with a new elite who are rewarded for their superior and 'innate' intelligence and effort. A meritocratic society produced through the formula of $I + E = M$ ('Intelligence combined with Effort equals Merit') would mean that the 'deserving' will 'rise to the top' and climb the 'ladder of opportunity' while others are left behind.

The Rise of the Meritocracy sought to expose how the myth of inherited difference enabled the elite to create and justify unfair divisions in society. Yet Young's warning has since been taken up 'not as a cautionary tale but as an ideological blueprint' (Bloodworth 2016: 2; see also Littler 2013). On coming to power in 1997, Labour Prime Minister Tony Blair declared: 'The Britain of the elite is over. The new Britain is a meritocracy' (Blair, in Bloodworth 2016: 29). Meritocracy was a defining feature of Blair's New Labour rhetoric which asserted a commitment to creating a 'new, larger, more meritocratic middle class', providing 'ladders of opportunity for those from all backgrounds. No more ceilings that prevent people achieving the success they merit' (Blair 1999 in Tomlinson 2005: 169). Similarly, as indicated in the quote that opened this book, the UK's Conservative government (who were in power as a coalition with the Liberal Democrats when we conducted this research), vigorously promoted itself as a 'party of equality in opportunity' (Cameron 2015). Cameron continuously reasserted this claim throughout his leadership:

> What I want to see is a more socially mobile Britain, where no matter where you come from, you can get to the top in television, the judiciary, armed services, politics. . . . You've got to get out there and find people,

win them over, get them to raise aspirations and get them to think that they can get all the way to the top. (Cameron 2013)

Despite subsequent shifts in government, including the move from Coalition to Conservative government in 2015, and changes to the Conservative leadership in 2016, this political obsession with aspiration and meritocracy shows no sign of abating. Since replacing Cameron as Prime Minister in 2016, Theresa May has said,

I want Britain to be the world's great meritocracy – a country where everyone has a fair chance to go as far as their talent and their hard work will allow. . . . I want Britain to be a place where advantage is based on merit not privilege; where it's your talent and hard work that matter, not where you were born, who your parents are or what your accent sounds like. (May 2016)

The political currency of meritocracy and aspiration is not confined to the UK. Discourses of aspiration featured prominently within US President Barack Obama's articulation of the 'American Dream' (Hill Collins 2012), and across Australian policy agendas (Kenway & Hickey Moody 2011). Meritocratic notions of success are central to China's education system (Waters & Leung 2016).

In the meritocratic ideal that suffuses political discourse, the capacity to aspire and work hard are located as the primary resources through which to overcome disadvantage. Just as former Labour Prime Minister Gordon Brown (2007) located educational inequality as the result of a 'poverty of aspiration' rather than a 'poverty of opportunity', Cameron (2012) criticized a 'toxic culture of low expectations . . . a lack of ambition for every child, which has held this country back'. Thus, policy interventions have sought to 'raise' aspirations among disadvantaged groups to reduce child poverty and increase social mobility in Britain (Cabinet Office 2011; Department for Work and Pensions and Department for Education 2011). A commitment to tackling a so-called 'aspiration deficit' has been 'embraced and understood by political parties of all persuasions', so much so that it has been 'ingrained into wider public consciousness as being an incontrovertible, self-evident truth' (Roberts & Evans 2012: 72).

As we demonstrate in this book, government policy constructs some aspirations as desirable, and others as valueless, establishing dominant notions of 'success' and 'happiness' that police young people's aspirations (Chapters 5 and 6, see also Allen 2013). The increasingly narrow set of destinations and pathways endorsed within policy (namely elite universities and professional careers) overlook the diffuse range of hopes that young people hold for their futures as these enmesh with local contexts, family histories, gender, class and race (Brown 2011). Aspirations policy rhetoric assumes that young people are rational subjects for whom the realization of their aspirations is free of external constraints. This individualized model constructs by default a deficit narrative that locates certain young people – namely working-class youth – as being held back by a 'lack of aspiration' rather than a lack of opportunity. This narrative has been repeatedly disproved by research demonstrating that across social class, gender and race, young people do aspire to higher education and professional careers (Abrahams 2017; Allen & Hollingworth, 2013; Archer et al. 2010; Bathmaker et al. 2016; Reay et al. 2001; Roberts & Evans 2012; St Clair et al. 2013). This research problematizes the focus on individual aspirations, emphasizing the structural factors that shape young people's sense of desirable and achievable aspirations, and their opportunities for realizing them.

The persistence of these inequalities illuminates a fundamental disconnect between the individualized policy discourses of aspiration and meritocracy and the opportunities available to young people. In this light, aspiration can be understood as a mechanism for obscuring deep-rooted structural inequalities that constrain young people's transitions, recasting them as individual deficits (Raco 1999). Aspiration becomes a 'rhetorical device that seeks to whitewash a neoliberal economic and political project and the staggering inequalities it produces' (Tyler & Bennett 2015: 6). Sociologists of youth and education have long been concerned about this tension 'between the meritocratic promise and the impossibility of "success"' (Sporher 2015: 414). It demands urgent renewed attention in the current landscape within which young people are imagining and materializing their futures.

Youth in a post-crash landscape: A lost generation?

Following the global financial crisis of 2007–08 and the bank bailouts, the UK, like many Western nations, saw a period of economic crisis and a subsequent period of 'austerity'. In the UK, austerity measures included fast and deep cuts to public services and working-age benefits, resulting in 'the deepest and most precipitate cuts ever made in social provision' (Taylor-Gooby 2013, see also Lupton et al. 2016). These were justified by political elites as necessary to reduce public debt and return the country to economic stability. At the time of writing, these goals have not been achieved, and austerity is set to continue into the next decade (Emmerson et al. 2017).

Austerity measures have accelerated neoliberal economic policies protecting the interests of capital, including through deregulation, tax breaks, and privatization (Bhattacharyya 2015; Harvey 2014). As Yanis Varoufakis (2015) stated on the BBC programme *Question Time*, 'The problem is that austerity is being used as a narrative to conduct class war. . . . To be talking about reducing the state further when effectively what you are doing is reducing taxes like inheritance tax and at the same time you are cutting benefits – that is class war.'

Despite claims that 'we're all in it together' (Osborne 2012), austerity has seen falling wages and increasing poverty among those at the bottom of society while the wealth of the richest has grown rapidly (Dorling 2014a; Sayer 2014). In early 2017, the British think tank Resolution Foundation warned that the UK is experiencing the biggest rise in inequality since the 1980s (Corlett & Clarke 2017). Austerity has had particularly severe and disproportionate impacts on already-vulnerable groups. These include children, black and minority ethnic populations, women (especially mothers) and, significant to this book, the young. Young people globally have been carrying a particularly 'heavy burden for many of the downstream effects' of the financial crisis (Kelly & Pike 2016: 8). In the UK, young people have experienced increasing poverty rates, including rising in-work poverty (Tinson et al. 2016). Despite youth unemployment rates beginning to recover from the very high rates seen following the 2010 recession (Powell 2017), young workers continue to face significant challenges. In particular the growth of insecure employment, including zero-hour contracts, has affected young people in particular, with many trapped in temporary and low-paid work (Greg & Gardiner 2015; Office of National Statistics 2015). Significantly, this includes growing numbers of graduates, with over half of employed graduates working in 'non-graduate' roles (Office of National Statistics 2013). Across Europe, the United States and Australia, young people are experiencing slow and frustrated transitions (Allen 2016; Antonucci 2016; Kelly & Pike 2016; MacDonald 2016). The 'graduate premium' (the expected increase in earnings accruing to a university graduate compared to someone without a degree) used by many governments to encourage young people to invest in higher education has dramatically reduced. Under austerity, the meritocratic promise – or 'opportunity bargain' (Brown et al. 2011) – that hard work and qualifications will guarantee upward social mobility and economic stability is increasingly being broken.

Austerity measures have escalated an ongoing marketization of education. In England this has included abolishing the Education Maintenance Allowance (EMA) designed to encourage young people from economically disadvantaged backgrounds to stay in education after 16. Other moves include the dismantling of the national careers service, the introduction and subsequent raising of university tuition fees, and the scrapping of university maintenance grants for disadvantaged students. Such moves militate against the achievement of government agendas for social mobility by reducing the role of the state in enabling access to (higher) education.

Dwindling opportunities within education and employment have been accompanied by challenges in other areas. Cuts in local spending have led to drastic reductions in youth services (Unison 2016) and young people have been disproportionately affected by the introduction of benefit sanctions (Watts et al. 2014). A growing housing crisis has left swathes of young people unable to buy or rent a place to live. A marked increase in the number of people aged 20–34 living with their parents (ONS 2016) has led some to label them 'Generation rent' (Dorling 2014b) or the 'Dependent Generation' (Malik 2014). Young people's mental health and well-being is suffering, as evidenced in higher reported rates of anxiety and depression (Frith 2016).

These socioeconomic conditions, and their impact on young people's lives, did not suddenly appear in 2007–08. As Gargi Bhattacharyya (2015: 3) warns, we must 'forgo the nostalgia that seeks to remake the world before austerity, not least because the pre-austerity world was also divided, unequal and unliveable for many'. Austerity is an acceleration of long-term global trends, including those unleashed by the neoliberal economic policies associated with the UK Thatcher and US Reagan governments in the 1980s. Neoliberalism as a political and economic project is characterized by, among other things, the fetishization of free-market economics, the privatization of public services, the rolling back of the state, and the replacement of manufacturing jobs with those in the service sector and in financial- and 'knowledge-' based industries. The socioeconomic changes ushered in by neoliberalism have had an impact on young people's biographies. This includes a shift away from the relatively predictable youth transitions of the post-war period following the collapse of the youth labour market in the 1980s, towards more extended and complex transitions (Furlong & Cartmel 2007). For many young people – particularly the most disadvantaged – experiences of precarity and unemployment existed well before the current crisis (Roberts 2009). Furthermore, Phil Brown and his colleagues (2011) have demonstrated how even prior to the crisis, the expansion of higher education and a 'global war for talent' had already begun transforming the neoliberal opportunity bargain into an 'opportunity trap' for many young people (Brown 2003).

While not entirely new, however, these processes have gained momentum since 2007/8 and their effects are being felt by a wider cohort of young people (MacDonald 2016). As Alan France and Steven Roberts (2015: 224) write, 'The current situation represents a blip in history because precarity is not new, just new to the middle classes' as uncertainty becomes the new normal. These transformations have unsettled the taken-for-granted assumptions regarding young people's transitions to adulthood and the milestones they are expected to achieve – degree, job, house, family. Burdened with private debt that most will never repay, facing a hostile labour market and with little hope of being able to afford a home, austerity has produced a more speculative orientation to the future among many young people (Allen 2016). Bhattacharyya (2015: 4) calls this a context of 'diminishing expectations'.

Such shifts are reflected in recent discursive constructions of youth oriented around a narrative of generational decline. With young people in Europe and the United States at risk of becoming the first generation ever to record lower lifetime earnings than their parents' generation (Chetty et al.

2016; Gardiner 2016) there have been growing concerns of an intergenerational divide between so-called millennials and older baby boomers (though such claims have been criticized for masking *intra*-generational inequalities (Roberts & Allen 2016)). Newspaper headlines in the UK describe young people as a 'lost' or 'jilted' generation, 'robbed of their futures' and occupying a state of 'suspended adulthood' (Quinn 2016, see Chapter 2). In 2014 the Council of Europe's Commissioner for Human Rights described youth unemployment as 'the most common pathology of many countries implementing austerity measures' (Muizneiks 2014).

Despite accusations of apathy, young people have taken to the streets to articulate their frustration. The surge in popularity of left-wing anti-austerity figures and social movements among younger (and older) generations – including Labour leader Jeremy Corbyn in the UK, Bernie Sanders in the United States, Socialist candidate Jean-Luc Melenchon in France and parties like Podemos in Spain and the Pirate Party in Iceland – has been attributed to their growing discontent and desire for an alternative to austerity. There has been a parallel rise in right-wing populism, from Donald Trump in the United States to the National Front in France, largely among older voters. Both these trends became apparent after our research and so we return to them in the conclusion, although their beginnings, such as in the Occupy, anti-austerity and anti-fees movements, are part of the context of this study (Nunns 2016).

Despite this sustained attack on young people's opportunities, the political rhetoric of meritocracy is stronger than ever and aspiration figures as a neoliberal imperative. As Jo Littler explains in her persuasive genealogy of 'meritocracy', aspiration has become not simply a moral virtue but a necessity:

> In Britain the powerful language of aspiration, social mobility and opportunity for all to rise through the social structure has not become muted, despite a double-dip recession, still growing inequality, and a historically unprecedented drop in living standards for the working majority. On the contrary: it has escalated. . . . According to Cameron's stated worldview, the ability to 'believe in yourself', and by extension, your child, is primary. . . . Hope and promise become more integral in an unequal society in which hard work alone has less and less chance of reaping the prizes. Through this rhetorical mechanism, instead of addressing social inequality as a solvable problem, the act of addressing inequality becomes 'responsibilized' as an individual's moral meritocratic task. This process devolves onto the individual personal responsibility not just for their success in the meritocratic competition, but for the very will to compete and expectation of victory which are now figured as moral imperatives in themselves. Not investing in aspiration, in expectation, is aggressively positioned as an abdication of responsibility which

condemns yourself – and even worse, your child – to the social scrapheap. (Littler 2013: 65–66)

In this bleak and punishing landscape, young people must nevertheless act as though they live within a meritocracy. This paradox speaks to Berlant's (2011) concept of 'cruel optimism' that opened this chapter and that we return to throughout the book. Cruel optimism is a vital attachment to the fantasy of the 'good life' (including the promise of upward mobility, happiness and economic security), despite living in 'compromised conditions of possibility'. It is this cruel tension that we capture in our concept of 'austere meritocracy' that lies at the heart of this book.

Making sense of austere meritocracy: Just neoliberalism as we know it?

While 'austerity' has come to dominate the ways in which many of us think and talk about the contemporary climate since the crash of 2007–08, its meanings are multifarious and contested (Bramall et al. 2016). In this book we consider austerity not simply as an economic project of fiscal management but also a sociocultural category and subject-making discourse (Jensen & Tyler 2012). It is a discursive object containing distinct subject positions, aesthetics and meaning-making practices (Bramall 2013). Austerity is not an abstract phenomenon operating at the level of policy but is made present in everyday life through cultural representations and people's lived experiences (Hitchen 2016).

Austerity is deeply entangled with neoliberal logics and rationalities (Allen et al. 2015b; De Benedictis & Gill 2016). Neoliberalism extends beyond the economic and political sphere so that its values infuse all areas of social and personal life. It governs individuals via forms of authoritative knowledge that work through our beliefs and desires (Dean 2009). In particular, neoliberalism promotes subjectivities organized around enterprise and self-responsibility (Brown 2005; Rose 1999), even though the ability to conduct one's life in this way is not equally available (Skeggs 2004). With the decimation of collectivized forms of social support, austerity intensifies this neoliberal injunction for individuals to respond to hardships by becoming even more enterprising and self-responsible.

The public narrative of austerity has relied upon establishing a 'common sense' (Gramsci 1977; Hall & O'Shea 2013). In this common sense, poverty – and a lack of social mobility – results from personal pathologies including irresponsibility, immorality and lack of aspiration (Pantazis 2016). As) The framing of austerity as a moral crisis, generated by failures of the behaviours and cultures of particular groups of people (namely the working class), 'serve[s] to obscure the structural conditions of a deep social, political and economic crisis, such that only the effects are visible' (Dowling & Harvie 2014: 872). These explanatory frameworks shape public perceptions about the causes of the crisis, and appropriate policy responses to them. They are embodied in the figures of the 'scrounger' and 'striver' that have circulated within policy and media since the global financial crash:

> When you work hard and still sometimes have to go without the things you want because times are tough it is maddening to know that there are some people who could work but just don't want to. You know the people I mean. You walk down the road on your way to work and you see the curtains drawn in their house. You know they could work and they chose not to. And just as maddening is the fact that they seem to get away with it. (Cameron 2010)

The scrounger and striver reflect the subjectivities that neoliberal austerity has made available. They are found not just in the soundbites of politicians. The scrounger appears regularly on the front pages of newspapers and within a controversial genre of popular 'factual' television programmes centred on experiences of the benefits system, such as Channel 4's *Benefit Street*.

In his analysis of Thatcherism, Stuart Hall (1988; Hall & Jacques 1983) identified two representational figures that circulated across political discourse and media and popular culture. The 'taxpayer' and the 'customer' embodied a set of values and practices aligned with Thatcherism, such as enterprise, hard work, and acquisitive consumerism. These ideal subject positions sat in contrast to their 'undesirable' others. As Anita Biressi and Heather Nunn (2013b: 8) write: 'The ethos here was that those who would thrive best were the self-starters, individuals motivated to improve their own lives. In other words, this was not about equality of outcomes or resources but of individual drive and resourcefulness.' The striver of austerity does similar work to Hall's taxpayer and customer, classifying individuals into ideal subjects and outsiders through a moral vocabulary of hard work, responsibility and deservingness (Clarke & Newman 2012). Pitting the feckless scrounger who prefers 'sleeping off a life on benefits' (Osborne 2012) against 'hard-working taxpayers', these representational figures invite identification and othering.

Yet, the scrounger and striver also reflect an intensification of neoliberal discourses within austerity. The striver clearly embodies Hall's taxpayer but also reflects a vigorous assertion of a meritocratic ideal that rewards 'those who strive to make a better life for themselves' (Cameron 2013). While the customer remains an important and constant subject position within neoliberalism, there are evident shifts in the framing of wealth and consumption since the financial crash. Austerity has ushered in a set of moral classifications around consumption through national and individual imperatives to 'tighten belts'. The rise of 'new thrift culture', with its wartime aesthetic of 'make do and mend' privileges 'responsible' and ethical consumption rather than non-consumerism (Bramall 2013; see Chapter 7). This emphasis on thrift sits next to an intensified stigmatization of excessive consumption. This was made hyper-visible in the summer of 2011 as riots broke out across cities in England. Rather than look at wealth inequality, unemployment and institutional racism as factors contributing to the unrest, politicians explained them as 'sheer criminality' (Cameron in Watts 2011) driven by abject greed and vulgar materialism (Jensen 2013). Accusations of immoral and undisciplined consumer desire – alongside the absence of an ethic of hard work – were levelled at young people in particular. This is evident in this explanation provided by the then Secretary of State for Work and Pensions, Iain Duncan Smith: 'X-Factor culture fuelled the UK riots. . . . Kids believe that their stepping stone to massive money is the X Factor. Luck is great, but most of life is hard work. We do not celebrate people who've made success out of serious hard work (Duncan Smith in Wintour & Lewis 2011).

While the enterprising, self-responsible and calculating subject of neo-liberalism remains constant, we can therefore also identify a set of regulative discourses that are specific to, and in tune with, the requirements of austerity. These include an intensified emphasis on 'hard work', 'optimism' and 'resilience' and a policing of relationships to consumption through discourses of 'un/deserving wealth' and 'thrift'. In the rest of this book, we tease out in greater detail what austere meritocracy is and how it operates in shaping young people's aspirations. To do this, we turn to the accounts of the young people who participated in our research and address the following questions:

1 What kinds of futures do young people imagine for themselves?
2 What is required of young people in the process of achieving these futures?
3 How are inequalities of social class and gender embedded and reproduced within these?

We illustrate how austere meritocracy governs young people's desires, sense-making practices and imagined futures in two ways. First we show how it establishes particular behaviours and orientations as the legitimate and desirable means through which young people are to pursue and attain their aspirations. Chapters 3 and 4 focus on these, looking respectively at work and authenticity. Second, we show how it designates some futures, pathways and destinations as socially desirable and legitimate, and others as those to be avoided. Chapters 5 and 6 look at the 'legitimate' goals of success and happiness and Chapters 7 and 8 at the 'illegitimate' goals of money and fame. In the next section we explain why young people's celebrity talk offers a productive and novel lens through which to prise apart austere meritocracy.

Turning to celebrity

This book examines how austere meritocracy is lived and negotiated by young people in England and how it shapes their aspirations. We do this through exploring young people's talk about celebrity. In this section we explain how we approach celebrity. First, it is a disciplinary technology regulating which ways of being are possible within austere meritocracy. Second, it is a sense-making resource though which young people negotiate this regulation – sometimes contesting, resisting and reworking it.

Neoliberal logics, values and assumptions infuse multiple sites and practices. These range from social institutions such as schools and workplaces, through to lifestyle television programmes and the apps we use on our smartphones to track our productivity. This book is based on the premise that media representations – including celebrity – are key sites upon which wider political agendas and crises are registered.

> Media representations can crystallise and express the key moments in relationships which define a period or type of society. In this sense images grow historically and are located in the material world. But they also extend, legitimise or comment on such relationships – they can celebrate or criticise. In this they have a crucial role in the winning of consent for a social system, its values and its dominant interests or in rejection of them. (Philo & Miller 2014: 13)

Media representations can prop up dominant ideas about the self, success, failure, opportunity and inequality. We have already signalled this in our discussion of the scrounger and the striver. Found across political and cultural arenas, these figures illuminate a powerful convergence between the political rhetoric of austerity and the values, narratives and subject-making discourses found within popular culture and celebrity. As Biressi and Nunn (2013b: 12) argue, neoliberal austerity values and discourses have extended into the cultural arena where they are 'deployed to marshal, harness and legitimize certain kinds of conduct and attitudes and to marginalise others – all in the service of sustaining the neoliberal project' (see also Bennett & McDougal 2016; Jensen & Tyler 2015). Building on such work, this book considers celebrity as a site that is central to austerity's cultural politics, and proposes that analysing celebrity representations and their 'use' helps us make sense of the current moment.

Since Richard Dyer's (1979, 1986) early work on stardom, celebrity has been studied as a particularly illuminating site through which to understand society:

We are fascinated by stars because they enact the ways of making sense of the new experience of being a person in a particular kind of social production (capitalism), with its particular organisation of life into public and private spheres. We love them because they represent how we think that experience is or how it would be lovely to feel that it is. Stars represent typical ways of behaving, feeling and thinking in contemporary society. (Dyer 1986: 16–17)

A substantial body of work identifies how celebrity representations articulate dominant and sometimes contradictory ideas about the self and society, including social mobility, competitive individualism and meritocracy (Biressi & Nunn 2004; Littler 2004; Marshall 1997; Negra & Holmes 2008; Tyler & Bennett 2010). This work also reveals how distinctions and hierarchies of class, gender and race play out within celebrity representations. In this book we build on these insights to consider how celebrity operates in the construction and circulation of austere meritocracy's discourses and subjectivities. In doing so, we respond to Nick Couldry's (2004) suggestion that rather than assume that the social function of celebrity is given, we must explore this empirically, investigating how celebrity operates within people's social practices in specific contexts.

Rather than dismiss celebrity as a trivial aspect of contemporary life, we take celebrity seriously as a social and cultural practice through which we work out and express our ideas about ourselves and others. The cultural meanings that they produce 'organise and regulate social practices, influence our conduct and consequently have real, practical effects' (Hall 1997: 3). We see celebrity as mediating how young people think about their future and take actions towards it. We demonstrate how celebrity representations regulate young people's aspirations by opening up and closing down certain ways of thinking, being and acting within austere meritocracy. And we expose how broader social divisions and hierarchies are reproduced within celebrity.

Celebrity as a site of 'new media governmentality' (McRobbie 2013) is not a coherent or straightforward project in which individuals passively consume its discourses. We draw on earlier work on media audiences which demonstrates how, far from being 'cultural dopes', people interact and make meaning from cultural texts within the context of their everyday lives (Ang 1996; Fiske 1992; Hall & Jefferson 1976; Radway 1984). Thus we locate celebrity as a site of struggle that is put to work by young people, informed by their own experiences and by their class, gender and race. As Bev Skeggs and Helen Wood (2012: 59) state, cultural texts generate 'different reactions, characterised by contestation and resistance . . . [our] judgments [of celebrities] depend on forms of connection between text and viewer, and how these thread back to our own identities and social positions'. These diffuse and varied reactions can include challenges to cultural representations that individuals consider inaccurate, reductive or damaging, and rejecting the norms, values and modes of subjectivity contained within celebrity. Looking at how young people make meaning from celebrity in contradictory, unpredictable and sometimes subversive ways, this book demonstrates young people's active negotiation of the dominant discourses and injunctions inscribed upon celebrity.

The book draws on and extends work within the cultural studies of education and youth (Buckingham & Bragg 2004; Cann 2014; Nayak & Kehily 2008). This includes studies concerned with the relationship between young people's mediated cultural practices and their transitions (Archer et al. 2010; Hollingworth 2015; Shildrick & MacDonald 2006). We locate young people's talk about celebrity as 'performative practices' (Duits 2010: 249) through which they position themselves and others. To put it another way: talk about celebrity is more than just talk about celebrity. Celebrity provides cultural resources or 'conceptual maps' that young people 'can, at different moments, "talk with" and "think with"' (Kehily & Nayak 2008: 330) as they make sense of their futures. However, this approach does not imply that young people's aspirations are projects of self-fashioning. Rather, as we demonstrate, these practices are informed by – and constitutive of – broader inequalities of class, gender and race.

Introducing the study

The research presented in this book seeks to disrupt dominant policy and media discourses about celebrity and youth. These either locate celebrities as 'role models' to 'raise aspirations' or, far more frequently, as a damaging influence that erodes young people's aspirations and fuels unrealistic expectations (see Chapters 2 and 8). Young people's voices are conspicuously absent from these discussions. Aside from a handful of small-scale surveys, there is a paucity of research exploring the role that celebrity plays in how young people think about themselves and their futures. Our study sought to address this. Rather than dismissing celebrity as antithetical to aspiration, or assuming that young people are passive and uncritical victims of celebrity, we offer a nuanced insight into how celebrity mediates young people's lives.

As such, the book is grounded in two key premises. First, that to understand the social function of celebrity it is essential to examine texts alongside their consumption. Second, that research on young people should be 'youth centred', seeing them as active meaning-makers and social agents. We wanted to ensure that our methods could capture the complexity of our participants' lives, and be oriented to their definitions and consumption of celebrity, rather than our own. In addition, we were interested in how young people collectively made sense of celebrity in their peer group, as well as exploring participants' own aspirations. These methodological commitments informed the research design.

From 2012 to 2013, we worked with 148 young people aged 14–18 in six English comprehensive schools in London, a rural area in South West England and Manchester, a city in Northern England. The schools were selected to ensure that the student cohort was broadly reflective of the ethnic and socioeconomic profile of the local area. At the start of the school year, we worked with gatekeepers in each school to recruit around twenty-four students – two groups each of around six students from Year Ten (aged 14–15) and six from Year Twelve (aged 16–17). Just prior to Years Ten and Twelve, students make key option choices about their futures and these cohorts are frequently the focus of public debates on celebrity (discussed above). Before taking part in the research, participants were given information sheets about the study and written consent was sought from them and, for those under 16, from their parents/guardians. Participants were also asked to complete a short biographical questionnaire. Of our 148 participants, eighty-one identified as female and sixty-seven as male; eighty-two were white British, sixty-two from a mix of black and minority ethnic backgrounds, including twenty-seven Asian (predominantly Pakistani and Indian), nine black (Caribbean and African), seven Somali, five Afghan and nine who identified as 'mixed'. We asked participants about their parents' or guardians' occupations and whether they had been to university. Our participants were roughly divided in half in relation to university education; sixty-three said that at least one of their parents had been to university, and sixty-four that none had. The remaining participants were not sure or did not answer. Participants were invited to choose pseudonyms, which have been used in this book. Many participants chose pseudonyms that related to celebrities that they liked or that they had discussed in the interviews.

The first stage of fieldwork consisted of four group interviews per school. These were carried out in school time, lasting between 40 minutes and an hour and were loosely structured to ensure that the research was led by young people's ideas and practices. In these interviews we examined the shared negotiation of meanings around aspiration and celebrity. Our interviews included questions about the celebrities the young people liked and disliked and why, which celebrities they would like to meet, who – if any – they would like to be and whose job they would most like to do. We asked young people to talk about what makes someone a celebrity, and asked participants to group their chosen celebrities, discussing the different ways that they evaluated and classified them. We also asked young people about how they learnt about celebrity.

Following these interviews, we identified twelve celebrities from among those who generated the most discussion among our participants – both positive and negative – and conducted textual analysis of their media representation. We selected men and women from a range of class backgrounds and fields. We analysed discourses of aspiration in each celebrity's coverage in three media outlets over six months and selected other material (for example, Twitter feed, autobiographies). The twelve selected were singers

Beyoncé and Justin Bieber, entrepreneur Bill Gates, actors Emma Watson and Will Smith, royals Kate Middleton and Harry Windsor, reality television stars Katie Price and Kim Kardashian, footballer Mario Balotelli, rapper Nicki Minaj, and diver Tom Daley. While this book focuses predominantly on data from the group and individual interviews, we also draw on the celebrity case study data to explore the key themes that emerged in our discussions with the young people. For example, in Chapter 2 on youth, we have included a case study of Justin Bieber.

We then returned to the schools at the end of the school year to conduct individual interviews with fifty-one of the participants (about eight per school). These interviews looked closely at how individual students' educational and career aspirations relate to celebrity and to their social class and gender. The individual interviews lasted between 35 minutes and an hour, and were held during school time. We developed good relationships with the gatekeepers at each school and worked with them in the selection of participants to encourage a diversity of interviewees at each school based on their earlier responses, rather than staff picking the 'best' pupils. However, the method of selecting students varied across schools, depending on the gatekeeper and practical constraints. In one school a teacher ignored our list of suggested participants, leading to some unexpectedly interesting interviews, such as with Person McPerson, whom we discuss in Chapter 6.

The individual interviews explored participants' aspirations in more detail. We brought along flash cards with images of the twelve case study celebrities and asked participants to imagine they were their age and attended their school. We encouraged them to think about what kind of students they would be, and whether the participant would try to befriend or avoid them. Asking young people to talk in general about celebrities enabled discussion about celebrity aspiration, but also offered a useful space to start conversations about success and happiness in general terms, before reflecting on their own lives. The individual interviews allowed much more detailed exploration of young people's aspirations, including a memory exercise in which we asked for the earliest memory they associated with their chosen career. This generated rich data on important people, life events and 'critical moments' (Thomson et al. 2002) in the development of their aspirations and unfolding biographies, that we discuss in Chapter 4. This also opened up space for young people to talk about influences, opportunities and constraints on their aspirations beyond frameworks of 'role models' and 'work experience', which enable only certain, authorized stories to emerge. Interviews capture our participants within a specific moment in their lives. The incidents and ideas narrated within their accounts can be read as provisional identity claims about what kinds of futures they imagine and desire, rather than as indications of whether these will be attained (Thomson et al. 2002).

It is important to recognize our role as (adult) researchers in generating the conditions of possibility for these young people's accounts. While we aimed to challenge dominant discourses of aspiration, our research cannot stand outside of these nor access a true experience of youth. Our own (professional, classed, gendered and raced) subject positions, the research questions we used and the contexts of the schools within which we conducted the interviews all shaped the research encounters. For example, the title of the research project may have set up expectations among participants, possibly reinscribing the normative power of the very discourses we set out to challenge. Asking young people to tell us about their lives can reproduce a wider autobiographical injunction that gives value to those who are able (and willing) to narrate themselves as reflexive, aspirational and enterprising. Reflecting on his research with children about television, David Buckingham (1991) wondered if, in taking up critical positions, including expressing disapproval of television advertising and racism, children were providing what they thought were appropriate responses to him as an adult who they assumed would also disapprove of these things. In asking young people about their consumption of celebrity – a topic loaded with discourses of pathological consumption and low aspirations – it is unsurprising that participants largely presented accounts that would garner our and society's approval. This demonstrates the strength of these discourses and the possibilities for selfhood within the contemporary moment. Although as we show, the individual interviews generated more opportunities to break out of these authorized discourses than was possible in the group setting.

While youth researchers can 'never "know" what it really means to be young . . . [this] has not prevented us from speaking for and about young people' (Griffin 1993: 26). This book, continuing a rich tradition of youth research, provides one story about young people growing up within the conditions of austere meritocracy.

Outline of the book

By foregrounding these young people's voices, this book aims to bring celebrity back 'from the margins of classroom life' (Marsh et al. 2005: 12). The chapters are organized thematically, and built around the words of our participants and how we made sense of them. Chapters 2 through to 8 include a short case study that examines the media representation of a celebrity who featured prominently in the young people's talk in relation to the chapter's theme.

Chapter 2, titled 'Youth', provides context for the chapters that follow, exploring the 'burden of representation' that young people carry as indicators of the state of society. Expanding on the discussion above, we explore two competing constructions of youth within austere meritocracy, where it figures as both a key resource essential to the nation's financial recovery and a site of 'moral panic', decline and loss. We look at how young people negotiate these discourses of 'potential' and 'risk' and illustrate how they use celebrity to talk about the difficulties of being young.

Chapters 3 and 4, titled 'Work' and 'Authenticity' respectively, explore the behaviours and orientations that young people saw as 'legitimate' ways to pursue their aspirations. In Chapter 3 we show that hard work is the idealized route to education and employment success in austere meritocracy. Our analysis of young people's talk about celebrities like Will Smith highlights a deep investment in stories of graft and resilience. We locate the investment in hard work within wider societal shifts that include the distinctions between scroungers and strivers discussed above. In Chapter 4 we show that alongside hard work, young people valued authenticity both within their own aspirations and their judgements about celebrities. We locate this focus on authenticity within broader social shifts, arguing that it supports capitalism. The chapter also shows how dominant judgements of celebrity authenticity reproduce inequalities of class, gender and race and explore the difficulties faced by young people who assert the authenticity of celebrities otherwise derided as fake.

Chapters 5 and 6, titled 'Success' and 'Happiness' respectively, examine the legitimized goals of austere meritocracy. Chapter 5 analyses two dominant discourses of success in young people's talk. The first is entrepreneurial success, corresponding to austerity's future-oriented and resourceful ideal subject. The second is the stability success discourse that figures in young people's pragmatic aspirations to 'have enough'. In Chapter 6, we identify and discuss three 'happy objects' that direct young people's orientations to the future: family relationships and friendships, career fulfilment and financial stability. In both Chapter 5 and Chapter 6, we explore case studies of two young people who break the social rules of success and happiness, in order to explore how far it's possible for those imagining their futures within austere meritocracy to resist neoliberal logics.

Chapters 7 and 8, titled 'Money' and 'Fame' respectively, explore the aspirations that are marked as illegitimate in austere meritocracy. Chapter 7 shows that young people feel a duty to financially support themselves but rarely aspire to be rich. We examine the central role that financial restraint plays in the cultural politics of austerity. The chapter ends by analysing how young people made sense of the extreme wealth of celebrities like Bill Gates, arguing that discourses of entrepreneurship and philanthropy inoculate such celebrities from accusations of greed and excess. Chapter 8 explores austerity's other illegitimate goal – fame. The chapter disrupts stereotypes of young people as fame hungry, showing how most distance themselves from celebrity aspirations. Fame can be legitimized through evidence of skill, hard work and authenticity, and enjoyed only as a by-product of these rather than as an end in itself. We show that YouTubers are austerity meritocracy's ideal celebrities, fitting with wider work subjectivities based on self-branding.

Finally, Chapter 9 brings together the book's key arguments about austere meritocracy, youth aspirations and celebrity, reflecting on the questions that framed our enquiry and that we listed above. We offer suggestions for how others might engage with our findings and we identify some of the transformations that have taken place since the time of the research, reflecting on the challenges and possibilities that these transformations present.

2

Youth

Over the last century, the 'condition of youth question' has assumed increasing importance as being symptomatic of the health of the nation or the future of the race, the welfare of the family, or the state of civilisation-as-we-know-it. For the last 50 years, young people have had to carry a peculiar burden of representation; everything they do, say, think, or feel, is scrutinised by an army of professional commentators for signs of the times.

(COHEN 2003: 43)

Youth is often presented as a 'natural' stage of development, a biological category. Yet it is a social construct, a highly 'contested and slippery concept' (Valentine et al. 1998: 4). It is a mix of contradictory discourses. On the one hand, growing up is seen as a time of risk and irresponsibility, and on the other, a moment of possibility and transformation (Sukarieh & Tannock 2015). Young people have historically been positioned as indicators of the state of society – sometimes feared as disrupting the present and a symptom of societal decline, and at other times a symbol of hope, entrusted with the responsibility to create a better future (Comaroff & Comaroff 2005; Harris 2004). This 'peculiar burden of representation', in the quotation from Phil Cohen above, means that young people are simultaneously framed as both a cause of societal problems and a solution to them. They figure as both threatening deviants and vulnerable, dependent not-yet-adults (MacDonald & Marsh 2005). While concerns about youth have existed for centuries, specific discourses of youth are shaped by and express the historical contexts out of which they emerge (Griffin 1993). Youth researchers have shown that such anxieties are heightened at times of social, cultural and political upheaval, during which fears about change are directed towards particular groups of young people as 'folk devils', manifest in 'moral panics' about criminality, sexuality, drinking and media use (Cohen 1972; Osgerby 2004).

In the last chapter, we outlined the particular configuration of forces within which young people are growing up. Public anxieties about young people and celebrity fit within wider concerns about the state of the nation. In the wake of the 2011 English riots, David Cameron spoke of a 'slow-motion moral collapse' and about how 'social problems that have been festering for decades have exploded in our face'. Young people were one of his primary targets: 'Irresponsibility. Selfishness. Behaving as if your choices have no consequences. Children without fathers. Schools without discipline. Reward without effort.' Here young people are constructed as selfish, but also vulnerable and 'at risk' from absent parents and bad schooling. Contrasted with this positioning of young people is that of young people as potential and hope. For example, at the 2016 Conservative Party Conference, UK Education Secretary Justine Greening spoke of the 'need [for] a world class education system that works for . . . all of our young people'. The goal is 'The Great Meritocracy. Opportunity Britain – a levelled-up Britain'; the post-Brexit project articulated by Prime Minister Theresa May (2016), who committed 'to giv[ing] ordinary, working class people the better deal they deserve'. Young people figure as the future and 'unlocking potential . . . is Britain's greatest generational challenge' (Greening 2016).

Such discourses filter down from policy rhetoric and into young people's lives, creating anxiety. As past research has shown, within high-stakes schooling, young people grapple with individualized imperatives to display excellence and 'fulfil their potential' (Jackson 2006; Lucey & Reay 2002; Walkerdine et al. 2001). The heightened uncertainty of austerity has further unsettled their relationship to the future. Discourses of meritocracy have taken on a new tone as young people are expected to manage the insecurity of transitioning to adulthood in a society with fewer jobs and less support, and where the failure to do so is presented as evidence of moral deficiencies (laziness, irresponsibility and selfishness). They carry a double burden: they are both held responsible for spearheading the national economic recovery *and* imagined as a 'lost generation' without hope.

In this chapter, we explore how our participants experienced these contradictory discourses. In the first two sections, we look in turn at the discourses of youth as troublesome/at risk and youth as hope/potential in our data. We also show how individual rather than collective orientations run through participants' ideas about youth and opportunity. We then look at how young people used celebrity talk to position themselves in relation to these discourses and navigate the tensions arising from them.

'You get all these like accusations': Negotiating the discourse of problem youth

Youth or adolescence has often appeared in public narratives as a time of deviance (Cohen 1972; Griffin 1993). 'Problem youth' is an enduring motif, but one revitalized within austerity through political rhetoric denigrating the 'troublesome rioter' as lazy, irresponsible and materialistic (Tyler 2013). As we noted in Chapter 1, mainstream reporting of the 2011 riots across England dismissed attempts to connect them to the effects of austerity (including cuts to youth services), institutional racism within the police force and escalating wealth inequality. Rather, the riots were explained as the 'mindless' criminal behaviour of 'feral youth' (BBC 2011; Harvey et al. 2013). Whether aimed at 'rioters', or the 'mods', 'rockers' and 'ladettes' of previous decades, such moral panics construct scapegoats at times of social instability. This othering is classed, gendered and racialized drawing on long-standing discourses which position young people outside white middle-class norms as dangerous and immoral (McDowell 2012). It plays out in recurring anxieties attached to 'chavs', 'yobs' and other representations of deviant working-class masculinity (Coward 1998; Nayak 2006), and between oppositions of high-achieving 'can-do girls' as 'exemplars of new possibility' (Harris 2004: 1; McRobbie 2008) and 'at risk' girls coded as failures – categorizations that are classed and racialized (Archer et al. 2010; Projansky 2014).

Our participants were aware of these dominant representations. They both critiqued them as inaccurate and stigmatizing stereotypes *and* dissociated themselves from these others of austerity, paradoxically reinforcing their truth status. This is part of a process in which subjectivities are constructed via 'establishing opposites and "others" whose actuality is always subject to the continuous interpretation and re-interpretation of their differences from "us"', and where this designation of others reproduces power relations (Said 1995: 332).

Talk of transition to adulthood ran through the data, as many conversations focused on hopes and dreams for the future. However, two questions specifically focused on their experiences of growing up. The first asked them to describe what it is like to be a young person as though to an alien who has just landed on earth. The second asked them to compare being a young person today to their parents' generation, something we explore in the next section. It was in their responses to the hypothetical alien question that the spectre or the 'troublesome teen' emerged:

It's rather oppressive really. I mean you get all these like accusations that young people are to blame, we're all in trouble, and like half of us don't even do anything wrong, we just keep to ourselves. Erm like it's difficult, because you've got to branch out from what you were to what you're going to become. (Archibald Brunel, SW, 16–17)

It's hard, because like we get stereotyped for being thugs, and like doing bad things, and like some of us actually work hard, sit at home, like don't go out every day. Some people smoke and that, like not everybody's the same. (Tim Jimmy, London, 14–15)

It's not what the other people think we are . . . because most of the people think oh, we just stand around smoking, and doing this and that. But that's not true. Dedicated. Confident. What else? Talented, I would say. [both laugh] Most of us [are] respectful. (Sasha, London, 16–17)

We see an explicit challenge to oppressive and narrow stereotypes of deviant youth (as 'thugs', 'in trouble', 'to blame', smokers). However, these extracts highlight struggles for meaning over the category of the 'young person'. The idea of *mis*representation draws boundaries around 'good' and 'bad' youth. Good young people are described as hard working, 'talented', keeping to themselves, dedicated and respectful. They are contrasted implicitly or explicitly to the lazy, unruly and disrespectful stereotype against which they find themselves being judged. These illustrate an attempt to challenge the all-encompassing and overdetermined nature of the 'troublesome youth' stereotype. However, rather than eradicate it, the stereotype is reaffirmed: that is to say, the 'good' young person (and speaker) claims legitimacy through invoking the spectre of the 'bad' young person. Such tensions speak to the difficulties of challenging negative stereotypes simply by replacing them with positive ones (Hall 1997).

Imogen Tyler (2013) has pointed to the visceral way that binary oppositions like these construct some people as more human than others. She argues that the casting out of particular groups is a central feature of neoliberal capitalism, enabling consent to be gained for repressive policies towards specific categories, such as working-class youth. The labelling of particular young people as deviants presents social problems as resulting from individual bad behaviour, directing attention away from structural inequalities (see also Griffin 1993). In the context of austere meritocracy's rhetoric of 'scroungers' and 'strivers' (discussed in Chapter 1), it is not surprising that hard work and dedication figure in young people's talk as they defend themselves against this stigmatized category and affirm their own position as 'good'.

The potential for 'bad' youth to disrupt and lead astray 'good' youth was also present in young people's accounts. This is manifest in a discourse of 'falling in with the wrong crowd', which appeared frequently as a potential risk to achieving their aspirations:

One of my best, well, she was one of my best friends, sort of strayed and ended up in a bad crowd. But my mum has always told me going, 'if people are gonna misguide you', she said, 'you need to have the initiative to, to step away and just be like I'm not comfortable with this'. And I did that at that point, but it's just like I feel like that's what hinders people a lot, it's they feel like, like immediate gratification like we need to have fun now. (Ginny, London, 14–15)

Like following the crowd, I mean following certain people that don't value what they have, like education and, and family and stuff; people who go out of their way to, to like encourage other people to do bad stuff as well, that maybe steers some people away from that. (Zayneb, Manchester, 14–15)

Youth still gets seen as gangsters, violent, everything else. Like say if we, a teenage girl, she's definitely, goes out partying and takes drugs, does alcohol, but they don't see the other side, how they study every night, help out with their parents, help out, do whatever, do chores, they don't see that side. (Sabeen, Manchester, 14–15)

The discourse of bad youth in the wrong crowd constructs the boundaries around legitimate ways of being young. Those in the 'bad crowd' are presented as motivated by 'immediate gratification'. They function as cautionary tales which prop up austere meritocracy's ideal behaviours, values and ways of being: thrift, responsibility and sacrifice as opposed to immediate pleasure, selfishness and irresponsibility. Making the right choices is not simply about planning responsibly and working hard, but also choosing the right friends. In later chapters we identify how these 'choices' relate to the aspirational goals and means of achieving them that are privileged within austere meritocracy. We show how these mark out some pathways and people as good and some as bad.

While Sabeen troubles the binary between good and bad youth, her claim to legitimacy still draws on discourses of hard work and personal responsibility. These stories about troublesome youth have an impact on young people at a time when they feel immense personal responsibility for – in Archibald's words – 'branch[ing] out from what you were to what you're going to become'.

'There's a lot depending on us': Bearing the burden of hope in austere meritocracy

As we briefly discussed in Chapter 1, one of the key discourses characterizing austere meritocracy is thrift, in which national resources must be deployed responsibly – by individuals and governments – for the sake of our future well-being. Such resources include the young, whose education and labour-market 'success' are deemed crucial to ensuring the nation's recovery. In this formulation, the enemy is 'wasted potential' – signalled by Justine Greening's comments above. There are multiple problems with the dominant conceptualization of potential that saturates the government's education and social mobility discourses, including how it serves wider economic agendas and is used to justify class inequalities (Beauvais & Higham 2016; Sellars 2015). The concept of 'wasting potential' is individualized, translated into a failure to plan responsibly, choose correctly and overcome obstacles. In this section we look at how young people negotiated this responsibility.

While participants depicted growing up as a space of fun and freedom, they also described their experiences as difficult and tough. Youth emerged as a time of negotiating an array of external pressures that shaped their transitions. When we conducted the research, participants were preparing for exams, making decisions about continuing in education and writing personal statements for university applications or college. While in some cases this was presented as an exciting time of new possibilities, there was a clear sense that they felt overwhelming pressure to make the 'right' decisions for their future. Mike (SW, 14–15) talks about feeling 'an awful lot of pressure on everything when you are at this age' and asks, 'Whose amazing idea it was to put all your exams in the space of three weeks?'

Homer (London, 14–15) similarly speaks about having a 'lot of responsibility even though you're young and you don't have to work, and you don't have a family, it's still quite a lot of responsibility getting your GCSEs [16+ examinations], the jobs that you want, erm living round bad estates'. Homer explicitly links passing examinations to getting a job as a solution to his current situation ('living round bad estates'). Investing in education emerges as a passport to 'the good life'. This notion of education as a driver of social mobility gained momentum over the course of the twentieth century as the provision of free mass state education and the expansion of higher education was framed by successive UK governments as opening up the possibility for individuals to 'scale the heights' of the social class system (Reay 2013: 665). Class is spoken of euphemistically in Homer's reference to 'bad estates', resonant of how working-class locales are commonly constructed and imagined as 'rubbish' and 'shit', 'contain[ing] the socially excluded, "unfit" and undesirable' (Archer et al. 2010: 2; see Lucey & Reay 2002). Within dominant rhetoric, social mobility requires escape from places that are deemed to lack opportunity. This narrative of social mobility acts as a powerful justification of class inequalities – the widening gap between rich and poor is acceptable if it is possible for anyone to become wealthy through trying hard. For Homer, talking about his studies above, the ability to get 'the jobs that you want' is a matter of individual work. This narrative obscures the difficulties and pain involved in 'getting out and getting away' for working-class young people like him (Lawler 1999). As we elaborate on in Chapter 5, Homer describes himself as 'not really clever'. Failure – to get high grades or secure unemployment – haunt his words: it is all down to him.

Fears about the difficulty of finding work surfaced in many participants' accounts. They were often articulated through discourses of generational change, in which their life felt more precarious than their parents. As Rick (London, 16–17) says: 'It's definitely got tougher to get a job, erm, and it's got tougher for people when they come out of university.' Alisha (London, 14–15) echoes this: 'There's a lot depending on us because they're worried about our future, and they've already had their chance to like achieve in life, and jobs are getting harder to like get nowadays.' Alisha refers to her parents' wish for her to 'do well in school' to secure her future. Thus the 'peculiar burden of representation' is felt as a generational responsibility: As Alisha explains, 'There's a lot depending on us.' Yet we see the immense difficulties of fulfilling this promise. While young people have typically been equated with progress – the beneficiaries of modernity and meritocracy – this is undermined by the contemporary discourse of youth as a 'lost generation'. Rather than locating their generation as beneficiaries of expanding opportunities, both Rick and Alisha draw on a narrative of generational decline and future uncertainty.

Across the dataset, the responsibility for dealing with the risks of future unemployment fell on individuals in the present – to study, work and gain skills, while making the most of their youth:

> To be a young person is basically you have to, it's basically learning the skills you need for erm adulthood, cos it's now competition for jobs has gone up a lot . . . and money isn't the greatest . . . from having the recession and everything. So I think it's more just learning the techniques you'll need for adulthood and just basically you want to have a good time in your childhood, well in being a young person, because you don't want to have bad memories . . . thinking 'oh I could have done so much more'. (John, SW, 14–15)

For John, the transition into adulthood requires work on his part in order to survive the current 'competition for jobs'. The 'skills needed for adulthood' are framed in terms of employability and financial security. John sees the recession as requiring a particular response from him, of self-work, upskilling and planning, in order to ensure he has a stable life – or at least to minimize the risks generated by current conditions. He does not look to collective provision in the form of the welfare state nor to collective strategies such as trade unionism.

The ways in which participants talked about their futures bear marks of austere meritocracy. But these were not explicit. The terms austerity and recession were noticeably absent from young people's talk (with recession appearing in only three interviews, and austerity in none). While explicit economic terms were used rarely, the context labelled by John as 'recession and everything' above – that of high youth unemployment, low pay and reduced public spending – featured implicitly across the dataset. This was particularly apparent in conversations about employment and money, which we explore in more detail later in this chapter and in Chapters 5 and

7. While a few young people mentioned structural reasons for these challenges and insecurities, they tended to be subsumed within individualized frameworks in which participants emphasized their own responsibility to achieve financial security.

Conditions accelerated by austerity, including the precarious labour market and the dismantling of the welfare state, are having profound and disproportional effects on young people. Our participants, still in school, are yet to feel the full force of these conditions. Yet concerns about austerity pervade their accounts. While the lost generation discourse opens up a space for locating dwindling opportunities within an account of structural transformations and austerity, the dominant political narrative proposes no changes to social organization. Instead, it frames hope for the future in terms of achieving one's potential. This powerful discourse is an instance of cruel optimism (Berlant 2011). Policy premised on the 'opportunity bargain' (Brown et al. 2011) of 'learning = earning . . . aims to produce optimism about the benefits of education' (Sellars 2015: 202). Even though conditions of austerity have (further) revealed this bargain to be fraudulent, young people must continue to invest in a hopeful orientation to the future and take responsibility for fulfilling their potential.

This is particularly apparent in how young people discuss the potential barriers to achieving their aspirations. We look at these throughout the book but offer one typical example here. Asked if anything stops people from achieving their aspirations, Syndicate (London, 14–15) focuses not on external structural barriers or resources but internal, psychological ones. Here he describes how other people's negative perceptions can shake young people's confidence to pursue their dreams:

> **Syndicate:** I guess for anyone to achieve their dreams it's mainly support, I reckon, so people telling you [that] you can't do something, like . . . it could like take down their confidence and they might go to something they completely don't like [when] they could have had the potential to do something they liked.
> **Interviewer:** Are there things, do you think, that make it difficult for you to do what you want to do?
> **Syndicate:** Erm, not really, because with me I just, if people say I can't do something it spurs me on more to prove to them that I can. Like I got told that I wouldn't be able to run 100 metres in under 13 seconds, and I did. (London, 14–15)

Other people's perceptions are presented not just as a barrier to overcome, but as a motivating force that propels him to success (it 'spurs me on more to prove to them'). We see again how something that could be understood as an injustice becomes subsumed within powerful discourses of individual responsibility and determination.

These young people's words show how difficult it is for them to negotiate the conflicting discourses that construct contemporary youth: those of despair and hope, blocked futures and unlimited potential, constraint and opportunity, risk and responsibility. In the next section we show how celebrity talk offers a space for them to articulate these tensions in their transitions to adulthood.

'Off-the-rails' child stars and 'exceptional' role models: Negotiating youth through celebrity talk

Our participants took a particular interest in celebrities who were close in age to themselves. These included singer Justin Bieber, actor Emma Watson and diver Tom Daley and others who had grown up in front of the camera. Although our participants are likely to have heightened exposure to these celebrities through the popular culture targeted at the teen market, this is not the only reason for their prevalence in young people's celebrity talk. As we show, participants' interest in young celebrities reflects their own concerns about growing up and demonstrates how child stars become condensations of contemporary anxieties around morality and adolescence (Projansky 2014).

A central argument of this book is that celebrity helps us make sense of what it means to be human. We see celebrities as embodying tensions and contradictions that arise from dominant discourses of the self and society at a given historical moment, particularly when these are under threat. In this section we show how celebrity offers our participants a set of cultural resources through which to tell stories about what it means to be young and so to work through some of the tensions highlighted so far. Specifically, we argue that the two dominant constructions of youth discussed above – youth as troublesome/at risk and youth as hope/potential – map closely onto the patterning of participants' talk about young celebrities.

Participants broadly discussed young celebrities through two sets of discourses: one focused on the failures and public downfalls of child stars, and another on the exceptional successes of those who have 'achieved a lot at a young age'. Both are defined by a sense of 'age inappropriateness' or precocity (Lesko 2001): of doing 'too much too young', whether engaging in risky adult behaviours or exceeding normal expectations through exceptional achievement. These are, respectively, labelled as 'uncivilized' and 'civilized' forms of precocity (Lesko 2001) and we see these play out in our study. In the uncivilized group, we have child stars, viewed as tragic 'crash and burn' figures whose 'innocence' has been sullied by fame. For example, in a heated discussion in one group (SW 16–17), Paris mentions Miley Cyrus: 'A child star' who 'went off the rails for a bit. They all do, child stars.' Joe follows this with the example of Macaulay Culkin and Tom expands: 'He's like a smack head now, isn't he?' Other child stars cited as having been ruined by fame include Michael Jackson and Disney stars Lindsay Lohan and Demi Lovato, who were variously discussed as experiencing addiction, poor mental health, eating disorders and – ultimately – rehab.

These discussions of child stars invoked moral evaluations around 'inappropriate' and 'risky' conduct, including substance abuse, casual sex, and lack of responsibility for their careers. These themes are not surprising. As Sarah Projansky (2014) illustrates in her analysis of celebrity girlhood, child stars have long been subjects of intense fascination and hostility, manifesting historically specific anxieties around adolescence, sexuality and femininity (see also Beer & Penfold-Mounce 2009). Young people's celebrity talk provides an important site in which they negotiate the moral regulatory discourses that govern their subjectivities and actions.

These celebrities were seen not simply as a risk to themselves but were criticized as negative influences on other people; usually younger children and girls. This was evident in discussions about boy band One Direction and singer Bieber – young male celebrities with a large fan base of teenage girls. These celebrities were regularly criticized for engaging in reckless behaviour that sets a bad example for their younger fans. For example, Joanna (London, 14–15) mentions One Direction's Harry Styles purportedly sleeping with older women: 'He's got these kids looking up to him and he's like in charge of them, and it's not fair that he's doing that.' Several groups discussed Bieber's well-publicized antics – examined in this chapter's celebrity case study – as irresponsible. These included taking drugs, missing concerts, and playing pranks on his management team. Kayda (Manchester, 16–17) states: 'He's really annoying. Just rude to people, like he locked his manager in the wardrobe, he punched a cake, like there's no need for that.' In these discussions, Bieber is charged with mismanaging fame at a young age – being attention seeking, selfish and ungrateful, and setting a bad example for others. One flashpoint that generated much discussion was the #cutforbieber viral phenomenon where young fans reportedly shared online pictures of themselves self-harming after receiving reports of Bieber smoking marijuana. This critique of Bieber's negative influence by Hibapottamus (Manchester, 16–17) is typical:

> I think he's a bit too influential on young people. . . . Like the time he took weed . . . and then there were like young people, young girls like slitting their wrists all over the place. . . . I don't think he uses his influence in a positive way really.

The figure of the young vulnerable female celebrity consumer emerged throughout young people's talk, both in reference to child stars and other celebrities. Dumbledore (SW, 16–17) complains, 'I know full well that there's people who are 11 or 12 or 10, or 9, or 8, cos they've all said to me stuff like this, they would be quite happy to go off and marry a footballer, because that way they're rich and trampy.' In one group interview, Alison (London, 16–17) remembers how at 'age 13, the Jonas Brothers . . . took over my life. I would just sit there for hours on a computer just looking at pictures of them . . . and now I'm like I hate them so much.' Alison produces herself as mature by placing her obsession with Disney stars in the past, associating this extreme fandom with a child self that she has now out-grown. Rick underlines the message that you are required to grow out of such things by warning that 'some people don't grow out of it'. This draws on ideas of female vulnerability, triviality and childishness, and the notion of girls as irrational cultural consumers (Projansky 2014; McRobbie & Garber 1977). We see this in Nishaan's (Manchester, 14–15) comments, in which he describes celebrity as an interest of younger people who have time for play, contrasted with his more adult preoccupation with the seri-ous work of study: 'This stage of time, . . . you're mostly like focusing on all your work you've got. . . . You don't really care what a celebrity does.' This distancing from celebrity influence is a way of presenting oneself as mature, rational and serious rather than distracted by the trivial, frivo-lous and feminine world of celebrity. Discussions about both appropriate and inappropriate celebrity tastes and consumption are closely intertwined with young people's performances of age and gender. In Chapter 8 we dis-cuss further how celebrity fandom was feminized and infantilized within young people's talk.

While they voiced disapproval of the reckless behaviour of young celeb-rities, participants also showed empathy for child stars. They positioned them as vulnerable and offered various justifications for their decline. In the following extract, participants discuss the negative effects of achieving celebrity at a young age:

Strawberry: Recently [Bieber] has become a slightly more cocky teen-age boy than he was. . . .

Pringles: I think he's going to become like, the fame's got to him a bit now.

Dr Lighty: Yeah, cos he's smoking weed, innit? He smoked weed. I heard about that.

Interviewer: Do you think fame changes you?

Pringles: Yeah, definitely. People take their actions too far.

Dr Lighty: They get too greedy. . . . The money changes you.

Strawberry: I think the younger you start the more likely it is to change you.

Dr Lighty: Yeah, that's true, because Adele. She's not really like that, and she started at an old age. Not old [laughter] but like twenty something. Whereas people like Justin Bieber or Willow Smith cut-ting her hair off.

Pringles: She's just gone crazy. . . . It's cos when they're younger they have more of an imagination as to what they want to do. As you grow up you just realize that – that's obviously not going to be good for my image.

Strawberry: Well if you were given like millions now you'd go crazy. If you were older you would be more responsible, hopefully.

Pringles: Civilized about it. It is tough like when you're young, and you are going through all this. (London, 16–17)

Bieber and singer Willow Smith appear as naïve celebrities. Their youth deems them incapable of handling the otherworldly amounts of money that fame brings and unaware of how to protect their image. There is an assumption that this is a stage that one outgrows in maturing from a vulnerable, irrational child to a civilized, responsible adult (Lesko 2001). Youth is characterized as a liminal space – between childish desires for fun, instant pleasure and self-absorption and adult orientations to personal responsibility, delayed gratification and consciousness of others. Within this talk there is sympathy with celebrities' off-the-rails behaviour as an understandable part of becoming adult.

Participants talked of young celebrities being under intense media scrutiny: 'To deal with stuff like that. I know they say like don't read it, and stuff. But if someone's writing stuff like that about me I'd want to read it' (Paris, SW, 16–17). Some discussed young stars being easily corrupted by the celebrity scene, exposed to drugs, alcohol and the 'wrong crowd': 'That sort of crowd where you take drugs. . . . They're influenced and even though they do have fans they are still humans, they still make mistakes' (Naomi, Manchester, 14–15). This leads them to 'grow up too fast': 'I think a lot of the people that start from Disney, then they try and act all older' (Jane, SW, 16–17). One group (London, 14–15) referenced Bieber vomiting on stage in a broader discussion about the public scrutiny of celebrities, with Tim stating, 'It's hard cos like you have a reputation and like you are always going to do good, but if like you mess up, then like everyone is like taking the mick out of you like forever.'

These concerns – huge workloads, the pull of the wrong crowd, constant surveillance and judgement – resonate with those concerns that young people speak about in relation to themselves, discussed earlier in the chapter. The intense visibility and unceasing scrutiny experienced by young celebrities resemble, albeit in hyperbolic fashion, the administrative adult gaze that governs youth in general (Lesko 2001). It is a gaze that is present in teachers' expectations, parents' hopes, and the media and politicians' unrelenting preoccupation with young people's 'successes' and 'failures'. Thus celebrity talk is not simply a mechanism for young people to construct themselves as mature subjects and good citizens through enacting moral disapproval of (young) celebrities. It provides a space to express empathy with them and offers a resource for articulating the shared difficulties of being young and becoming an adult.

The second dominant discourse drawn upon by participants in their talk about young celebrities is that of celebrities who have achieved a lot at a young age. This discourse was less common than that of the failed/vulnerable child star. Participants mobilized it in expressing admiration for celebrities whom they associated with extraordinary success as teenagers, based on talent and hard work. This included Indian badminton player Saina Nehwal, who was praised for representing her country at 19, singer Ed Sheeran and the *Harry Potter* stars, including Emma Watson, who played Hermione. We discuss Watson's image as a hard-working, high-achieving 'can-do' girl in Chapter 8. The young celebrity who was most regularly positioned through this discourse was diver Tom Daley. Daley was praised by a number of participants for his sporting achievements, deemed extraordinary and especially inspirational because of his youth. Babatunde (London, 14–15) explains, 'He's young as well, so he's kind of representing the younger generation in the celebrity world.' John (SW, 14–15) labels him a 'good role model' because 'he inspires people, and he's like decided to show people like you don't have to be like a grown-up to be able to do certain sports, because he like started when he was eleven or something'. Sabeen (Manchester, 14–15) calls him 'an amazing diver . . . he was like [an] Olympic athlete at the age of fourteen anyway, which was pretty good'. As we discuss in Chapter 5, Daley epitomizes the entrepreneurial form of success that is privileged within austere meritocracy.

There is a sense in young people's talk of these young celebrities as role models who map out 'proper' ways of being young. As Projansky (2014: 79) illustrates, young sports celebrities tend to be coded through nationalistic discourses of spectacular achievement, 'national darlings, loved, and when necessary protected'. Daley, carrying the nation's hopes on his shoulders every four years as an Olympic athlete, is constructed through these discourses. Further, he figures as austere meritocracy's exemplary subject of fulfilled potential, hope and progress. Significantly, these young celebrities appear as self-made, their exemplary success a product of their hard work and determination (examined in Chapter 3). There is little talk of the role of luck, privilege or collective social provision or support in contributing to this success (other than perhaps the adoration of the British public). Daley has benefited from state funding for diving, and public services from swimming pools to coaching to the BBC (resources that have been subject to public spending cuts under austerity (Conn 2015)). Yet such support mechanisms are absent from the young people's accounts of how he achieved so much at such a young age. In Daley's celebrity, as in the participants' discussions about their own futures, success and failure are spoken about almost exclusively through the individualizing discourses of meritocracy. The impact of these discourses is evident throughout this book. In this section we have begun to demonstrate how celebrity both perpetuates dominant discourses, and provides a resource for their negotiation. This analysis is developed in the chapters that follow.

Conclusion

In wider society, the dominant view of age is chronological, a measurement of one's time on earth that is associated with a biological and psychological process of growth. However, age is a social construct. It is produced through the stories we tell about it and the meanings we make of it, including through celebrity. In particular, we have identified two powerful constructions of youth: youth as a cause and symptom of social disintegration and moral decay (youth as troublesome/at risk); and youth as social and economic salvation (youth as hope/potential). Through both these positions, young people are held responsible, tasked with ensuring their own and the nation's success through their determination, entrepreneurialism, frugality, resilience and optimism. As we have demonstrated, these positions structure young people's talk about celebrities who function as cultural resources through which to articulate and negotiate the difficulties of growing up.

CELEBRITY CASE STUDY: JUSTIN BIEBER

Justin Bieber is a Canadian teen singer and songwriter who was discovered on YouTube. He released his first single at 15, and has since become a global success. Echoing the fervent discussions of his antics by our participants, a dominant theme within Bieber's media representation is his reckless behaviour: partying and drug taking, excessive spending (including purchasing a pet monkey), dangerous driving and playing pranks. Such behaviour attracted criticism and hostility, particularly online. Bieber appears within these stories as a troublesome/at risk teen, engaging in the wrong kinds of behaviour and making the wrong choices: favouring hedonism over hard work, childish fun over adult responsibility.

There were two key flashpoints during the case study period that exemplify this positioning. The first was Bieber appearing ninety minutes late at a concert in March 2013. This generated much criticism from his fans, their parents and the media for his lack of responsibility (resonating with our participants' discussions above) (Brown 2013). The second was the revelation that Bieber wrote in the guest book at the Anne Frank House that she 'would have been a Belieber'. This was widely criticized as tasteless, disrespectful and a sign of stupidity (Harless 2013). Through linguistic and visual devices, Bieber is positioned as an uncivilized child

FIGURE 2.1 *Justin Bieber, photograph by iloveJB123,*
no changes made. Licence https://creativecommons.org/
licenses/by/2.0/.

who is failing to mature appropriately. For example, he is described as a
'toxic toddler' (Furtado 2013), and a 'teenage brat' (Robertson 2013) who
needs a 'babysitter' (Smart 2013). This was most evocatively captured in
an image – circulated online as a meme – of Bieber lashing out at a paparazzi photographer that was photoshopped to show Bieber wearing a
nappy and sucking a dummy.

   These stories not only generated ridicule and hostility but also concern, where his 'erratic' behaviour was positioned as an understandable
response to growing up in the limelight. For example, celebrities including
Robbie Williams and Jada Pinkett Smith defended Bieber, drawing attention to the pressures of coping with exposure at a young age. In a piece
in *The Mirror* newspaper, Tony Parsons (2013) emphasized the burden of
young fame:

We all know that Justin is at that difficult age when we all have a genius for making fools of ourselves. He is also at that point in his celebrity where it is all becoming a burden – the endless touring, the gawping paparazzi, the interior of another hotel room in a city that looks just the same as the last one.

Parson's words echo our participants. There is a sense of youth as a time of experimentation and self-development, and thus empathy for the difficulties of doing this under the policing gaze of 'the gawping paparazzi'.

Bieber's representation rehearses a well-worn tragic story of child stars sullied by fame. A piece in *The Independent* newspaper speculates on whether Bieber is on the 'verge of a meltdown' (Fekadu 2013). It compares him to other 'off-the-rails' child stars, such as Britney Spears and Michael Jackson, and is littered with motifs of the train wreck celebrity (drug taking, rehabilitation). Constructions of child stars as 'at risk' are underlined by psychological discourses that position their erratic behaviours as symptoms of childish irrationality, manifestations of 'emotional bleeding' (Clark 2013) that express the difficulties of growing up in the spotlight. Bieber appears as a cautionary tale in which transitions to adulthood can by derailed by excessive wealth, success, absent parents and bad company:

A lack of parental guidance, combined with the emerging pull of his worrying new circle of friends in the wake of the star's split from girlfriend Selena Gomez in November, is now raising serious questions about Bieber's increasingly erratic behaviour and state of mind. (Graham & Gould 2013)

Bieber's responses to these controversies appear within media articles and interviews and in his Twitter feed. These are oriented around repentance and defiance, as this extract demonstrates:

Everyone in my team has been telling me, 'keep the press happy' but I'm tired of all the countless lies in the press right now. Saying I'm going to rehab and how my family is disappointed in me. My family is beyond proud. . . . If Anyone believes i need rehab that's their own stupidity lol I'm 19 with 5 number one albums, 19 and I've seen the whole world. 19 and I've accomplished more than I could've ever dreamed of. . . . I know my talent level and i know i got my head on straight. I know who i am and i know who i'm not. . . . My messages have been to never say never and believe, not to believe in me, but to believe in yourself. . . . I'm a good person with a big heart. And don't think I deserve all of this negative press. I've worked my ass off to get where I am and my hard work doesn't stop here. I'm growing up finding myself while having people <u>watch</u> me and criticise me everyday I think im doing pretty damn good. (Bieber in Cubarrubia 2013, original emphasis)

Bieber's response not only draws on the discourses of the child star explored in this chapter. It also represents a familiar ritual of celebrity confession found in talk shows and autobiographies – what Barry King (2008) calls the 'para-confession' and describes as a highly mediated performance of self-disclosure. Even when defending against judgement by asserting that he is a 'good person', Bieber reinforces powerful ideals of neoliberal selfhood. As we have seen in the accounts of participants earlier in this chapter – and which will be developed throughout this book – such techniques are central to constructions of the 'good' young person. Bieber can only rescue himself from the denigrated position of the troublesome teen through asserting his exceptional achievement, constant striving and positivity. As Syndicate said earlier, negative judgements are positioned not as constraints but as motivational tools for growth: hurdles to be overcome and disproved through individual effort and resilience – ideas we explore in more detail in the next chapter. Bieber's representation communicates a 'grammar of conduct' (Beer & Penfold-Mounce 2009) about growing up, in which making the wrong choices and engaging in the wrong kinds of behaviour risk blocking the fulfilment of potential. Failure must be avoided and hope redeemed through engaging in self-reflection, hard work and personal responsibility.

3

Work

In this chapter we show how hard work emerges as the 'correct' way for young people to attain the endorsed goals of austere meritocracy: success and happiness. Across both the individual and group interviews, hard work dominated the data. We will show that it threaded through young people's talk about their current examination anxieties and their plans for the future. Young people's taste in celebrities offers a way of expressing and policing their own and other people's commitment to hard work. Their investment in hard work in their own lives and the value they give to 'hard-working' celebrities challenge dominant media and policy discourses about young people. As we discussed in Chapters 1 and 2, young people are frequently portrayed as a lazy, 'get-rich-quick' generation, epitomized by their alleged attraction to fame. This narrative of lazy youth draws attention away from the discursive role of hard work within their accounts which is our focus in this chapter.

Hard work and aspiration are the key moral imperatives of austere meritocracy. When US President Trump's wife Melania Trump spoke at the 2016 Republican Party Convention, her plagiarism of one of Michelle Obama's previous speeches was widely reported and criticized (McCarthy & Jacobs 2016). Yet, the actual content of the plagiarized section of her speech passed unnoticed: 'Because we want our children – and all children in this nation – to know that the only limit to the height of your achievements is the reach of your dreams and your willingness to work for them.' Shaun Spicer, later briefly White House Press Secretary, responded to the plagiarism accusations and attempted to quell criticism by pointing out how common such sentiments are (see Meyers 2016). He cited voices as diverse as musicians John Legend and Kid Rock and Twilight Sparkle – from global toy phenomenon My Little Pony – as speaking about the value of dreaming big and working hard. The United States, with its myth of the American Dream, is the original 'aspiration nation', one in which, so the story goes, immigrants can rise to become president through their dedication and application. Yet, political dynasties and billionaires from the Clintons to Donald Trump dominate the presidency, as hundreds of millions are spent even before you get your name on the ballot. Eddie Glaude Jr. (2015) discusses how belief in the American Dream has intensified under neoliberalism, highlighting the spread of a prosperity gospel within black churches which 'blunts criticism of durable inequality, precisely because wealth and the aspiration for upward mobility are tied to individual spiritual considerations'. Hard work here is a spiritual goal but remains individualized.

Similarly, hard work saturates UK political rhetoric. The strapline for the 2013 Conservative Party Conference was 'for hardworking people'; and in the 2015 General Election, the two main political parties competed to position themselves as the ones standing up for 'hardworking families'. Jo Littler (2013), in her analysis of the shifting meanings and uses of meritocracy, identifies hard work as central to how it operates within recent UK government policy. In particular, she identifies hard work as at the heart of David Cameron's claim that Britain is an 'aspiration nation':

> 'Aspiration Nation' as a rhetorical strategy, and as an expression of meritocratic feeling, connects self-belief and aspiration with the trope of hard work. It is striking how, again and again, 'hard work' combined with self-belief is employed by an unprecedentedly privileged cadre of politicians and millionaire elites to justify their position and success and to prescribe this as the route for others. 'Working hard and wanting to get on' is the way to progress. (Littler 2013: 67)

This developed in the 1990s, marking a shift from 1980s Thatcherism, when there was a 'meritocratic appeal to consumerism as a general mode of participation in public life which invited people to identify with the notion of themselves as consumers rather than as workers or citizens in a range of public settings' (Littler 2013: 63). The emphasis on hard work within recent articulations also represents a shift in emphasis from intelligence to effort in the meritocracy formula discussed in Chapter 1: $I + E = M$ ('Intelligence combined with Effort equals Merit').

In the United States, the UK and much of Western Europe, this focus on hard work sits alongside increasing youth unemployment, and growing student debt. The appeal to hard work by these nations' elite politicians is deliberate. It 'helps to erase any image of over-privileged indolence from the speaker's persona whilst interpellating the listener as able to achieve a similar social status' (Littler 2013: 67). However, the possibility of most people attaining this level of wealth and social status is very low and is getting lower, as brutal cuts to social support systems make 'the distance aspiration needs to travel that much further and far less likely to be traversed' (Littler 2013: 68). Yet this failure is constructed as an individual one, for the idea of 'hardworking people' constructs a binary opposite: lazy people, those who do not work hard or perhaps do not work at all. As we discussed in Chapter 1, this opposition is encapsulated in the frequent UK political soundbites pitting 'strivers' against 'scroungers', recycling older distinctions between the 'deserving' and the 'undeserving' poor (Reid 2013). In this context, young people's concerns to locate themselves as hard working are unsurprising. This is cruel given that falling wages and rising rates of in-work poverty mean that working hard is even less likely to guarantee financial security.

In the first two sections of the chapter, we show how young people are strongly invested in hard work. We look first at how the discourse of hard work structures their own aspirations. We then consider how they evaluate celebrities in relation to their perceived hard work, with fame and success positioned as justified if they have been earned by determination and tireless effort. In the final two sections of the chapter we critically examine this positioning of hard work. We explore how stories about celebrities as hard working – or not – are classed, gendered and raced, and consider the implications of discourses of meritocracy for young people given the persistence of such oft-unspoken inequalities. We end by examining disputes between participants over who they consider hard working and consider how these are informed by young people's own social positions. We draw mainly on the group interview data to show the negotiations that take place over who is hard working, but we begin with a brief look at the individual interviews.

'I know if I work hard, I can do anything I want to do': The centrality of work to aspiration

Young people's deep investment in hard work as a route to success runs through their talk about success, which we examine in Chapter 5. There we discuss two dominant success discourses: entrepreneurialism and stability. *Entrepreneurialism* imagines a future of ceaseless striving and *stability* contains the hope that such striving will end, but both are based in determination and graft. We will meet Ginny, who imagines opening the envelope containing her examination results as the moment when all her hard work will pay off, and Mariam whose grandmother, through working hard for her children, provided inspiration on how to be a 'good woman'. In Chapter 2 we identified how educational success represents an obstacle between young people and their dreams. Their talk about this tended to be individualized, focused on hard work and motivation. Work figures as an investment enabling you to 'get a good head start' on your competition (Mat Power, SW, 14–15).

Across these data we see that hard work is a powerful discourse through which young people are positioned as able to make their dreams a reality *if* they invest sufficient effort. As Zayneb (Manchester, 16–17) says, 'I think everyone has the potential to achieve their dream. They just have to put the work in, and some people may need to work harder than others but if you want to achieve your dream then you still have to deal with it and do it.' For Tim Jimmy, it enables him to reject negative views of his capabilities:

> People told me before like 'you won't be able to do this, you won't be able to do that'. So that annoys me, because like I know like they're not, they can't plan my future. I know if I work hard, I can do anything I want to do. . . . If I prove someone wrong it gives me a good feeling, cos I know that I was right, and they wasn't. (London, 14–15)

Thus, in some senses, this is a hopeful discourse, in which the world is open to young people if they 'put the work in'. However, there is a danger in the way Tim sees hard work as a route past all obstacles: '[If] I try my hardest in like everything . . . other people will be fighting for a job, like I'll be having a good job, and like living a good life, where people have like a rough life.' As Mariam puts it, the only barrier to realizing your dreams is yourself:

> I tend to be lazy and I don't apply [myself] to exams, I don't do my coursework, I tend to do it the day before always, my homework. So I think the only one that's helping me is myself. If I, if I want to do something, I will do it, I just, I need to mentally just reach into myself and then just have a mind of 'I will do this, I can do this'. (Manchester, 16–17)

In our conversations about the barriers young people face, participants talked about other people's perceptions of them – as we saw with Syndicate in Chapter 2, the risks of falling in with 'the wrong crowd' and economic inequality – as we also discussed in Chapter 2. Yet, as they do for Tim and Mariam, determination, work, motivation and personal resolve appear as the primary means of overcoming these obstacles. Olivia Bolt describes herself as working class, and hopes to have a career as a solicitor. In a discussion about whether social class has an impact on being able to work in law, she draws on the powerful discourse of hard work:

> I think once you can prove to someone that you're like, you're good at your job and you're worth it, they won't think about where you went to school or anything like that. I think that people won't really notice that, and if they do I'm just going to have to work a bit harder to prove that I'm better than that, so. (SW, 16–17)

While reflecting on the policy trends discussed earlier and historically embedded narratives of meritocracy, this intensive focus on hard work among our participants was initially surprising to us. This was partly because of the extent to which it saturated our data, but also because research in secondary schools in England has consistently shown that 'effortless achievement' is the most valued way of producing academic success. In particular, Carolyn Jackson's (2006) study of laddish behaviours in schools documents the effort that goes into performing effortless achievement by young men and women, as all work must be concealed from view. In this context, 'hard work' is devalued: the province of the 'less intelligent', placed in opposition to 'effortless achievement', and generally attached to female and working-class students by teachers and peers (Walkerdine, 1990).

While some studies have found female and/or working-class students building learner identities based in hard work – from Paul Willis's (1977) 'ear'oles' to Máirtín Mac an Ghaill's (1994) 'academic achievers'– this has not displaced effortless achievement from its dominant position. Louise Archer and Becky Francis (2007: 66) identify a trichotomy of Western education discourses of students shown in Table 3.1. 'Ideal' students are naturally talented, innovative, active, independent, leaders and 'normal'; 'pathologized' students are diligent/plodding, conformist, passive, dependent, followers

TABLE 3.1 *Trichotomy of discourses about pupils*

'Ideal' pupil	Other/pathologized pupil	Demonized pupil
Naturally talented	Diligent/plodding	Naturally unintelligent/ lacking ability
Innovative/initiative	Conformist	Peer-led
'Outside culture'	Culture-bound	Victim of 'bad' culture
Leaders	Followers	Anti-social/Rebels
Enquiring/engaged	Deferent, unquestioning	Problematically challenging and disengaged
Assertive	Unassertive	Aggressive
Independent	Dependent	Ungovernable
Active	Passive	Anomic
'Normal' sexuality	Asexual/oppressed/ repressed	Hypersexuality
Normal	Other	Other/abnormal
(White)	(Asian/Oriental)	(Black/white working class)
(Outside class/middle class)	(Deserving poor)	(Underserving poor/ underclass)
(Masculine/ masculinized)	(Feminine/feminized)	(Hypermasculine/ Hyperfeminine)

Source: Archer, L. and Francis, B. *Understanding minority ethnic achievement: race, gender, class and 'success'* (Abingdon: Routledge, 2007: 66).

and 'other'; 'demonized' students are naturally unintelligent/lacking ability, peer-led, anomic, ungovernable, anti-social/rebels and 'other'/abnormal. These three categories align with class, gender and race, with the ideal student position mapping to middle class, masculine and white; the pathologized position to deserving poor, feminine/feminized and Asian/Oriental; and the demonized position to undeserving poor, hypermasculine/hyperfeminine and black/white. The valuing of hard work within our study changes this typology, offering the possibility that different learners can experience success. However, there are limits to this, as evaluations of 'hard work' often reinscribe rather than unsettle existing classed, gendered and racialized distinctions. We explore this in the rest of the chapter by looking at how hard work features in young people's celebrity talk, and mapping its relationship to class, gender and race.

Obama shows us that 'we can get everything we want if we try hard': Hard work and celebrity talk

The young people in our study also showed a strong investment in hard work as central to, and necessary for, future success and happiness, through their celebrity talk. We can see this in the next extract:

> **Dave:** I think it can go two ways: you're either a celebrity who's earned what you have, or you're a celebrity who got lucky.
> **Interviewer:** . . . So for those who've earned what they've got, what's that through, do you think? Is it talent or hard work?
> **Dave:** It's talent. Talent, obviously. Like Usain Bolt, he is, he has a lot of talent for running, but he also has to train that talent for – I think it's been twelve years that he's competed.
> **Jerome:** Do you remember that thing we watched in German, where the, *The Life of Usain Bolt*, and he trained so hard that he actually vomited. (Manchester, 14–15)

The opposition with which Dave starts, between 'deserving' celebrities ('who've earned what you have') and 'undeserving' celebrities ('who got lucky'), was pervasive across our data (see also Allen & Mendick 2012). Although Bolt's talent is important for Dave, it is through working hard day in, day out that Bolt is judged to have earned his success. Vomiting appears as a sudden visceral manifestation of the extent of his training. It serves as evidence that he has pushed his body to its limits and it demonstrates his worth. Here, as elsewhere in our data, hard work has a temporal dimension: it needs to be regular and maintained over long periods of time.

Our most popular celebrity figure was actor Will Smith, with thirty-eight of the fifty-one participants who took part in individual interviews saying that if he attended their school they would want to befriend him. He was uniformly seen as happy and successful: 'The coolest person on earth' (Rick, London, 16–17), 'a legend' (Lewis Johnson, London, 16–17) and someone whom 'everyone loves' (Mat Power, SW, 14–15). Smith's appeal is intimately connected to hard work, both through representations of his own life and in the lives of the characters he plays. Schmidt (London, 16–17) admires how, 'everything about him, . . . it's like he wants to do well in life, like he wants to achieve something'. Anonymous (Manchester, 16–17) was 'moved' by Smith's role in the film *The Pursuit of Happyness,* in which he struggles against adversity to become a successful stockbroker: 'The part I liked the most was him suffering and how he handled it, like yeah, that desperation, that will to survive. . . . I just could see that like the fire that was burning within him.' In such talk, participants are picking up on a key feature of Will Smith's media representation, as we explore in the case study for this chapter.

In young people's celebrity talk, as exemplified in Anonymous's comments about Will Smith, hard work is repeatedly spoken of within a broader rhetoric of individual strength, resilience and agency. It figures as a way of overcoming obstacles, as when working-class Somalian Anjali (16–17, Manchester) explains that she likes the then-US President Barack Obama because he shows us 'that we can get everything we want if we try hard'. Similarly, Roman, a working-class British Pakistani young man, talks about how the life of African-American singer Etta James showed him that 'you always have to stay strong':

> If you've watched the new *Cadillac Records* [film], Beyoncé starred as Etta James and she just showed her life and how it was for her as a young woman trying to get into the music business . . . and how men would just like think 'oh yeah women, all these women can't do what we can do and all'. And it's just like, that really like showed me that no matter what comes in your way, you can always get past that, and you always have to stay strong. (Manchester, 14–15)

In these and other extracts individualized practices of 'working hard' and 'staying strong' figure as ways to overcome structural disadvantages just as they did in the extracts in the previous section about young people's own futures. As Roman puts it, 'No matter what comes in your way, you can always get past that.' The talk of Obama and James references and draws on struggles for race and gender equality, but in ways that depoliticize them, eliding wider inequalities by emphasizing the heroic individual who succeeds against the odds. So while we want to acknowledge young people's commitment to hard work, and its possibilities, we also want to look at it critically.

In young people's talk about hard work we can see them negotiating their investments in the dominant discourses of austere meritocracy, where success can be achieved regardless of one's background. As we see throughout this book, popular culture has a pedagogic and disciplinary role in propagating these dominant discourses, both drawing from and exceeding policy:

> Neoliberalism has been engaged in constructing new entrepreneurial identities and re-engineering the bourgeois subject. . . . [W]e detect similar tendencies: in consumer and celebrity cultures, the drive for instant gratification, the fantasies of success, the fetishisation of technology, the triumph of 'life-style' over substance, endless refashioning of the 'self', the commercialisation of 'identity' and utopias of self-sufficiency. These 'soft' forms of power are as effective in changing social attitudes as are 'hard' forms of power. (Hall et al. 2013: 19)

As Stuart Hall et al.'s use of scare quotes suggests, distinctions between soft and hard forms of power are problematic. However, they do indicate how consumer and celebrity cultures are often dismissed (in academia, as elsewhere) in contrast to the 'hard' powers of the legal system and the economy. One of our aims in this book is to show the significance of celebrity talk as a space in which dominant discourses are reproduced, as collectivist stories of social support and solidarity are replaced by individualist ones of hard work and authenticity. In these, struggle features as something to be overcome, located in the past, rather than something to be lived with and through in the present. These discourses construct inequality as part of the old world, with only 'melancholic migrants' or 'feminist killjoys' remaining hung up on discrimination, fixated on finding racism, sexism and class inequality where they 'no longer exist' (Ahmed 2004; Gill 2016).

Celebrity encourages and celebrates the figure of the agentic, autonomous, individualized neoliberal subject who is free of constraints. As discussed in earlier chapters, poverty, unemployment and other forms of 'failure' are increasingly understood as the result of individual pathologies (laziness, irresponsibility and so on) and poor 'choices' rather than inequality and discrimination (Gillborn 2010; Tyler 2013). The distinction with which we started this section – between 'deserving' and 'undeserving' celebrities – is central to these processes of individualization.

A discussion of UK musician Ed Sheeran's journey to fame in a group of middle-class young women concluded that 'he worked his way [up] by just playing all the time in gigs and on the streets, and then, he got signed' (Bella, SW, 16–17). Scarlett added, 'I think he actually deserves to be famous, because he worked really hard for it. Whereas someone like Justin Bieber has never really had to work for it.' As noted earlier, such comparisons and juxtapositions of the 'deserving' and the 'undeserving' occur often in the data. The sense of injustice directed at celebrities, like Bieber, gaining fame and wealth when they 'never really had to work for it', and the sense of justice associated with Sheeran's fame, reflect wider discourses circulating within austere meritocracy.

We have shown both the prominence and value given to hard work in young people's talk, and how this downplays the structural inequalities which shape their own and celebrities' education and career trajectories.

However, as we show in the next section, these very structures, notably of class and gender, shape what gets counted as hard work, and so who gets seen as hard working and who can be dismissed as following easy, and so valueless, routes to fame.

'What did she do to get famous?' Class, gender, race and the uneven ascription of hard work

In this section, we attend to the uneven practices of evaluation within young people's celebrity talk around hard work. We argue that female and/or working-class celebrities are disproportionately denied access to the privileged and celebrated position of the 'hard-working celebrity', and suggest that this has implications for how young people's aspirations are formed and valued.

The working-class young women in Louise Archer and colleagues' (2010: 70) study of 'at-risk' London school students largely produced 'glamorous' working-class hetero-femininities. By this, Archer et al. mean that they adopted a look combining 'elements of Black, urban US styles (notably "bling" fashion) with "unisex" (although often coded as "male") items of sportswear (such as Nike trainers or tracksuits) and hyper-feminine "sexy" clothes, make-up and hairstyles'. These served as a form of capital within their friendship groups but were constructed by teachers 'as both overtly and *overly* sexual and . . . positioned as antithetical to educational engagement and success' (Archer et al. 2010: 71, original emphasis). We found similar judgements operating in relation to celebrity.

Female celebrities adopting 'glamorous' working-class hetero-femininities were usually named as worthless and 'famous for nothing'. They typify the 'chav' or 'white trash' celebrity (Tyler & Bennett 2010; Yelin 2016) – generally (though not exclusively) working-class female celebrities associated with reality television and other devalued routes to fame (Williamson 2010). The placement of these figures within celebrity hierarchies is captured by Dave: 'Reality TV stars and models like Kim Kardashian, they're at the bottom of the celebrity pit . . . they've done nothing.' Later he explains:

> The Kardashians are only famous for really stupid reasons as opposed to athletes who are famous because they worked really hard for four years; and they come from another Olympics, they compete and work really hard against other athletes . . . and then they get some kind of recognition. (Dave, Manchester, 14–15)

By implication, Dave constructs the reasons for the Kardashians' fame as 'stupid' because they do not involve hard work. As in the next extracts, the Kardashian family, particularly its most visible member, Kim, was frequently referenced as the epitome of 'undeserved' fame:

> **Edward:** Isn't she only famous cos of the whole thing?
> **Interviewer:** Sex tape, yeah.
> **Edward:** Yeah. [laughs]
> **Sasha Fiers:** I can't stand her. (London, 16–17)

> I just think that there's people who work really hard to become someone . . . say like a really famous actress she's not just become famous she's had to work to be. . . . It's not just about the famous part, but she's had to work to be known that she's good at something. . . . Whereas they are just famous for being who they are really: being a Kardashian. (Naomi, Manchester, 14–15)

Similarly, we see below how UK reality television star Kerry Katona is derided for her illegitimate fame alongside Kardashian:

> **Julia:** Kim Kardashian, but like the whole Kardashian family, because they just sort of are out to go on TV and shout at each other a lot and it just winds me up.
> **Dumbledore:** People who are famous for being famous, who haven't actually got any talent whatsoever.
> **Julia:** She's famous because she walks around half naked, that sort of thing.
> **Jinny:** What's her face, Kerry Katona. What did she do to get famous? (SW, 14–15)

While most of the women judged in this way came from working-class backgrounds, Kim Kardashian's intersectional position is more complex (explained further in Chapter 4's case study). She is incredibly wealthy and part of a well-known dynasty and so lacks the humble beginnings of Katona or Price. However, her cultural capital is devalued within dominant discourses of work and success. She is associated with excessive and immoral sexuality through her high-profile relationships with black men, a sex-tape scandal and her curvaceous body. The association of her work with her body – through the sex tape, photo shoots in revealing clothing and via performing herself on a range of reality television shows – renders this 'non-work'. Kardashian was also talked about in terms of nepotism and unfairness in a way that members of the royal family and 'respectable' celebrity-child Jaden Smith (son of Will Smith) were not.

As we explore in Chapter 4, Kardashian, along with working-class women such as Katona, UK reality television star and model Katie Price and US musician and talent show judge Nicki Minaj, attracted disapproval which was linked to their perceived inauthenticity. Price's negative evaluation by participants was commonly made through talk about her over-the-top dress, inadequate mothering and multiple relationships with men, and Minaj's to her artificial and excessive body. In the next chapter, we show how authenticity is a critical element of becoming successful and happy within austere meritocracy. These stars are famous for, as Naomi puts it, 'being who they are'. Yet, as these data show, authenticity has no value for them as they do not represent the right kind of hard-working self (see also Allen & Mendick 2013). The only male celebrity who was regularly viewed as undeserving of his fame was Justin Bieber (as above); he was often feminized, with young people identifying his 'girlie' sound and 'soft voice'(Anzyi, Manchester, 16–17), 'scrawny' body and 'little muscles' (Mat Power, SW, 14–15) (Allen et al. 2015a). As discussed in the last chapter, he is also associated with young female fans.

Thus, young people's constructions of hard work mean that the labour involved in producing one's physical appearance (Skeggs 2004), or in nurturing family relationships (Reay 1998) is devalued. Our aim is not to argue the respective merits of these celebrities, or to compare activities as diverse as running a country, modelling, parenting, competing in the Olympics and starring in reality television, in relation to the work involved. Rather, we want to call attention to the significance of class, gender and race – and specifically the classed, gendered and racialized body – to these evaluations of hard work and deserved success. We also emphasise how celebrity reproduces powerful normative ideals of 'respectable femininity', through which black and white working-class women are constructed as sexually immoral, excessive and deviant (Skeggs 2004; Weekes 2002). They are the 'constitutive other' to the ideal subject of neoliberalism in that they represent the moral limit of propriety (Skeggs 2004). Throughout this book, but particularly here and in Chapter 8, we show how the working-class female celebrity, constructed as 'famous for nothing', plays a key role in sustaining wider social hierarchies (Allen & Mendick 2013; Tyler & Bennett 2010). As we elaborate on in Chapter 8, these hierarchies are also built into some academic writing on celebrity.

Returning to Archer and Francis's trichotomy of discourses of students in Table 3.1, these celebrities align with the 'demonized' category. Those hard workers examined in the last section map to the middle group of diligent workers, which contains many women and people from working-class and minority-ethnic backgrounds, the 'good' girls and 'deserving' black and/or working-class boys of celebrity. In addition to those mentioned earlier, this group includes Beyoncé, Emma Watson and Tom Daley. While their position is established via continual comparisons (such as that between Ed Sheeran and Justin Bieber cited above) and so perhaps carries an ever-present possibility of failure, this represents a significant shift, for they are not pathologized. Indeed, participants frequently cited them as 'ideal' celebrities.

However, Archer and Francis's 'ideal' group have not completely disappeared. One name came up more often than any other when we asked young people to discuss their ideal celebrity: US billionaire, technology entrepreneur and philanthropist Bill Gates. Across the data, white middle-class men, including many technology and social media innovators like Gates, were prominent within the talk about celebrities who had achieved success for the 'right' reasons and through the 'right' routes. They were associated with success achieved on the basis of intelligence, skill and passion (Mendick et al. 2016). Their fame and wealth were seen as a deserved by-product of their skill and talent rather than an aim in and of itself. These comments are typical of those about Gates: 'He's more famous for what he's like built, rather than for doing anything else so, yeah . . . I would say he is talented' (Stephano, Manchester, 16–17) and, 'He created one of the most used things in the world, and the amount of money he's given away to charity is just ridiculous' (Shane, London, 16–17). Female celebrities are completely absent from this elite group, and talk of 'talent' and 'creativity' signal discourses of natural intelligence that continue to exclude women and those from working-class backgrounds (Mendick 2006). Female participants were also markedly absent from discussions of these entrepreneurial celebrities. Hard work takes a background role in this talk, but even here their achievement is not valorized for its effortlessness.

So far, we have focused on mapping the dominant discourses of hard work, showing how, even as they make available successful subjectivities to those previously excluded from them, they simultaneously reproduce dominant distinctions around class, gender and race. However, discourses are never deterministic, as Michel Foucault (1976: 95) said, 'Where there is power, there is resistance, and yet, or rather consequently, this resistance is never in a position of exteriority in relation to power.' Indeed, we did find moments of ambiguity and contestation over what and who could be the subjects of hard work, but these were, as Foucault's words suggest, always constructed within, and in relation to, the dominant discourses of hard work. In the next section we explore in detail one such moment in order to ask, 'How can we work the power relations [around hard work] by which we are worked and in what direction?' (Butler 1997: 100).

'I don't think you can judge people': Struggles over hard work

In this section, we analyse one instance of dispute within the data in order to explore the limits of hard-work discourses, and the routes through which the demonized can gain value. We also point to a relationship between these challenges to dominant discourses and the classed, gendered and racialized positions of those participants speaking them. Here we draw on Bev Skeggs and Helen Wood's (2012: 59) study of women's class-differentiated readings of reality television which showed that popular cultural texts generate 'differently resourced reactions, characterized by contestation, ambivalence, resistance . . . judgments depend on forms of connection between text and viewer, and how these thread back to their own narratives, social positions, investments and the capitals they bring' (see also Allen & Mendick 2012).

Despite the general derision, we found that some participants valued celebrities like Kardashian, Katona and Price for being astute businesspeople and making it against the odds, recognizing their labour as good mothers and sisters. In these instances, participants refused the dominant judgements of hard work, mobilizing alternative readings which recognize and value forms of labour usually disregarded or degraded. The discussion we look at below is typical of these in the positions constructed. We have chosen it for its atypical length since this allows us to unpick overlapping strands within the same extract. The extract comes from a discussion about Katie Price that took place between 16- and 17-year-old students in London. Here, white working-class young women Mavie and Luigi dispute white middle-class Ally's rendering of Katie Price as 'not talented in any way' and 'one of the worst people I've ever seen':

Ally: She's one of the worst people I've ever seen in my life.
Luigi: But doesn't she help people that have got disabilities, like [her son] Harvey? . . . She was helping get a school back for people like, cos he had a school, or something, and it got closed down.
Ally: To be honest I don't think she even looks after him properly, let alone other people, so.
. . .
Luigi: She's got a busy life as well.
Ally: Yeah, but if she, er, she goes on holiday leaving her kids at home with a babysitter. I don't think that's really fair when they're growing up.
Mavie: She needs a break. . . . She's a single mum with three children.
Luigi: She only goes on holiday to do like, to promote her stuff.
Ally: Not really. Well, that's her fault, isn't it? Well that's her fault. . . . It's not like they're going to do it to go out there and earn money, are they? She's going out there just to go and get drunk with her friends.
Luigi: No, she might be promoting. Like I know she went abroad recently to do a modelling trip and stuff.
Mavie: But all her money does go to the kids.
Luigi: But to get money.
Ally: Yeah. And how did she used to do modelling? What did she used to do? Oh, just lift up her top, simple.
Mavie: Yeah, but I'm not being funny, you always bring in *The Sun* newspaper [containing topless photos] and flash that around anyway.

Ally: I don't mind, no no, not really. I mean that's one of the worst ways you can earn money. It's a rather sad way of earning money as well.

Mavie: I don't think you can judge people.

Ally: She's not talented in any way, is she?

Mavie: She's got a good business.

Ally: Huh?

Mavie: She's got a good business.

Luigi: Yeah, she's made a lot for herself, even though she –

Ally: Yeah, she's got a good business, but is it her that created it? And is it her that done all the stuff? No.

Mavie: Yeah, for her kids.

Ally: She's not a businesswoman, I'm telling you now, Katie Price is not a businesswoman.

Mavie: She owns Mamas and Papas. . . .

Ally: Yeah, she can own it, but, I think, oh, she's not a businesswoman, she's pathetic, honestly.

David: Did she make, or did she buy it?

Mavie: No, she made it all. (London, 16–17)

In evaluating whether Katie Price could be seen as 'hard working' or a 'good mother', participants both create categories and actively dispute their boundaries (Billig 1992). The persistence of Luigi and Mavie in the face of Ally suggests the collective possibility for claiming value in glamorous working-class femininities. But above all, we would argue that it is their positions as working-class and female that supports their defence of Price, connecting to Skeggs and Wood's (2012: 231) findings that some working-class women valued Price as part of defending 'their choice of full-time mothering against aspirational futures for the intrusive relational affective value it offered'.

After Ally denigrates Price, Luigi's opening attempt to defend her focuses on presenting her as a hard-working 'busy' mother and campaigner. Ally's response does not devalue mothering but seeks to reposition Price as an irresponsible mother to her 'growing' children who 'goes on holiday leaving her kids at home with a babysitter'. In the face of Ally's sustained resistance to their attempts to classify Price as a 'deserving' celebrity via campaigning and motherhood, Mavie and Luigi emphasize her commitment to working for her children ('all her money does go to the kids') and her entrepreneurial skills. This is the beginning of a shift in which Mavie and Luigi work to position Price as a businessperson, who's 'made a lot of herself', citing her ownership of Mamas and Papas as evidence. Mamas and Papas, a UK-based business catering for new parents and parents-to-be, has no connection with Price. Although factually incorrect, this claim functions in the group to give credibility to Price occupying a successful subjectivity. Mavie's response to David's question 'Did she make, or did she buy it?' with 'She made it all' finally ends the discussion. While it is likely Ally's feelings towards Price remain unchanged, he is effectively silenced in the group, as David, who normally sides with him, appears convinced.

However, we can see limits to what is possible within this dialogue. Mavie and Luigi are not able to position Price as successful through revaluing her modelling or reality television work, but only by making a claim to her being a creative businessperson. This claim is tentative, based on an inaccurate assertion that she has built a business based on her mothering, albeit a credible one given her success as an author of children's books and her equestrian clothing brand for adults. Policy rhetoric often positions working-class mothers as failures of aspiration and the antithesis of the ideal post-feminist subject who, combining motherhood with paid work, does not need support from the state (Allen et al. 2015b; McRobbie 2008). Only by converting the unpaid labour of motherhood – in this case working-class Price's mother-work – into the paid labour of business *does* motherhood get to count.

The strategies the young women use suggest that while they value motherhood and position Price as a striver for her children, they are required to frame this in relation to entrepreneurship and paid employment if they want to win the argument. Thus key distinctions around class, gender and hard work remain in place even as they are challenged. Again, our point is not to debate the merits of modelling as an aspiration for young women to pursue, but to call attention to the ways that hard work and deserved success get read off some bodies and forms of labour and not others. We return to these arguments in Chapter 7, which focuses on money. There we identify how some celebrities, from technological entrepreneurs to members of the royal family, are seen to deserve their wealth and status through a combination of their hard work, philanthropy, responsible consumption and societal impact.

Conclusion

As we outlined in Chapter 1, youth unemployment and underemployment is common to all economies implementing austerity measures, including the UK. As graduates are increasingly taking non-graduate posts, the rewards of a degree are less even as, with growing fees, the costs are higher. It is against this backdrop of the broken contract between the economic and education systems that we have seen an emerging focus on hard work.

In this chapter we have argued that, in contrast to previous research into young people's talk about learning, our data reveal young people's strong investment in the ethics and ideals of working hard as crucial to achieving and enjoying success. We mentioned earlier that this shift parallels one in policy. We can see other parallels, perhaps constituting a 'hard-work zeitgeist'. Although the near-elimination of coursework from public examinations in England could be seen as a move away from rewarding hard work, schools are increasingly 'preoccupied with policies of achievement, particularly public examination results' (Perryman et al. 2011: 179). This, alongside the introduction of high-stakes testing at ever-younger ages, may explain young people's increasing orientation to hard work. Alongside this relentless focus on credentialism, there have been wider cultural shifts. Malcolm Gladwell's (2008) book *Outliers* made available a narrative of hard work as the ultimate source of success, as he used diverse examples, from the Beatles to Bill Gates, to argue that it is 10,000 hours of labour rather than 'natural ability' that lies behind success. Similarly, our analysis of celebrity biographies shows that they rely on backstories that include hard work. For example, the opening page of a biography of 'self-confessed workaholic' (Vaughn, 2012: 56) Beyoncé tells us:

> Beyoncé possessed two very rare talents. The first was an innate ability to sing and dance, but the other was probably more important. Beyoncé knew that talent alone was never enough. Practice, dedication, and sacrifice were every bit as important as raw talent. That she sits on top of the world today validates her sacrifices, even if she's sometimes wistful for the lost years of childhood. (Vaughn 2012: 7, emphasis added)

As we discuss in the case study in Chapter 6, Beyoncé is a happy object: an object towards which we are drawn by the promise of happiness (Ahmed 2010a). The case study in this chapter is of actor Will Smith, another happy object. These celebrities' cultivated associations with hard work are central to their promise of happiness within austere meritocracy. In an era of narrowing opportunities and widening inequalities, we need to believe that hard work will be rewarded.

This investment in hard work operates as a key element within austere meritocracy, which celebrates entrepreneurialism and individualism while obscuring inequalities within education and the labour market. Celebrity narratives of individual achievement via hard work facilitate a shift from structural frameworks for understanding 'success' and 'failure' towards intimate, personal and individualized ones. Thus, while this opens up successful subjectivities to more people, exclusions remain. Women and the working class continue to be excluded from the realm of intellect and reason, which is coded as masculine, middle class and white; and white and black working-class women remain constrained in how and to what extent they can inhabit success. The fantasy that hard work is rewarded can be read as a form of cruel optimism: part of an attachment to objects whose realization is impossible within our current conditions. Young people's investment in hard work reflects the 'centrality of optimistic fantasy to reproducing and surviving in zones of compromised ordinariness' (Berlant 2006: 35).

CELEBRITY CASE STUDY: WILL SMITH

FIGURE 3.1 *Will Smith, photograph by Vanessa Lua,*
no changes made. Licence https://creativecommons.org/
licenses/by/2.0/.

Given the value attached to hard work, many celebrities project an image of themselves as dedicated and determined. US actor and musician Will Smith offers an extreme example. Smith came to mainstream public attention through the US 1990s sitcom *The Fresh Prince of Bel-Air,* in which he plays a character also called Will who was raised on 'the streets of Philadelphia' and is sent to live with wealthy relatives in their Bel-Air mansion. Two decades after its finale, this series airs daily on UK television and our data attest to how powerfully it influences how young people see him, as do his many films and well-publicized family, particularly his teenage children, son Jaden and daughter Willow, and their music and acting ventures. Further, as discussed below, Smith circulates as an inspirational figure via social media. Throughout these representations, hard work is integral to his public and 'private' persona.

Smith's 'sickening work ethic' is the central theme of Lisa Iannucci's (2010) official biography, featuring on most of its 127 pages. Iannucci describes how, in childhood, through his parents' efforts and values, 'Will finally learned the meaning of the words work ethic' (2010: 6). She quotes extensively from interviews in which Smith discusses his hard work, rejecting the distinction between talent and skill:

> The separation of talent and skill is one of the greatest misunderstood concepts for people who are trying to excel, who have dreams, who want to do things. Talent you have naturally. Skill is only developed by hours and hours and hours of beating on your craft. . . . I've never really viewed myself as particularly talented. Where I excel is ridiculous, sickening work ethic. You know, while the other guy's sleeping, I'm working. While the other guy's eating, I'm working. (Legacy Education Resources undated)

Earlier we identified an opposition between effortless achievement and hard work. Smith positions himself against effortless achievement not just as something inaccessible to him but because hard work is morally superior: in austere meritocracy, achievement has the most value if you have worked for it.

The most striking example of Smith's work ethic is his commitment to die on a treadmill: 'The only thing that I see that is distinctly different about me is: I'm not afraid to die on a treadmill. You might have more talent than me; you might be smarter than me. But if we get on a treadmill together, there's two things: you're getting off first, or I'm gonna die' (Legacy Education Resources undated). Less dramatic but no less powerful is his assertion that determination can overcome even the certainty of mathematics:

> Two plus two only equals four if you accept that two plus two equals four. Two plus two's gonna be what I want it to be. . . . There's a redemptive power that making a choice has, you know, rather than feeling like you're an affect to all the things that are happening. . . . You really can make what you want. (iManifestWealth 2010)

Smith prefaces these remarks by saying he wants to 'be an idea' and to 'represent possibilities'. He is austere meritocracy's ideal celebrity, representing the power of individual freedom and choice over constraint: 'You just decide what it's gonna be, who you're gonna be, how you're gonna do it.'

These statements on motivation, success and happiness circulate widely online. They are compiled into inspirational YouTube videos with uplifting backing music. Many such videos have hundreds of thousands or millions of views. While Smith does not have his own Twitter account, his quotations circulate as memes, exemplars of self-help, entrepreneurialism and motivation. They foreground the power of self-belief and hard work: 'Tough times don't last, tough people do', 'The first step is you have to say that you can.' The characters that Smith plays in his films are central to his representation and quotations from them sit alongside his own words, barely distinguishable from each other as his on-screen persona and 'private' self blur. 2013's *After Earth* had one line that resonated, on the power of choice: 'Do not misunderstand me, danger is very real, but fear is a choice.' In *The Pursuit of Happyness*, Smith plays Chris Gardner, a poor salesman who loses his wife, job and home, but who becomes, through his will and determination, a stockbroker, embodying the American Dream. At one point Will Smith (as Chris) tells Jaden Smith (as Chris's son):

> Hey, don't ever let anybody tell you you can't do something, not even me. You got a dream, you got to protect it. When people can't do something themselves they wanna tell you you can't do it. You want something, you go get it. Period.

Smith's representation is a source of inspiration for many. Yet we find its individualism troubling. In insisting on the power of hard work, Smith denies constraints: fear can be overcome, dedication eclipses talent. Smith's success philosophy leaves little space for considering structural inequalities, including racism. This is explicit in his response to Barack Obama's election as America's first black president:

> When Barack Obama won, it validated a piece of me that I wasn't allowed to say out loud – that America is not a racist nation. I love that all of our excuses have been removed. . . . There's no white man trying to keep you down, because if he were really trying to keep you down, he would have done everything he could to keep Obama down. . . . If Barack Obama can win the presidency of the United States, you can absolutely be the manager at Saks.

This 'post-race' narrative belies the persistence – and indeed entrenchment – of racialized inequalities in America across the realms of education, employment, housing, political participation and criminal justice. The US system of mass incarceration is the reason why 'a black child born today is less likely to be raised by both parents than a black child born during slavery' (Alexander 2012: 26). Successes like Obama's and Smith's do not only coexist with racism but enable racism by concealing it and legitimizing Smith's position that 'America is not a racist nation.' As Eddie Glaude Jr (2016: 6) argues, the deaths of African-Americans at the hands of the police, and the disproportionate loss of wealth by black America following the financial crisis have 'shattered any illusion we might have had about a post-racial America'.

4

Authenticity

Within austere meritocracy, success must not only be arrived at through effort but through authenticity. It has become a moral imperative that we know – and express – who we *really* are through our actions and relationships, from what we write on our Facebook pages to our choice of furniture. As Nikolas Rose writes,

> Humans are addressed, represented and acted upon as if they were selves of a particular type: suffused with an individualised subjectivity, motivated by anxieties and aspirations concerning their self fulfilment, committed to finding their true identities and maximising their authentic expression in their lifestyles. (Rose 1996: 169)

Increasingly, our relationship to work is governed by this ethical ideal of authenticity. Work is no longer something we do simply to earn money to live, but a space of self-realization and an expression of our 'true selves'. This makes work a site of optimism, as a source of personal fulfilment. Yet, this is another example of what Lauren Berlant (2011) calls a cruel attachment. The promise of authenticity, like the promise of hard work, is that it will overcome disadvantages that cannot be overcome. The investment in work as a site of authentic self-realization legitimizes the declining material and psychological rewards of labour under global capitalism which is characterized by burgeoning low-paid, casualized and unstable work (Shildrick et al. 2012; Standing 2014). It places responsibility onto workers to shape their careers in line with their 'inner selves', reducing the responsibility of employers to provide secure and 'decent' employment. Work is part of a wider 'fantasy of "entrepreneurship"' (du Gay 1996: 70) in which we must create our own opportunities.

In dominant discourses, young people's aspirations are understood to emerge from within, driven by self-knowledge. Across policy and popular cultural discourses, young people are encouraged to 'follow their dreams'.

However, government policy imposes a hierarchy of aspirations based on a middle-class model, privileging some pathways and denigrating others. As such, young people are compelled to express their 'authenticity' through aligning themselves with socially sanctioned aspirations. Our participants, like those in Elsa Davidson's (2011: 103) US research, 'sought to cultivate themselves and define their authenticity through their career aspirations and individual tastes while simultaneously struggling to measure up to social and academic standards that conflicted with ideals of self-cultivation through freedom of expression and creative exploration'. As we will show, for some young people, the demand to aspire implies becoming 'someone else'. These young people must take the risk that their aspirations are judged as failing the additional demand to remain true to oneself.

Celebrity talk offers a space for young people to negotiate these demands. Authenticity is an enduring trope within celebrity, as stardom unites 'the spectacular with the everyday, the special with the ordinary' (Dyer 1979: 35). While traditional media have long promised behind-the-scenes insights into the real person behind the image, reality television and social media extend these promises, revealing to us the seemingly banal, candid and authentic aspects of celebrities' private lives (Allen & Mendick 2012; Marwick & Boyd 2011). Consumers are encouraged to engage critically with these aspects, actively 'test[ing] out their own notions of the real, the ordinary, and the intimate against the representations before them' (Murray & Oullette 2009: 8; see Gamson 1994). These practices of testing out 'the real' and their relationship to young people's aspirations are the focus of this chapter. In the first two sections, we show how young people are strongly invested in authenticity, exploring how it features in their individual aspirations and how they evaluate celebrities in relation to it. We show how fame and success are positioned as justified if they have been earned by remaining 'true to yourself'. In the next section of the chapter we explore how stories about celebrities as authentic – or not – are classed, gendered and racialized, focusing on judgements of their philanthropy and appearance. In the final section, we discuss how stories and disputes about celebrity authenticity have an impact on young people from different backgrounds.

'I can't really remember like a day where I decided I wanted to do it': Career pathways as self-realization

Earlier research has shown that young people's career aspirations balance intrinsic factors, such as enjoyment, and extrinsic factors, such as pay and status (Ball et al. 2000; Hodkinson 2008). We, too, found this, however, intrinsic factors dominate across the full range of pathways. For example, Archibald Brunel (SW, 16–17), who wants to work in either the police force or the army ('to keep some order'), speaks about how, from being part of the local Cadets Force, 'You get this sense of satisfaction, like you can use a weapon and you can strip it down, assemble it backwards, and like you get all these other people that have just joined and you feel like, "oh yeah, you know, I can do this better than people."' Louise (Manchester, 16–17) plans to become a nurse, a route with government funding for her higher education fees (through a bursary programme that has since been cut). But her decision predates the tripling of university tuition fees that made this funding significant. Louise relates it to childhood experiences of asthma during which she spent a lot of time in hospital. She recalls, 'I know like a nurse said something to me and I liked it, but I don't remember what it was she said, because I was little, but like I thought I want to do this job.' Archibald and Louise are typical in aspiring to careers through which they can express a sense of self, whether they find this in managing a weapon or nursing patients.

In the individual interviews, we asked participants about their career plans and their reasons for them. We also asked them for any memories attached to these careers. In asking them to connect aspirations and memories we were more likely to generate emotional accounts of self-realization than had we simply asked them why they wanted to do what they did, a question that generated more rational, pragmatic accounts. Yet, these memories appeared easily in most cases, suggesting that participants saw them as part of their decision making. We discuss this more in Chapter 6, where we show that career fulfilment is an anticipated site of happiness for young people. There, as here, the discourse is not totalizing. Person McPerson (London, 16–17), discussed in Chapter 6, and Lolita (SW, 16–17) do not offer any career aspirations to their interviewers. Rick (London, 16–17) feels, 'I have to get some more life experience before I can decide . . . really what I want to do' but talks about pursuing a job related to his enjoyment of reading. Dumbledore (SW, 16–17), discussed in Chapter 5, recalls his childhood fascination with cocaine and aspires to pleasure through rejecting authorized career pathways. A few young people held specific aspirations without associated memories, focusing on their interest in a subject: Aliyah (Manchester, 16–17) in medicine, Herbert (SW, 14–15) in geography, and Schmidt (London, 16–17) in law. Olivia Bolt (SW, 16–17) recalls at around 14 being given a 'big careers book' by her mum with 'every imaginable career in it. . . . And when I had finished going through it I realized all the jobs, most of them I'd pointed out were like law-related.' Others focused on external goals. Zayneb (Manchester, 14–15) is studying mathematics and science to get a good job and support her mum. Kirsty (Manchester, 14–15) talks about the money and status of dentistry. Manjula (Manchester, 16–17) remembers: 'I started researching . . . and then finance come up, and then financial managers are good because I heard they're top paid and stuff.' As we explore in Chapters 5 and 7, having enough to get by matters but very few young people prioritized money. The remaining forty-one participants discussed memories – often poignant ones– that oriented them towards their future employment as a mode of self-realization.

The discourse of self-realization constructs careers as a reflection and a development of an essential self. We can see this in the interviews with Mike, a young woman who wants to be a wildlife photographer, and Will Smith, a young man who wants to be an outdoor instructor.

> I've always wanted to do like animals and stuff since I was little. I've always been into photography and stuff, so I can't really remember like a day where I decided I wanted to do it. I just always remembered liking animals and I remember when I was younger though, think it was the first year we moved here my brother brought me like a great big thick animals book and I read it cover to cover and I made a list of all the endangered species, [both laugh] when I was like 7 it took me like four hours. (Mike, SW, 16–17)

> I climbed my first mountain when I was about 3 or 4. . . . I remember standing on top and standing on the tree point and just being like, 'I'm here. I've done it'. Like because I've been up and like mum had carried me up and dad carried me up in a rucksack thing before and it – since I was crawling around on the floor but then it was just – like I just remember the achievement of doing it and being up there and like I found a picture the other day of me and I looked quite good, . . . a massive toothy grin on my face. I was soaking wet as well. (Will Smith, SW, 16–17)

Mike and Will talk of desires dating back to early childhood. Mike repeatedly says 'always' in relation to her interests in animals and photography, interests that she combines in her career choice. Will remembers not just climbing his first mountain but that 'mum had carried me up and dad carried me up in a rucksack . . . since I was crawling around on the floor'. Both describe feats that mark them out from other children: spending hours listing endangered species at age 7, or climbing a mountain 'soaking wet' at age 3 or 4. Their accounts suggest that it is the 'authenticity' of these activities – their emergence from and reflection of an inner self – that sustains the hard work needed for success.

Self-realization, while an individualized resource, expresses relationships with others. As in Louise's aspiration to be a nurse, it is often accomplished through helping others. Participants offered memories of being helped by dieticians, dentists and doctors as sources for their own aspirations. Sasha (London, 16–17) is one of many who talks about giving back to her parents, being true to her family through her work. Sasha wants a career as a businesswoman in the creative arts: 'For me it's more about my career, and my parents, my family, cos like they do a lot for me, so I just want to do the same for them.' She combines this with a memory of getting her nursery teacher to take her to every performance of an event by saying,

'Miss, why don't you take me? I am better than the other students, so take me to it, because I want to do it'. . . . And then apparently the teacher goes, 'Oh, she's the first child I've seen who speaks like this'. [both laugh] I've always been into creative stuff like that. If there's a crea – like something performance going on, like even in school, like you can ask like any of the teachers, I've always been involved.

This memory is part of Sasha's family narrative as she explains that 'yesterday, my mum was speaking to my dad about this'. Sasha – like Mike and Will – positions herself as 'naturally' drawn to the arts. Like them, she tells of a feat that distinguishes her out from other children, accomplished at a young age. Like Mike, she uses the word 'always' to suggest that there has never been a moment when she was influenced towards creativity, even as she describes a pivotal event that did just that, creating a story that has been told and retold to cement the dream.

Social constraints are missing from these accounts. They appear only in a few instances where people held multiple aspirations, some more pragmatic and not spoken of as routes to self-realization. Peter York (SW, 14–15) wants to pursue a musical career and associates this with powerful memories going back to his early years at school. He feels the only viable route is via the Royal Marines Band, which offers secure employment and 'you get one-on-one tutoring. . . . The only problem is . . . I'm not really one for like going out and shooting lots of people.' His fall back is biology, about which he shares no memories, but talks of an interest 'mostly to do with the body'. In her interview, Dory (SW, 16–17) shares memories of football: 'Me, my brother and my dad have loved it since I was four.' But she is resigned to how 'my future's kind of like the same as mum's to be honest, I want to go into childcare route'. Peter York and Dory's talk indicates the possibilities of sociological understandings of their choices as embedded in processes of social reproduction and unequal opportunity structures. Yet the dominant discourse of authenticity makes such understandings difficult: if your career choice is a manifestation of your essential self it cannot also be socially constrained. Louise's choice of nursing, presented as freely made and authentic to her, is a common one for working-class young women seeking social mobility and 'respectability' (Huppatz 2012; Skeggs 1997). All four of those who, like Archibald, spoke of aspiring to the army came from rural schools and – apart from Peter York – linked this to experiences of Ten Tors, an annual hiking challenge for teenagers in South West England. Will's rejection of university and his desire to be outside rather than inside are narrated by him as a way to 'just carry on being the way I am'. Yet, they fit a more general orientation to earning over learning that research has found to be common among white working-class boys, and is discussed in Chapter 5 (Archer et al. 2010; Ward 2016). While authenticity, like hard work, is enormously enabling for young people, its erasure of the social conditions of such choices mean it needs critical interrogation.

'she had faith in what she'd done, and she believed it could go somewhere, and it did': Celebrity, authenticity and making it against the odds

Our participants viewed fame as a space where desirable opportunities were undercut by risks to authenticity. As Joanna (London, 14–15) warns, celebrities can 'get caught up in their own life, . . . they lose who they are'. Participants placed great value on those celebrities whom they perceived had 'stayed true to themselves' within the extraordinary circumstances of extreme wealth and media scrutiny. Reflecting previous research into audience engagement with authenticity in popular culture, they took pleasure in seeking out and evaluating instances of 'the real' (Gamson 1994).

Young people's ideas of celebrity authenticity involve a constellation of traits: genuineness, ordinariness, relatability and humility. For example, Ginny (London, 14–15), speaking of the qualities that make a good role model, says, 'They need to be genuine, like they need to be relatable.' Similarly, Somaya (Manchester, 16–17) explains 'being real' as 'if they're not that rich then they shouldn't show off themselves as being really rich, and as higher than other celebrities. They should accept and just live with what they have. . . . You don't have to be so selfish.' 'Show[ing] off', through announcing your wealth, is deemed arrogant, selfish and inauthentic. In contrast, mundane or embarrassing behaviours were offered as evidence of authenticity: talking off the cuff, making mistakes and doing what 'ordinary' people do (Billig 1992; Harvey et al. 2015). US actor Jennifer Lawrence was the archetypal celebrity praised for resisting the artifice of the celebrity industry, exemplified in well-publicized actions, such as ordering a burger at the Oscars, tripping up on live television and resisting the pressure to be skinny. Typically, Strawberry (London, 16–17) likes Lawrence and sees her as 'sending out a positive message' because 'she's just normal. Like she was on the red carpet and she was ordering McDonald's. . . . And then she tripped and just laughed at herself.' Lawrence is rendered 'just normal' despite how the act of drawing attention to these events marks them as out of the ordinary.

Thus, as with hard work in the last chapter, through their celebrity talk and in their own aspirations, participants showed a strong investment in authenticity as central to, and necessary for, future success and happiness. As with hard work, authenticity recurs in young people's talk of individual strength, resilience and agency – as in Mike and Will's memories above. Across the dataset, young people drew upon backstories of celebrities escaping poverty and overcoming oppression via the realization of their true self, achieved by cultivating their talent.

South American footballers like Ronaldinho, for example, I know him, er, he just like spent every day kicking a ball of socks around to start with, and then he got scouted and became possibly the best player in the world, and maybe one of the best players ever. And then, he still spends lots of money on like, like loads of the slums in Brazil to try and help them have better living conditions and stuff like that. (Herbert, SW, 16–17)

Harry Potter had been rejected 12 times before it actually got published, and the fact that [J. K. Rowling] kept going, and kept sending it back after it had gotten rejected just shows like she had – she had faith in what she'd done, and she believed it could go somewhere, and it did. (Ginny, London, 14–15)

[Stephen Hawking's] disabled and he's that amazing, and normal people just think that because you're disabled you're like stupid. But he's got some sort of like brain condition, and he can still, he's still like the cleverest person in the world. (Timothy E, SW, 14–15)

These extracts convey that, whether your talent is for sport, writing or science, dedication to this and remaining true to it will triumph in the end. This narrative of perseverance is one of pursuing an authentic dream, rather than changing paths when faced with obstacles to that self-fulfilment. A 'ball of socks' is a symbol of ordinariness, poverty and the capacity for someone's inner drive to tackle adversity. Ronaldo de Assis Moreira's – aka Ronaldinho's – ongoing focus on the 'slums of Brazil' where he came from is further evidence of his authenticity, giving back to where he came from. Eleanor-Marie (London, 14–15), in the same London school as Ginny, says of Rowling, 'She was poor. She used to write on scraps of paper at cafés, she literally had nothing, and now look at her.' Like Ronaldinho, Rowling's backstory serves as proof not just of her 'ordinariness'. It also suggests that success can be achieved through having 'faith' and not accepting others' judgements of you (despite the poverty symbolized by the meagre 'scraps of paper'). Alongside Ronaldinho, other South American footballers, such as Lionel Messi and Luis Suarez, and a few working-class UK footballers, such as Steven Gerrard and David Beckham, were valued as 'real' people who had 'come from nothing' (Syndicate, London, 16–17). These classed backstories of celebrities overcoming humble origins through dogged persistence serve as powerful evidence of their authenticity. However, working-class celebrities occupy a perilous position in relation to judgements of authenticity. As we show below and in later chapters, they are often deemed inauthentic through their associations with 'excessive' bodies, wealth or consumption.

Indeed, while some footballers were celebrated for their ordinariness, as we elaborate on in Chapter 7, there was far more talk of how footballers' wealth was an indication that they had failed to stay true to themselves and their working-class roots. In contrast, the immense wealth attached to royalty did not prevent members of the royal family being seen as authentic. Alongside Kate Middleton (the subject of Chapter 7's celebrity case study),

Harry Windsor was positioned as ordinary and liked by almost all of the participants. Central to this construction of Harry are his laddish antics (such as playing strip poker in Las Vegas), and his military role. As with Lawrence, Prince Harry's ordinariness is deemed to be *out of the ordinary* and thus praiseworthy. As Joe (SW, 16–17) says, 'Even if he is in the royal family, he's just a normal guy. He fights for our country. He's just trying to be a normal bloke, he wants to go out and have a good laugh.' Paris agrees with Joe, 'He's young. Like, I'd say that's like what every young person would be doing.' Britney responds by underlining that this shows his authenticity, 'People like him for what he is, and not for what he like pretends to be.' Both 'hav[ing] a good laugh' and joining the military help construct him as staying true to himself. Tom describes this as (almost) inspirational:

> Obviously he's in the royal family, he should have some form of like restraints but like that whole Las Vegas thing when he went out [laughs] like that's just who he is. Like he's young. He's gonna – although he's in the royal family it doesn't like necessarily stop him from doing what he wants to do. I think that's quite, I wouldn't say inspirational but I'd say he's staying true to who he is, and I think that's what you need to do.

There are similarities between this and the discussions of young celebrities in Chapter 2 – such as singers Justin Bieber and Willow Smith – who also attracted empathy for the pressures of growing up in public. Young people's celebrity talk provides a space to articulate the difficulties of 'staying true to yourself' while navigating others' (parents, teachers, the media) hopes and expectations of you which you may not share. Yet, as we have argued in these opening sections, authenticity figures as an individualized resource for tackling problems and inequalities. It downplays distinctions of class, gender and race, even while, as we show in the next section, it reproduces them.

'Fake means that they're literally not themselves, like some of their body parts just aren't real': Class, gender, race and inauthentic celebrity

Participants were highly critical of those celebrities they judged as fake. Sometimes young people applied this label to celebrities in general. For example, Kadija (Manchester, 16–17) feels that celebrities 'have their own culture and they sell it because that's how they make money. So then I start questioning: I don't know them as a person, so is that the real them?' But accusations of inauthenticity were largely targeted at *specific* celebrities: namely working-class, female and black celebrities. We can see this in talk about philanthropy. Normally, as we show in Chapter 7, philanthropy is admired by young people. Yet this relies on young people assessing charitable acts as authentic. Of the twenty-four men mentioned for their charity work in the group interviews, just one – the child abuser Jimmy Saville – was talked about as fake. This compares to two out of fourteen women whose charity work was labelled fake: singers Madonna and Tulisa. Most of the other attacks on male celebrities' charity were directed at footballers, depicting their actions as publicity stunts. For example, when Steve (SW, 16–17) says that 'there are footballers who do give their wages away to charity, Jinny responds, 'They do that because they're in the press.' This echoes the classed distinctions discussed above. Overall, more than twice as many men's philanthropy as women's was spoken of solely as authentic. This reflects a wider pattern that judgements of inauthenticity are overwhelmingly directed at women. As we demonstrate, their bodies are central to these judgements.

In the exercise where young people imagined that our twelve case-study celebrities attended their school, participants distanced themselves from celebrities they deemed fake, usually Katie Price, Kim Kardashian and Nicki Minaj.

> I'd avoid them because they come across as very fake people, erm, and the only reason that they're famous is because of their looks. They have no talent whatsoever, and that bugs me, erm, and I can't, I can't, I couldn't like them. They don't deserve what they've got. That's how I feel, especially Katie Price. She's the worst out of all of them, erm, and I don't know, they just, they're famous for the sake of being famous. (Rick, London, 16–17)

> [Price] is way too fake, and I don't like the way she, how she's become famous. So if she was our age I could just see her being very up herself, and arrogant. . . . [She became famous] purely because of her body and like it wasn't because she had a special talent. (Izzy, SW, 14–15)

Inauthentic celebrity is deemed undeserving. It is achieved through exploiting your body rather than through the legitimized means of talent and hard work. Becoming somebody through 'illegitimate' means involves arrogance, selfishness and betraying one's 'true self'. Such evaluations of inauthenticity draw on discourses of corporeal excess. The 'fake' body – via cosmetic surgery or 'over-the-top' make-up or dress – constitutes evidence of inauthenticity and provokes disapproval. Saafi (Manchester, 14–15) puts it succinctly: 'Fake means that they're literally not themselves, like some of their body parts just aren't real.' As Alexandra Sastre (2013: 123) argues, Kim Kardashian's 'curvaceous body' is 'a site where both her "realness" and artificiality lie'. The following extract about black US musician and *American Idol* judge Nicki Minaj also exemplifies this:

Strawberry: I don't like Nicki Minaj. I think she is a bad role model.

George: If you look at her message, it's horrible, innit?

Lewis J: She's fake. She's fake.

Pringles: She is completely fake, but she tries – like I've seen documentaries and stuff about her, but she just – it looks like she's trying to be really nice, but then behind the scenes you don't know what she's like. . . .

Lewis J: She had implants in. . . .

Pringles: She puts on a fake accent, like –

Taylor: She puts on a fake Jamaican accent. . . . Like a Caribbean accent.

George: She's from Trinidad, that's it.

Pringles: It's like 'you're never from there'. She's completely fake and she puts on a fake image.

Lewis J: Maybe she doesn't like who she is.

Pringles: She doesn't show who she really is.

Strawberry: Well obviously, she got butt implants.

Pringles: But then you can't really –

Taylor: Nose job.

Lewis J: You don't – then how are you going to know if she's a good person? She's hiding behind an image that makes her look like a good person, then she must be a bad person. (London, 16–17)

Minaj's cosmetic surgery and accent are taken as attempts to project inaccurate images of her as 'a good person'. This talk is performative. By expressing disapproval of those they deem fake, young people demonstrate their own investment in the moral imperative to 'show who [you] really' are.

Judged according to this moral imperative, working-class female celebrities fall short, marked as either too authentic or not authentic enough. Price, Minaj and Kardashian's hyper-feminine bodies – 'big boobs, and fake hair and fake make-up' (Paris, SW, 16–17) – break the codes of idealized, 'natural', restrained white middle-class femininity (Skeggs 1997). Their bodies not only carry signs of effort but celebrate them, representing deliberate desires to be looked at (Yelin 2016). These performances of femininity are coded working class, even when taken up by celebrities from privileged backgrounds such as Kardashian, as we explore in the case study at the end of this chapter. Such spectacular bodies contrast with the seemingly effortless beauty of actors like Emma Watson, Ginnifer Godwin and Jennifer Lawrence. For example, Isabella (SW, 14–15) favours Watson's 'natural beauty' and Lolita (SW, 16–17) sees her as 'genuinely a nice person. . . . Like they all go kind of arrogant, she's stayed quite true to herself.' Ginny (London, 14–15) commends Godwin's boyish haircut as a sign of her resisting social pressure and being authentic: 'She doesn't want to change for anyone else. She's her for her.' Value is attached to naturalness and this is central to bourgeois respectability, while artifice is 'de-valued for being made visible' (Skeggs 2004: 101). Mocked for her behaviour and voice, or vilified for her failed attempts at class passing, the 'celebrity chav' (Tyler & Bennett 2010) or 'white trash' celebrity (Negra & Holmes 2008) is marked as deviant.

Black and white working-class celebrities carry a special burden in relation to investments in authenticity. A proliferation of celebrity biographies and autobiographies emphasize their backgrounds, fetishizing humble beginnings and rags-to-riches journeys, circulating the powerful backstories we glimpsed earlier in talk of Rowling and Ronaldinho. Meanwhile, reality television constructs working-class people as 'ordinary' and 'signs of the real' (Biressi & Nunn 2008: 4). Graeme Turner (2010) identifies a 'demotic turn' in celebrity. Demotic is defined by the Oxford English Dictionary as 'denoting or relating to the language used by ordinary people'. Turner applies this to celebrity to describe the increasing visibility of 'ordinary' people and 'everyday' acts, either through creating celebrities out of ordinary people (through shows like *Big Brother* and *X-Factor* contestants) or by emphasizing celebrities' ordinariness (such as *Keeping Up with the Kardashians*). However, this is not a sign of wider social levelling or a democratic public sphere. Rather, Turner (2006: 157) demonstrates, as we do, that celebrity 'remains a systematically hierarchical and exclusive category'. So being working-class can propel some to celebrity – as a sign of their ordinariness, bolstering media-driven fantasies of social mobility. But their class also limits the value that they can acquire (Allen & Mendick 2013; Williamson 2010), risking accusations of pretension, 'a charge levelled at people . . . in whom there is a gap between being and seeming' (Lawler 1999: 17). Similar dynamics operate in relation to race. For example, young people who are seen as not behaving in ways authentic to their blackness are labelled Oreos or coconuts to signal they are black on the outside but white on the inside (Chun 2011; Ellis forthcoming). In the final section we show how this uneven distribution of authenticity has an impact on different young people, creating clashes – for some – between the demands to aspire and to be authentic.

'You should have another role model': Clashes between authenticity and aspiration

In Luigi and Mavie's discussion of Katie Price in the last chapter, we demonstrated how dominant ideas around hard work and 'deserving' celebrity are subject to contestation. Similar disputes occur in discussions of celebrity authenticity, manifest in disagreements about stories of celebrities' philanthropy, addiction, relationships and illnesses. For example,

Louise: Demi Lovato, because like she was like in rehab, and everything, and she had like loads of problems, and she like overcame it,
and stuff. And like people can like look up to her. . . . She had like
eating disorders, and everything. And like she cut herself. And then,
and that was like, people who have like –

Lexus Lewis: Would you not class that as attention seeking?

Louise: No, because she was actually ill.

Lexus Lewis: Oh right.

Louise: Like normally you'd think like, oh, they're just putting it on,
but she was actually ill.

Lexus Lewis: Because you can, like you can, you can just prevent
things like that yourself.

Louise: Yeah, but –

Lexus Lewis: If you think of – if you're strong enough minded then
you can, you can just overcome it yourself.

Louise: Yeah, but if you're not strong minded, then. . . . And she's like,
she's not really made a fuss about it. She sort of like stays like out
of the limelight. (Manchester 16–17)

While Louise agrees with Lexus that stories of celebrity mental health
problems are 'normally' manufactured instances of 'attention seeking' and
'putting it on', she excludes Lovato from this, stating repeatedly that she
was 'actually ill'. Lexus disagrees, asserting the power of the individual to
'overcome it yourself' and so questioning the need to share this publicly.
While Louise in part agrees, her response suggests a more empathetic reading of celebrities' vulnerability to mental illness. She again counters claims
of attention seeking and reasserts the reality of Lovato's illness by citing
how she has 'not really made a fuss about it'. In this extract, as in the debate
about Price in Chapter 3, we get a sense that those on each side have different investments in the outcome. Louise is invested in Lovato's authenticity,
presumably because she feels a connection with her. In the individual interview, she reasserts Lovato's position as a 'role model' to people with eating
disorders and selects her as the celebrity with whom she most wants to go
to school. As discussed earlier, Louise was often in hospital as a child and so
the narrative of Lovato's vulnerability and strength in recovery may be part
of this connection and investment in Lovato's authenticity.

In this instance, Louise can find authorized discourses through which to
defend Lovato. But what of those young people who feel a connection with
those celebrities derided within the dominant value system? This question is
raised for us when Snoop (London, 16–17) explains why he would like to
meet the late African-American rapper Tupac Shakur:

Cos I genuinely like him and ah, he's real, and like, he talks about the
struggles that people go through, and he's not just saying that he's a thug
or where he came from the streets. He just explains, whereas the other

rappers, they just talk about what they've done. . . . Even if there is some
people don't like him, I want to say he is my role model. . . . When I went
to my work experience, one of them said to me, they go 'who's your,
who's your role model'? I said: 'Tupac'. She goes: 'right'. And I explain
everything to her, she just couldn't, she said: 'I think he shouldn't be your
role model, you should have another role model'.

What Snoop values about Tupac is his authenticity ('he's real') which
he links to his humility and altruism, explaining that Tupac gave voice
to 'the struggles that people go through' rather than focusing on himself.
Snoop's investment in Tupac as authentic is informed by his social positioning, sharing Tupac's black working-class background and his Islamic faith.
Yet, as this encounter on his work experience shows, both Tupac and the
pathway he represents are not socially valued as aspirational. The rejection of Tupac as Snoop's role model can be understood to be embedded
within a long-standing moral panic surrounding black and working-class
young men's underachievement in education and employment, and circulating through media and policy sites (Francis 2006; Roberts 2014). Within
this rhetoric, underachievement and unemployment are primarily located
as resulting from a lack of 'positive male role models' within working-class
and black communities, presenting positive 'role models' as a solution to the
underachievement of 'problem boys' and a perceived 'crisis in masculinity'
(Alexander 2017; Gunter 2010). This reductive response negates the role
of structural disadvantage and discrimination within young men's lives and
transitions (Tarrant et al. 2015). It is also a deficit model, drawing on historical discourses of working-class and black masculinity as deviant and in
need of repair (Hamad 2014).

The boundary drawing around 'good' and 'bad' role models parallels the
opposition between youth as hope/potential and youth as troublesome/at
risk identified in Chapter 2. It also parallels the distinctions discussed in
Chapter 3. Like the ideal pupil of austere meritocracy, the good role model is
hard working, entrepreneurial and authentically talented. The classification
of Tupac as an unsuitable role model for Snoop contrasts starkly with the
dominant representation of another African American celebrity, and occa-
sional rapper, Will Smith, whose case study is included in Chapter 3. While
Smith presents a 'non-threatening' black masculinity, Tupac's status as a
hip-hop artist positions him within wider classed and racialized discourses
preoccupied with the link between violence and rap music (Rose 1994).
Smith, as we saw, brushes aside 'unhappy' talk of racism, projecting the message that anything is possible if you try hard enough. In contrast, Tupac's
'talk about the struggles that people go through' cannot be safely contained
within austere meritocracy's discourses of social mobility, hard work and
optimism. Rather, Tupac's music directly connects these struggles to race
and racism. Snoop does not abandon Tupac as his role model. However, as
he recalls this encounter we see him struggle with the disjuncture between

the ways of being he values and those approved by teachers and employers. We can see similar negotiations throughout our data when the dual demands to aspire and to be authentic clash.

In one group interview, most participants reproduce the dominant reading of Minaj as inauthentic, as discussed in the last section. They emphasize her over-exposed body ('only famous because she doesn't wear any clothes') and equate this with 'attention seeking', echoing Lexus's critique of Lovato using her illness to build her fame (above). Yet one participant – Sabeen (Manchester, 14–15) – interjects, defending her as 'an independent female'. When Dave says: 'She speaks about how good she is all the time, like she's just the best thing to ever happen to earth', Sabeen is supported by Maajida: 'But she is a celebrity, so you have to like make yourself stand out, you can't let other people beat you. You have to, obviously sometimes you're going to have to be attention seeking.' Maajida empathizes with Minaj's 'attention seeking' as a pragmatic response to a competitive industry, repositioning her through alternative discourses of self-defiance and determination. Dave dismisses this: 'But there are other ways of making yourself stand out other than . . . insulting other people and being naked on videos' and shifts the discussion to white male entrepreneur Bill Gates who 'stands out for the right reasons'. We look in Chapter 6 at how such strong women celebrities become a resource for Sabeen in positioning herself against the social goods of marriage and motherhood. Through this group discussion, we get an insight into the struggles that Sabeen has in being authentic to her aspiration to become an independent and 'difficult' woman like Minaj.

Sabeen and Maajida's interjections are fragile, mocked and refuted by others. But, like Snoop's, they show how dominant discourses of authenticity can be reworked as participants' own classed, gendered and racialized identities are brought to bear on who and what they come to think of as real. Roman's (Manchester 14–15) challenge to his peers' construction of the Kardashian sisters as inauthentic – as, in Naomi's words, 'making drama just to be famous' – is different. As a young man defending them from attacks by young women, we see – as we do elsewhere in this book – that identification often crosses boundaries of class, gender and race. Roman positively values the Kardashians' perseverance and self-belief in the face of criticism and 'a lot of hate'.

> I disagree about the Kardashians [laughter from group] because I just find them, they don't really influence me but I just love the way they are. They wouldn't let anyone get to them, cos they do receive a lot of hate from people. And still they're not afraid to come out into the public eye and they don't let anything to get to them.

In Chapter 8, we discuss Roman in more detail, including his experiences of bullying. Roman's reading of the Kardashians as 'not afraid to come out' and not letting 'anything to get to them' can be understood as refracted through his own struggle for acceptance. Roman's position generates mocking laughter, illustrating again the difficulties of aligning oneself with 'fake' celebrities. He follows the group's laughter with the disclaimer 'they don't influence me'. By positioning himself as a media-savvy consumer rather than a vulnerable celebrity fan, Roman may be attempting to ward off criticism. Roman's challenge – like Louise, Snoop, Sabeen and Maajida's – does not involve abandoning authenticity. He praises the Kardashians for 'the way they are', illustrating that it is possible to judge such celebrities differently (as real not fake) but not to escape the demand to be authentic.

Erin Meyers (2009: 901) contends that what matters is not what is 'true' but rather 'how notions of truth and authenticity are used by both [celebrities] and the celebrity media as a means to convey social norms and values'. We argue that as well as exploring how celebrities and celebrity media operationalize notions of authenticity, equal attention should be paid to how audiences *use and contest* notions of truth and authenticity within celebrity. Mobilizing alternative readings of 'the real' provides ways for young people to rework the norms that shape their transitions to adulthood.

Conclusion

In this chapter, we have shown that young people actively and critically evaluate celebrities for their authenticity, praising those who they feel have stayed 'true to themselves' and criticizing those they deem inauthentic. This is part of a broader investment in authenticity within their own lives, which is central to their aspirations. This investment can be understood as part of what Luc Boltanski and Eve Chiapello (2002: 2, original emphasis) call 'a *"spirit of capitalism"* the ideology that justifies people's commitment to capitalism, and which renders this commitment attractive'. They argue that capitalism is able to transform itself by incorporating past critiques. Locating work as a site of authenticity is central to a new spirit of capitalism that emerged in the 1980s, in response to 1960s criticisms that work under capitalism was routine and meaningless.

Susanne Ekman (2013: 292) notes that responses to this new role of authenticity have been polarized between those who celebrate the possibility of fulfilling work and those who see it as a mechanism for 'more refined profit maximisation based on the colonization of employee souls'. She, like us, uses empirical evidence to show the complexity of what people do with authenticity and how it is not easy to dismiss people's desires for work that enables 'limitless existential growth' (2013: 311). Indeed, as academics, we all value having jobs that offer possibilities for self-realization. Authenticity increases workers' expectations and the demands they make of employers. Yet, even though commitments to authenticity can be enabling for current and future workers, it has a huge downside. As 'authenticity is largely defined precisely by its absence of strategic and monetary concerns' (Ekman 2013: 297), it supports wage cuts and worsening working conditions. Feelings and personality traits are commodified as authenticity is given exchange value. Privacy is lost and anxiety grows as 'emotional labour' takes a toll on people's physical and psychological health (Hochschild 1979). Further, there is no evidence that there are indeed lots of high-skill 'fulfilling' jobs waiting for applicants. As already discussed, since the financial crisis, there has been an increase in young people taking up precarious and insecure work, including graduates. This suggests that for the majority possibilities for self-realization through work will remain, increasingly, out of reach.

Across the data, we find that authenticity, like hard work, is used to assign value to celebrities and so to associated pathways and ways of being. This reproduces the wider inequalities that mark our austere meritocracy as dominant discourses are more likely to construct middle-class, male and white celebrities' behaviours and bodies as authentic. While the visibility of female working-class white and black celebrities helps sustain myths of a meritocratic society through representing diversity and ordinariness, it reveals limits to social mobility. Aspiration rhetoric encourages young people to 'dream big', endowing special significance to those who follow non-traditional pathways. Working-class and minority ethnic young people are encouraged to follow educational and career pathways towards elite universities and high-status professions from which they have typically been excluded (Kirby 2016; SMCP 2015). There have also been many policy drives to increase the participation of women and ethnic minorities in sectors such as science and computing (Elias & Jones 2006; Phipps 2008). Young people who pursue and succeed in non-traditional pathways are declared exceptional, held up as aspirational role models who can inspire others. This celebratory policy rhetoric obscures the tensions between aspiring on these terms and staying true to a self that may not fit into the spaces where it is being incited to go.

CELEBRITY CASE STUDY: KIM KARDASHIAN

Kim Kardashian is a globally famous reality television star, socialite, businessperson and model. She appears in the reality television series *Keeping Up with the Kardashians,* alongside her mother Kris Jenner, stepparent Caitlin Jenner, four sisters and their partners. She has a large following on social media and runs a lucrative lifestyle brand with her sisters, including books and a fashion label. Following a stream of high-profile relationships, Kardashian married African-American rapper Kanye West in May 2014, having given birth to their child, North West, in July 2013.

Of Armenian heritage, part of an already-wealthy family and having attended a prestigious private school in Los Angeles, Kardashian's racial ambiguity and lack of humble beginnings mark her as different from Katie Price and other 'chav' or 'white trash' celebrities. However, as discussed in

FIGURE 4.1 *Kim Kardashian, photograph by Eva Rinaldi, no changes made. Licence https:// creativecommons.org/licenses/by-sa/2.0/.*

the previous chapter, like them, she is located outside of respectable, white middle-class femininity (Allen et al. 2015b). Kardashian is arguably more proximate to blackness than whiteness due to her Armenian heritage, high-profile relationships with black men and the centrality of her large bottom within her media image – a powerful racial signifier (Pramaggiore & Negra 2014; Hill Collins 2005). Her association with reality television and a sex tape subject Kardashian to charges of stupidity, bad taste and sexual immorality. In this chapter, and in Chapters 3 and 8, we see participants align Kardashian with an illegitimate and 'undeserving' celebrity and deemed lazy, talentless and artificial. News articles frequently refer to her as 'famous for being famous', a publicity-generating machine whose celebrity is built on controversy not merit, and who 'has to raise a few eyebrows every now and then to pay the rent' (Hardie 2013). The respected *Guardian* newspaper branded her an 'attention-obsessed numbskull'

(Benedictus 2013). On social media platforms, Kardashian is the subject of mass-circulated memes and jokes which position her as unworthy, in tweets such as: 'That awkward moment when Kim Kardashian's kid grows up and asks her why she's famous' and 'You know Kim Kardashian is bad when you miss Paris Hilton.'

Inauthenticity is central to her celebrity representation, carried in her alignment with 'undeserving' celebrity and through corporeal failure and excess. Kardashian's body, in particular her bottom, is a site of fascination, disgust and derision (Allen et al. 2015b). Subject to a punishing gaze, Kardashian is regularly criticized for inappropriate and risqué dress and poor taste, especially during her pregnancy:

> Always prone to the odd fashion howler, the reality star seems to have gone to pieces during pregnancy. Too tight, too short or just plain trashy . . . her recent outfits are a daily reminder of how not to flatter a bump. . . . If you want to get it wrong, follow Kimmy's golden rules. (Ross 2013)

Kardashian is not only vilified for her supposed excess but also for her artifice. Media scrutiny of her curvaceous body is oriented to questioning its realness, through repeated suggestions that she has had cosmetic surgery. The media also read her as inauthentic in her conduct, values and morality. A dominant narrative in Kardashian's mediation is that she projects an artificial image of herself, motivated by pathological and immoral desires for attention and fame. Her relationship with West has been positioned as a PR stunt (Hardie 2013). Appearing on *The Oprah Winfrey Show* in 2012, Kardashian was asked if her previous 72-day marriage to basketball player Kris Humphries was a sham to increase her show's ratings. While speculation over strategic celebrity marriages has been a staple of Hollywood (Peterson 2014), it is mobilized here to serve a narrative of Kardashian as fame hungry and fake. This narrative circulates online in memes and joke tweets, such as: 'I want to pull a Kim Kardashian – I want a huge fun wedding but I have no interest in actually being married' and, 'Congrats to Kim Kardashian on the birth of her publicity stunt.' Since the study ended, this remains a dominant discourse in Kardashian's representation, including allegations that she fraudulently claimed she was the victim of an armed robbery, staged as a 'publicity stunt' (Agence France-Presse in Los Angeles 2016). Kardashian is frequently criticized by other celebrities who associate her with undesirable forms of fame, as we see in the case study of Emma Watson in Chapter 8. Will Smith (in Hoffman 2013) who, as we saw in the last chapter, presents his celebrity as achieved through effort and determination, distances himself from 'the idea of fame or exploitation or orchestrating the media' that he associates with the Kardashians.

We end this case study by examining a flashpoint in Kardashian's media representation: the purported and controversial attempt by *Vogue* editor Anna Wintour to ban her from attending the 2013 Met Gala, a high-profile annual event attended by 'the great and the good' of high society. This provides insights into the alignment between authenticity and 'deserving' celebrity, and how these operate through classed and gendered judgements of taste and propriety that structure which aspirations are legitimate and for whom. This event, and the controversy over Kardashian's attendance, was covered across the media, with reports that she 'didn't fit the bill' and was not 'suitable for the magazine's aspirational tone' (Daily Mail Reporter 2013). Kardashian's attendance was followed by more negative coverage and tweets about her 'garish' dress. Constructed as an unwanted celebrity guest and vilified for her fashion faux pas, Kardashian appears as a tragic figure and trespasser. Attempting to enter the world of privilege, represented by the Met Ball and its elite hosts and guests, Kardashian is positioned as desperate and overreaching. While she may possess immense wealth and symbolic capital though her fame, she is judged and derided for her excessive and sexualized body, poor taste and eagerness. She cannot successfully perform modest, restrained femininity, nor the relaxed, disinterested aesthetic of the upper classes. In this failed Pygmalion story Kardashian becomes a figure of pretension – a 'class drag act . . . an unconvincing and inadvertently parodic attempt to pass' (Tyler & Bennett 2010: 381).

5

Success

At the 2014 Academy Awards, Matthew McConaughey, on receiving his best actor Oscar, spoke about needing three things in life. These were 'something to look up to' (God), 'something to look forward to' (family) and 'something to chase'. Expanding on the latter, he explained:

And to my hero. That's who I chase. Now when I was 15 years old, I had a very important person in my life come to me and say 'who's your hero?' And I said, 'I don't know, I gotta think about that. Give me a couple of weeks.' I come back two weeks later, this person comes up and says 'who's your hero?' I said, 'I thought about it. You know who it is? It's me in ten years.' So I turned 25. Ten years later, that same person comes to me and says, 'So, are you a hero?' And I was like, 'not even close. No, no, no.' She said, 'Why?' I said, 'Because my hero's me at 35.' So you see every day, every week, every month and every year of my life, my hero's always ten years away. I'm never gonna beat my hero.

At this peak of professional achievement, McConaughey seems to refuse the label of success. Instead he speaks of heroism as something he is relentlessly chasing. Any present success is never enough, 'not even close'. It can and must be exceeded. Chasing is his ideal existential state: 'I'm not gonna obtain that. I know I'm not. And that's just fine with me because it keeps me with somebody to keep on chasing.' McConaughey's moving target is constructed not as external to him but as coming from within. His hero is his forever-receding future self.

McConaughey's 'chasing' parallels dominant constructions of aspiration within austere meritocracy. As we argued in Chapter 1, aspiration is a disciplinary technology that shapes and directs our actions, hopes and dreams. It invokes young people to plan their futures in relation to socially approved pathways. It demands that they orient themselves towards what counts as legitimate success. It keeps them chasing their forever-receding dreams.

While externally structured, it must appear, as in McConaughey's speech, as an internal drive: a desire to improve. As we also noted in Chapter 1, we have seen an intensification of talk of aspiration and social mobility despite the ongoing economic crisis, and increasing inequality. In this chapter we look at young people's talk about success in relation to both celebrities' lives and their own futures, exploring how they negotiate dominant discourses of success that are key to aspirational selfhood within austere meritocracy.

The chapter is organized into five sections. The first sets out the dominant understanding of celebrity success. This is entrepreneurial, corresponding to the future-oriented, flexible and resourceful individual at the centre of austere meritocracy. In the second, we look at how the entrepreneurial success discourse manifested in young people's accounts of 'aiming high' and 'controlling your life'. These accounts downplay obstacles to success, including how social class, gender and race shape choices and opportunities. Yet, as we show, talk of social constraints remains alongside this discourse and in tension with it. In the third section we look, in contrast, at the stability success discourse that emerged in accounts of 'having enough' and 'getting by'. These convey a more pragmatic approach to what is possible and impossible for young people. These two success discourses – of entrepreneurialism and stability – intermingle in young people's accounts. Both are based in determination, authenticity and hard work. They reproduce dominant ideas of success which align with the goals of a 'good job' and financial security. However, there are also differences, for, as we show, one focuses on constant striving and the other on (eventually) being able to stop striving. These ideas of success can only exist through explicitly and implicitly evoking a spectre of 'failure'. It is to this that we turn in our final sections, looking at two young people who respectively 'aspire' to pleasure rather than deferring gratification, and to manual trades rather than a professional career.

'He's really successful because of what he created': The entrepreneurialism success discourse

We included two specific questions about success in the individual interviews, although the subject also arose elsewhere in discussions of their schooling, families and imagined futures. We asked what young people feel makes our case-study celebrities successful and what defines success in their own lives. We asked these same questions about happiness. Happiness is our focus in the next chapter, where we explore how this orients young people towards a 'good life' of family and a fulfilling career. For some young people to be happy was to be successful but for most success was articulated as distinct from, and even in tension with, happiness. This tension arises from dominant notions of success being tied to competitiveness, for to be success-ful means exceeding the achievements of other people. Rick puts this expli-citly, explaining that success requires going *beyond* basic happiness:

> I think to be successful you have to be able to sort of pass beyond every-one else. . . . If you can like break the average that's success. If you can afford more. . . . If you've got a job which is good and you like your job and it's something you've always wanted and you've worked hard for, that's success. (London, 16–17)

Rick is drawing on the dominant entrepreneurialism success discourse, which parallels the American Dream 'of a better, richer, and happier life for all our citizens' regardless of circumstances of birth (Adams 1931, in Meacham 2012). In Chapters 3 and 4 we looked at work and authenticity which – as Rick's words suggest – are the socially approved ways of chasing success. In this section, we focus on the three key features of this dominant discourse of entrepreneurial success that we see in Rick's (and McConaughey's) words: it involves having a *significant impact*, is *future oriented* and *individualized*. As Anita Biressi and Heather Nunn (2013a) note, within austerity, 'success is increasingly characterised as only achievable through the deployment of one's personal, private resources of passion and drive'.

This entrepreneurial success discourse dominated participants' celebrity talk with a focus on achievements and recognition. Although most young people viewed all our case-study celebrities as having some degree of suc-cess, diver Tom Daley and entrepreneur Bill Gates stood out as the most suc-cessful. Their feats – sporting and technological – were positioned as more significant than those of the other celebrities. As Mat Power (SW, 16–17) remarks: 'I'd like to see any of these others do about five flips off a diving board backwards.' In Chapter 2 we demonstrated how Daley's success was deemed particularly exceptional because of his young age.

Daley was repeatedly described as successful through reference to his sustained and individual effort. Harry Styles (SW, 16–17) sees success as a process of 'determination to just stick with what you're doing instead of giving up half way through'. He uses Daley to exemplify this: 'That's prob-ably the best success when you kind of, you don't fail but you don't do as well as you'd hoped for and then next year come back fighting.' Alisha (London, 14–15) draws attention to 'his effort, like he's been training long hours, so this has made him successful'. In this way young people are pick-ing up on his media representation, discussed in this chapter's celebrity case study. As we saw in the discussion of Usain Bolt training 'so hard that he actually vomited' in Chapter 3 and of Ronaldihno 'kicking a ball of socks around', the idea of success coming from perseverance, ongoing work and self-realization applied to sports people more widely.

Success is future oriented, based on sacrifice in the present to attain later rewards. John P (SW, 14–15), a keen basketball player and trampolinist, said that celebrity does not engage him 'because I'm basically constantly doing sport there isn't much time for doing much other things'. Yet his account is filled with sporting celebrities who inspired him, often because they had overcome disadvantage. For example, he mentions a Brazilian surfer who became a professional despite his 'manky house, it's like no, sort of one solid bed, not very many sheets, the bathroom's just like black plaque on the walls and stuff'. While John sees a role for other people in facilitating these celebrities' sporting success, he limits this to family, particularly parents. As with Daley in Chapter 2, success remains an individualized accomplishment rather than one embedded within a social context impacted by patterns of funding, access to facilities, and ideas about sport as a competitive activity aligned with masculinity (Clarke 2009).

Beyond sports people, it is technological entrepreneurs, epitomized by Bill Gates, who exemplify success across our dataset. Business celebrities featured in most of the group interviews and in five of the six schools. Apart from Richard Branson (Virgin) and a passing reference to the adventure tourism company Bungy, all of those whom young people primarily associated with business are drawn from the field of technology. Even Branson is increasingly connected to technology through many of his high-profile personal and commercial ventures, including space tourism, Virgin's broadband and digital empire and his multiple world-record attempts in balloons, boats and amphibious vehicles. Alongside Branson, Alan Sugar (Amstrad), Bill Gates (Microsoft), Burnie Burns and Gavin Free (Rooster Teeth Productions) and Steve Jobs (Apple) were named, alongside 'the guy who created Twitter' (Jack Dorsey), 'the guys who made Google' (Larry Page and Sergey Brin), 'the Facebook guy' (Marc Zuckerberg) and 'the Farmville guy' (Mark Pincus). All are white men and all but Sugar come from professional middle-class backgrounds (Sugar's working-class roots being central to his public persona, see Allen & Mendick 2013).

Gates was discussed as a 'good role model' and an 'inspiration', along with these other technology entrepreneurs (Mendick et al. 2016). As noted in Chapter 3, they were often cited as 'ideal' celebrities. Bob2 (London, 14–15) aspires to Gates' lifestyle, partly for his wealth, but also 'because he created like a whole new generation to technology, and that's something I want to do. Cos he's really successful because of what he created.' One young woman says of Jack Dorsey, 'I owe him an awful lot, which is life. … He invented Twitter' (Mike, SW, 14–15). These responses reflect the role of technology – namely digital and social media – in young people's lives (see Chapter 8). Here success is intertwined with discourses, not just of celebrity, but of business acumen, enterprise and individual brilliance. Through the alignment of success with these celebrities, it is associated with the entrepreneurial, future-oriented traits of initiative, innovation and impact. In the next section we look at how young people negotiate this entrepreneurial success discourse within their own aspirations.

'We're not people who can fly': Negotiating the entrepreneurial success discourse

Edward is studying chemistry, mathematics and physics, a combination chosen to prepare him for a degree in electronic engineering. He identifies as Black African. Speaking about his school friends, he says, 'We're just filled with weird people . . . who are weird in their own little way. A lot of the groups actually depend on race around here. . . . My friends are kind of mixed.' In this way he marks his friendship group and behaviour as independent of his ethnicity, and different from those around him. This independence runs through his discussion of success:

> I'd say the only thing that stops you from achieving your dreams is you. . . . You have to constantly believe in yourself. . . . Like you need to know where your weaknesses are. . . . I can happily say that my weakness would be writing my Personal Statement [for university application]. It's hard. Like I am finding it hard to write a whole page about myself and what I've done, and stuff like that. But I am pushing through it, like I'm learning how to do it. I'm learning all my mistakes. . . . And there are people would say, 'Yeah. But then what about the people around you? What if they're pulling you back? Blah blah blah.' The only reason they're pulling you back is because you're letting them pull you back. If they were really pulling you back, it's still on yourself, because you can be smart enough to walk away, or you can just be stupid and just stand there, while they ruin the rest of your life for you, and then end up blaming it all on them. When really it was just yourself. (London, 16–17)

This passage reads like a motivational speech. For Edward, the key to success is the individual who knows their weaknesses, pushes through difficulties, learns from mistakes and walks away from negative influences. He summarizes: 'The only thing that gets in the way of success is yourself.' He cites Gates as an inspiration: 'He's made Microsoft and Windows, and all these amazing things. So I'd love to be friends with him.' The other celebrity he would like to befriend is Will Smith who, as we saw in Chapter 3, makes motivational speeches that carry a sentiment that is remarkably similar to Edward's words above. But for Edward and other participants, enacting this entrepreneurial success discourse is far from straightforward.

Individualism places a burden on Edward evident in the passage above and when he recalls his trepidation before opening the envelope containing his examination results. It also conflicts with Edward's association with his 'rough' locality and the 'normal' school he attends which lead him to identify as working class despite having parents in professional occupations. Although Edward constructs 'your dreams [as] like something you have to climb towards and grab yourself', he sees them as constrained by this context:

You don't necessarily have to make dreams that are impossible. . . . So like if someone were to just say to you 'I'm gonna be the first person to fly. I'm gonna be like superman.' 'Fine. Go ahead. Try it.' They'll be trying their whole lives to fly and they'll never get it, because it's not in our nature, we're not people who can fly.

In this analogy, 'flying' is a metaphor for attending one of the UK's two 'top' universities: 'Oxford and Cambridge, around here we don't even look at them.' Like flying, 'it's not in our nature': 'Even if we are getting amazing grades and stuff, we're not coming out of a grammar school or one of those like private schools . . . so we're less likely to get a place.' Edward later says that he would not expect to meet the grade requirements for a place at Oxbridge. However, the statements above show that it is not simply lower results that preclude Edward from going to Oxbridge, but a more elusive sense of what is appropriate for 'people like us' (Bourdieu 1984; Reay et al. 2005). While class and race are not named explicitly by Edward, his words reflect those of 'non-traditional' students in other research who feel a sense of alienation from elite universities that privilege whiteness and middle classness (Loveday 2015; Mirza 2015). Elsewhere in the interview he dismisses Oxbridge, discussing superior facilities at another university, perhaps attempting to reconcile the entrepreneurial success discourse with his sense of his own possibilities. The tension between this sense of his own possibilities and his belief that 'the only thing that gets in the way of success is yourself' is unresolved. He ends by suggesting school and locality constrain him but insists that 'it's not holding me back to the point where I can't do what I wanna do'. In Edward's account, what holds him back becomes that which is 'not holding me back'. It is such contradictions that reveal the difficulties of young people's attempts to speak themselves through the entrepreneurial success discourse.

Mariam, originally from Somalia, has been a refugee in Western Europe for most of her life. Aged 2 she arrived in Holland with her mother and sister where she grew up, moving to Manchester in her teens. She describes her social class position as 'in the middle' but we define her as working class based on her parents' employment and education (her mother is a part-time cleaner with no experience of higher education). Mariam talks of wanting 'a good and steady life', to achieve in school, university and employment:

I don't care about having like millions of pounds and stuff in my bank account. If I have children, just to give my children a normal and stable life, like my mum gave with all, with all of the power give it to us. Because she was a single mum, and she still is, and I want to prove to my father's family like 'I grew up well without your help.' (Manchester, 16–17)

Mariam's aspirations are rooted in her family history, including her precarious position as a refugee, estrangement from her father, and her mother raising her children alone. Here she draws on the stability success discourse that we discuss in the next section, but Mariam's account also contains a sense of striving, drawing on the entrepreneurial success discourse. She is attached to its meritocratic promise: 'If you work hard and try hard, you will be secure. A future, your goal: you will achieve it. I guess, I need to change myself and be more determined to get what I want.'

Mariam admires her mother and grandmother as strong, independent women who 'did it on their own': 'My mother showed me how to be a good mother without having a job and an education, and my grandmother showed me how to be a good woman and mother with a job because she worked for [her children].' The feminist sensibilities that suffuse Mariam's account of her maternal role models are echoed in her relationship to celebrity. While Mariam defines herself as uninterested in celebrity, she sees Beyoncé as a role model: 'Beyoncé shows that women can like do a lot without a male. . . . She fired her father as a manager, and then she decided to manage herself. . . . She uses only females on stage.' She speaks about Beyoncé and other strong female celebrities as people who can motivate her to achieve her dreams: 'I would look up to them because they are important people and have achieved a lot. I would think that if they can do it, I can do it as well.' Her aspiration to work in fashion promotion is inspired by watching *The Hills*, an MTV scripted-reality series set in Los Angeles about young women who are fashion interns for *Teen Vogue*. However, celebrity lifestyles and the associated opportunities are very different from her own as a refugee.

We could read Mariam's account and her investment in these celebrities as evidence that she has been 'captured' by dominant discourses of meritocracy and neoliberal postfeminism. We might follow bell hooks's reading of Beyoncé as 'anti-feminist' and embodying 'a populist and anodyne post-feminism oriented around individual choice' (hooks, in Sieczkowski 2014). However, we could also draw a different interpretation in which Mariam is using celebrity as a resource through which to refuse some of the classed, gendered and racialized expectations that seek to place limits on her transitions. Yet, even here there is little space to acknowledge external constraints. Like Edward, Mariam is left feeling she must change herself and 'be more determined' if she is to achieve her aspirations. In the next section we look at those who attempted to maintain a focus on stability despite the dominance of entrepreneurial success discourses.

'A good and steady life': The stability success discourse

References to stability and security recur through young people's talk about their future success. Their aspirations are imbued with 'the desire for emotional well-being and stability' (Brown 2011: 16). We can see this in

Mariam's words above, and in Syndicate (London, 16–17), who hopes to 'have a steady, stable life' by the time he reaches his thirties. Within austere meritocracy, in which striving is valorized, stability is often denigrated as a low aspiration. This criticism comes not just from the political mainstream but from left critiques of neoliberalism. As Sara Ahmed (2014) explains, '"Getting by" or "making do" might appear as a way of not attending to structural inequalities, as benefiting from a system by adapting to it, even if you are not privileged by that system.' She instead reads such self-preservation as resistance: 'It is about finding ways to exist in a world that is diminishing.'

Money is central to the stability success discourse, as its central concerns are not aiming high and continually improving but having enough and getting by. Throughout the data, participants express a concern with paying bills, *not* becoming rich, with ordinariness, *not* excess. For example, Mat (SW, 14–15) talks about wanting 'not so much money, but I'd like to have a lot of money, obviously to like support a family. . . . Just a normal life really.' Similarly, Dave (Manchester, 14–15) does not aspire 'to be mega-rich. . . . Because of the world we live in right now, you kind of need money. So I want enough money to live on and use and some money left over to use for stuff for leisure.' Several participants, such as Manjula (Manchester, 16–17), link these goals with their parents' experiences or their current situation: 'My dad said if you work hard you'll become successful, but if you don't you end up struggling to pay bills and stuff.' The rarity of expressed aspirations to become 'mega-rich' suggests that such desires provoke moral judgements: 'you kind of need money' but must want only 'enough' (Harvey et al. 2015, see Chapter 7). The stability discourse, like the entrepreneurial discourse, occurred across our dataset, but was weakest in London and strongest in rural areas where limited local employment opportunities meant most participants saw no option but to move away to find work. By contrast, the entrepreneurial discourse was strongest in London. This stability discourse, unlike the entrepreneurial discourse, was barely present within young people's celebrity talk. It is striking that this discourse appears so strongly in young people's imaginations despite this lack of cultural support.

To understand its presence, we must see the stability success discourse as a product of the current insecure economic and labour market conditions within which saving money (thrift) and hard work (graft) have greater significance in political rhetoric and young people's talk (Allen et al. 2015b; Mendick et al. 2015). 'Getting by' does not feature in Paul Willis's 1977 study of young working-class men and schooling, because there were then many well-paid jobs not dependent on educational success. While insecurity intensified following the post-2008 global financial crisis, as we argued in Chapter 1, it predates this. In the late 1970s a neoliberal shift began, characterized by Zygmunt Bauman (1998) as a move from 'solid' to 'liquid' modernity. No longer can we rely on the solidity of a job, home or relationship for life. Work, housing and even love have become liquid. As the next two examples show, in the stability success discourse, we can see a yearning for solidity. It offers partial resistance to the cruel optimism of the entrepreneurial success discourse.

Ginny, a working-class British Indian young woman, wants to go to university and become a writer. Like Edward, she speaks of results day, something which lies ahead of her – 'My mum has always talked about that day' – describing how the family will drive to school to collect her results:

> I was like, 'But mum, I'm being truthful, if I pass I'm gonna cry, if I fail I'm gonna cry, I'm gonna cry either way.' And then she was like, 'You know what? I'm proud of you in general.' So she's just like, 'I will be smiling no matter what happens that day.' So I guess just the smile on like my family's face just when I know all of this hard work over these two years have paid off. (London, 14–15)

Ginny will recognize her success relationally through 'the smile on like my family's face'. Although Ginny's mum reassures her she 'will be smiling no matter what', Ginny links this smile to success, arising from her enduring individual effort. This focus on results day – still over a year away – is future oriented. Although this day will be when her 'hard work over these two years have paid off', it is also the beginning of a new struggle towards employment and financial security. Ginny hopes for a day 'that I don't have to struggle for a mortgage, or struggle to pay off things . . . just knowing you could, you could live in that moment'. She sees success in stability, not striving. She admits that she is currently 'not living in the moment. I'm not. I'm thinking about, you know, exams and working for that.' Ginny yearns to adjust her temporality to the present, rather than always orienting to examinations and other future goals: to be able to 'treat my, my friends and my family, and . . . go out and have a good time, and . . . do what I love'. This will be possible when 'I'm sort of secure in a way. Like I have things to fall back on, and at this point I have nothing to fall back on.' Ginny's engagement with popular culture through Tumblr becomes a site of happiness for her, a space for sharing her passions in fan fiction, perhaps as it offers instant, not deferred, gratification. The entrepreneurialism discourse is focused on process, continually working on the self, always chasing. Ginny's desire for security and freedom from struggle is focused on escaping that.

In Chapter 4 we met Archibald (SW, 16–17), who is from a white working-class background and wants a career in the army or with the police force. Failing that, he says he could do accountancy 'because I'm good at business. . . . But I will just try and get a decent job really, going into work.' Archibald presents a contrast between people, typified by celebrity technology entrepreneurs, 'that like develop and push themselves to make themselves successful', and those, like him, who prioritize happiness: 'Just being able to get a decent job, erm like being able to get a decent income, being able to support a family or something'. He speaks of his generation as 'brought up on a false point' – a statement that signals the narrative of the 'lost generation' discussed in Chapters 1 and 2: 'We were born in like the 1990s which was a good time, it was brilliant, the economy was great, everything was wonderful, no weather problems, no global warming yet.' Then, 'in 2000 everything just starts to go downhill. . . . It's just been getting worse and worse.' He sees himself as middle class but suggests that recent socioeconomic conditions have unsettled the taken-for-granted transitions previously enjoyed by middle class youth:

> In a triple-dip recession . . . with the jobs people are getting recently, money isn't going to be plentiful. . . . It's putting a lot of people in the same position. . . . All the benefits that people are getting are being slashed repeatedly. It's not going to help in the future, I mean it's just going to cause a riot. You take enough from people there's going to be trouble. (Archibald (SW, 16–17))

These data were collected before the intensification of public sector cuts under the Conservative government's programme of austerity measures. However, university tuition fees had tripled, there was growing youth (including graduate) unemployment and a media narrative of generational decline was already circulating. While few participants were as explicitly political as Archibald, many raised concerns about lack of jobs, higher education costs and cuts to youth provision.

In Ginny and Archibald's take up of the stability discourse, we see how they use it to articulate the importance of survival in conditions of adversity. In the next sections we look at two people who resist the entrepreneurial discourse not through stability but through expressing desires that are often rendered illegitimate within hierarchical constructions of aspiration: to instant pleasure and vast wealth. Dumbledore is a white, middle-class young man from the rural South West. He explicitly rejects success defined by a 'good' career, property ownership and a nuclear family in favour of hedonism. Homer is a white working-class young man from London. He aspires to traditional working-class occupations and extreme wealth. Through their words we continue to explore the limits and tensions of the dominant entrepreneurial discourse.

'Maybe the best I can isn't what I want to do': Hedonism and resisting success

Dumbledore describes himself as lower middle class. His parents hold professional jobs, although his mother is a teaching assistant and his father has recently been made redundant, introducing insecurity into his family's future. He presents himself as having effortlessly achieved good grades, doing 'no work' during earlier schooling, when he spent time partying. He is now studying pre-university qualifications, which he finds more challenging. He talks critically in the interview about pressure from his teachers and parents to 'aim high':

> If I didn't have the ability to get good grades . . . none of this would be here. I would be expected to just try and scrape a job and just try and scrape through, you know, I would be expected to do that. And then if I managed to find some way to break out of that, then fair play on me. . . . That option isn't available to me. It is, but it's not. . . . At any point of my life, I couldn't have turned around to my parents and say I'm not going to university. (SW, 16–17)

Dumbledore captures how he, like many middle-class young people, is trapped on an educational 'conveyor belt . . . they must be kept to that path at all costs'; their lives are 'rigidly circumscribed by the expectations of academic success' (Walkerdine et al. 2001: 175, 179). He becomes agitated when talking about expectations to attend university and get 'a good job' that are 'hammered into me by so many people including parents, relatives, dozens of teaching staff'. His desire to be in a position where he can 'just try and scrape through' ignores the economic difficulties that entails, and the pain of being judged as someone lacking the 'ability to get good grades'. Its attraction reveals the burden he experiences from the narrow expectations society attaches to success.

Instead of hoping for and celebrating 'good grades' as Edward, Ginny and others do, Dumbledore sees them as the source of 'stigma around me' – something marking him out for intervention by his teachers and parents. This 'stigma' closes off the stability success discourse, leaving entrepreneurial success his only apparent option. On the one hand, he rejects university: 'I don't want to go. . . . [Parents, teachers etc] go along with the whole sort of "but we're just trying to make you do the best you can". But maybe the best I can isn't what I want to do.' On the other hand, university offers him a chance to leave home and broaden his experience: 'I do kind of want to go, it's just I don't want. I don't know, I don't know what I want.' His teachers have identified him as 'a potential Oxbridge candidate'. Unlike Edward, he does not question if he belongs within these elite institutions. However, he says he is 'a hell of a lazy person', but 'I kind of feel one of the reasons I don't try is because . . . I don't want to go to Oxbridge, and even if I could I wouldn't go. I don't know why.'

In contrast to this uncertainty about his future, Dumbledore expresses clear ideas of success, centred on fame and wealth: 'I'd love to be famous and I don't care what anyone says.' His qualification 'I don't care what anyone says' indicates he knows this aspiration is deemed illegitimate (see Chapter 8) and perhaps one he can give because his class position provides greater protection from judgements about respectability that are levelled against working-class people (Skeggs 1997). Dumbledore recalls enjoying the attention he got arriving to his school prom in a limousine and imagines 'someone asking you a question and actually caring about your opinion', a scenario that contrasts with widespread disregard for young people's voices (Hadfield & Haw 2000). He is drawn to aspects of celebrity lifestyles labelled bad, and that operate as cautions against celebrity for other young people. When asked about his aspirations he discusses his 'fascination of the drug cocaine, even in primary school': 'For all these people to have been going off the rails on it, and then be harping on about how bad it is for us, there must be something amazing about it to make people take all these risks.' This contrasts with the moral disapproval most young people expressed towards drug taking, exemplified in the discussions of child stars analysed in Chapter 2.

Dumbledore's desire, not just for fame but for a hedonistic lifestyle, is a rejection of striving and requires wealth beyond the level of 'getting by': 'My ideal lifestyle would be I'd do something I love doing and I'm passionate about, and get away with, you know, good partying.' He is aware of the impossibility of pursuing pleasure inside *and* outside of work: 'You can get a job you enjoy if it's low pay and you haven't got the money to live that kind of lifestyle.' Instead, he will take a year out between school and university to 'earn as much money as I can and then blow the money on the rest of the gap year doing all the things I want to do that I see I won't be able to do later on in life'. Although he has largely conventional ideas about celebrity success, he is also drawn to the idea of 'letting go' exemplified in stories he recounts of footballer Mario Balotelli and musician Liam Gallagher:

[Balotelli] just sounds like he doesn't care. . . . Like setting fireworks off in your bathroom, because you can. Driving around in your car with £10,000 . . . in his own words, because I am rich, and then throwing it to people because he can. It's just I'd love to be able to do that.

Similarly, he tells the interviewer that Gallagher bought drinks for everyone in a pub before 'just chilling for hours with his fans, just talking. Because he just enjoys it.' Bev Skeggs et al. (2008) discuss a form of controlled or calculated hedonism or risk-taking as a middle-class disposition 'where people work out the limits to their hedonism so that they are not late for work the next day'. It is future-oriented pleasure seeking concerned with economic exchange rather than 'not caring' about your future. Through his celebrity talk, Dumbledore expresses desires for the opposite to such calculated hedonism – represented by Gallagher's 'just chilling in the pub because he enjoyed it'. Yet he is unable to fully escape a middle-class orientation to the future. Despite these desires, Dumbledore seems resigned to his 'worst-case scenario' as he imagines his future self:

I get stuck in maybe a well-paid, it's an alright-paid job maybe, but it's like eight you know or nine in the morning to like five or six at night, and I commute away from wherever I'm working to my little family house and my little family. A stereotypical family with a little stereotypical family portrait on the wall, and we sit down and have dinner together, maybe watch a bit of TV and then go to bed. Wake up in the morning and the next, same thing. In a little suburban house. . . . And then you retire and you're too old to have any fun, and then you die.

This is a bleak rendering of the socially approved future of 'stereotypical' family, suburban home and well-paid professional employment. Here, as when he rejects Oxbridge, he rebels against middle-class, normative expectations of his success. Through Dumbledore, we can see how 'success' constrains even relatively privileged young people. Our next case study, Homer, shows how 'illegitimate' aspirations to wealth play out differently in the lives of working-class youth. Their accounts provoke the question: Does hedonism offer a pragmatic response to austere meritocracy given that realising 'high' aspirations are only possible for a few?

'My granddad's a welder. . . . He's quite a successful man': Manual labour and resisting 'success'

Homer (London, 14–15) was one of just six of our fifty-one participants who aspired exclusively to traditionally working-class occupations. Others held some such aspirations but they, like Archibald above, presented these alongside (or as a back-up to) aspirations for professional careers. Homer, like many working-class young men, is committed to earning over learning (Archer et al. 2010). Although both his granddad and his aunt are trying 'to convince me to go to university and college', 'I want to like work straight away. . . . Experience is better than knowledge, because if you've experienced it you'll remember it more than just learning about it in school.' He continues, 'I don't know whether to be a plasterer, a plumber, an electrician or a welder. . . . My dad's a plasterer. My granddad's a welder.' Although he does not know any electricians and plumbers, 'my dad does'. Here we see the significance of social capital for imagining employment trajectories. Although Homer has an interest in celebrities, celebrity discourses do not connect to, or feature in, his aspirations, suggesting that they do not provide resources for his working-class transition to adulthood.

Given the focus on professions in current policy that we discussed in Chapter 1, Homer's range of traditional working-class occupations may figure as 'low' aspirations or a sign of an aspirations deficit. This shows how policy devalues some young people's families and experiences through judging negatively the choices that arise out of them. Similarly, Homer's granddad has 'always been a role model': 'He's quite a successful man. Erm, wife, three kids, grandkids, and he's still alive at the age of 70 and he smokes. . . .

He's got quite a lot of money, he's got a nice house, car, van, and he's kind.'
The aspects of his granddad's life that inspire him – his working-class job for
life, kindness, material possessions and capacity to defy the risks of smoking – are neither endorsed nor sanctioned by policy.

As with Dumbledore, Homer wants to enjoy his work, be 'rich' and
escape the relentless demand to orient to the future. Danger and excitement
are part of Homer's attraction to welding: 'You get to play with fire.' They
are central to his electrician aspiration: 'Electricity's always interested me
because it's like dangerous.' Homer recalls his earliest memory associated
with this:

> When I was at work with my dad, I touched a plug and I got an electric
> shock. I stood there like just shaking for like two seconds, it was weird. . . .
> It was good though. . . . It doesn't like hurt, it just makes you like shake
> and you can't control your body.

This is reminiscent of the working-class 'lads' in Paul Willis's classic
1970s study *Learning to Labour*. Like Homer, 'having a laff' and friendship were important to Willis's lads. But it is in their attraction to fighting
that the similarities are strongest. Fighting provides a source of excitement,
a means of escape from the everyday world, through which 'the dialectic
of time is broken' (Willis 1977: 34). Homer finds a way of being in the
moment, not through inflicting violence on others but through the personal
risks of working with electricity. We can read his attraction to this as resistance to the imperative to orient to the future, something we can also see in
his relationship to getting older.

Discussions of maturity and immaturity recur in Homer's interview. His
parents' separation last year comes up early in the interview:

> I remember it like it was yesterday. . . . I was at my nan's and my mum like
> just came knocking on my nan's door and like said mum and dad had had
> an argument and then I said, 'Oh why? I leave you two kids alone for two
> minutes and you squabble.'

Homer presents himself as the adult, positioning his parents as 'two kids'
who cannot be trusted without him. His adult role is also clear when he
explains, 'I feel like the man in the house now. . . . Sometimes this involves
getting money, like I have to work with my dad. . . . It involves like just
mowing the grass, or tidying up sometimes, looking after my little brothers.'
The identified tasks relate to the adult-male family role, including earning
money through assisting in his dad's working-class occupation. However, he
also enjoys childish pranks, for example, filling his mum's hair dryer with
flour and successfully blaming the ensuing mess on his younger sister. He is
ambivalent about growing up. When he discusses his aspirations, he says
that even thinking about the future 'makes me think how old I am, even
though I don't really feel it. I still feel like I'm like ten.'

Homer, like Dumbledore, unashamedly expresses a desire for huge wealth. However, there are two distinctions between them. First, Homer wants wealth for his family, to ensure their safety:

> I wouldn't bother spending the money on me, I would bother about my family and putting it in a safe place. And then I would probably move my entire family, if I was that rich, and then we got, live in a nice estate . . . in central London, busy and stuff. But like not on a highway, so that we can go to like shopping centres a lot. . . . I'd probably buy them everything they wanted, because I'd have that much money I suppose. But that won't happen.

The second distinction between Dumbledore and Homer is suggested by Homer's final sentence. Both young men feel that their dreams of wealth and pleasure are unattainable. But while Dumbledore is successful in school and ascribes any failures to laziness, Homer feels he cannot be wealthy 'because I'm not really clever'. Dumbledore can follow the middle-class pattern of combining rebellion with educational success via effortless achievement, maintaining a 'balance between cool/rebellious and studious/good student' (Hollingworth 2015: 1247). Homer cannot. He has failed against the standards of school success having not 'got an A in one subject yet'. When the interviewer suggests alternative measures of intelligence, for example in skills not taught in school, Homer rejects this, saying 'I count clever as . . . things that you learn in school. . . . Like physics, that's hard, so people that do that are clever.' Homer is unable to identify and align himself with the dominant notions of success, intelligence and achievement found in schooling's value system. Through Homer's story we see him attempting to assert an alternative value system and ideas of success drawing on the lives of his dad and granddad, whose entrepreneurialism is unacknowledged by the entrepreneurial success discourse. We see the difficulties of this when dominant notions of success are institutionalized within schooling.

Conclusion

Within austere meritocracy, '[t]he ability to "believe in yourself" . . . is primary. This is a discourse which vests not only power but also moral virtue in the very act of hope, in the mental and emotional capacity to believe and aspire' (Littler 2013: 65). The entrepreneurial success discourse is central to this and, as we showed in this chapter, it dominates celebrity representations and young people's celebrity talk. It is individualistic and future oriented. We analysed its psychological costs and their uneven distribution across social class, gender and race, as individuals are given the moral responsibility to address inequality through aiming high. We can see the tensions this creates in the accounts of Edward, Mariam, Ginny and Archibald, who experience constraints in their life but feel that they must rely on themselves to overcome them.

We have identified cracks in this dominant discourse. There are tensions between discourses of entrepreneurialism and stability, and between the individualistic, autonomous and asocial imperative that Littler describes above and the relationships which shape and the constraints which bear down on young people's sense of who they are and who they can become. Yet, currently nascent anger at social inequalities, such as Archibald's, tends to be directed not outwards but inwards at themselves. Lauren Berlant (2011: 28, original emphasis) implicates the requirement to orient to the future in this, highlighting 'the "technologies of patience" that enable a concept of the *later* to suspend questions about the cruelty of the *now*'.

In this context, the only legitimate way to acknowledge failure is retrospectively, as something through which we have learnt how to make ourselves more successful. Yet, in an austere meritocracy, where there are fewer jobs (or at least fewer jobs offering 'good work') and where those that exist tend to be less financially and psychologically rewarding, more of us – especially young people – are experiencing 'failure' in relation to society's expectations. Thus, we also explored interviews with two young people whose imagined futures represent 'failures' in relation to the orientations that are endorsed by the contemporary politics of aspiration. Dumbledore and Homer represent 'failure' because they resist a success that has been reduced to constantly chasing your future self. In a context where success is narrowly proscribed and increasingly out of reach, there is hope in such 'failures':

> Failure allows us to escape the punishing norms that discipline behavior and manage human development with the goal of delivering us from unruly childhoods to orderly and predictable adulthoods. Failure preserves some of the wondrous anarchy of childhood and disturbs the supposedly clean boundaries between adults and children, winners and losers. (Halberstam 2011: 3)

In exploring failure we do not lose sight of the 'disappointment, disillusionment and despair' (ibid.) that accompanies it and that are apparent in Dumbledore and Homer's talk. But these interviews offer 'the opportunity to use these negative affects to poke holes in the toxic positivity of contemporary life' (ibid.), with its entrepreneurialism success discourse, and to fracture the relations of cruel optimism that inhabit us.

Our analysis shows that we urgently need to find ways of working with, and making policies for, young people that embrace a wider range of ways of being, encompassing young people as valued members of society rather than as citizens-in-the-making. We need policies and practices that give them space to explore, rather than requiring them to narrowly imagine their futures around their economic productivity. A focus on happiness rather than success appears to promise this. It is to this goal that we turn in the next chapter.

CELEBRITY CASE STUDY: TOM DALEY

FIGURE 5.1 *Tom Daley, photograph by Jim Thurston, no changes made. Licence https://creativecommons.org/licenses/by-sa/2.0/.*

As outlined above, the dominant discourse of success is entrepreneurial, focusing on future orientation, individualism and impact, and this is pervasive within celebrity representations. In this case study we exemplify this through UK diver and television presenter Tom Daley. We introduced Daley in Chapter 2 as exemplifying the discourse of 'youth as potential/ hope' through his associations with extraordinary success and nationalistic achievement (Projansky 2014).

Daley came to public attention when he competed at age 14 in the 2008 Olympics and in 2010, when the BBC screened a reality-television-style documentary about his life, *Tom Daley: The Diver and His Dad*. Just months before we began collecting data, Daley won a bronze medal at the London 2012 Olympics. He featured heavily in the UK publicity for these games, and in the run up to the Olympics there had been an autobiography, unofficial biography and a second BBC documentary. His first venture into television presenting, the celebrity-diving show *Splash!*, aired at the same time as some of the group interviews.

Daley's media representation focuses on him as a (British) national success: someone who has overcome obstacles – school bullying, his father's death from cancer – to achieve through hard work and passion. Central to this is the idea that he holds high aspirations that he has pursued from a young age, making sacrifices along the way. The opening of *Splash!* shows us Daley about to make his medal-winning dive, his voice-over saying: 'This is my dream and I only get one shot.' Accounts of Daley's life repeatedly cite the time in 2002 when, as a young child, he drew a picture in response to hearing that London was to host the 2012 Olympics. His picture, called 'my ambition', shows a young man wearing Union Jack Speedos doing a handstand alongside the Olympic rings (Daley 2012: 28; *Tom Daley: The Diver and His Dad*). There are frequent references to how hard he works and what he is missing, including typical teenage activities, such as drinking alcohol, young romance and hanging out with friends. His mother, Debbie Daley (2013), defending him against attacks from David Sparkes (British Swimming's Chief Executive) for his media work, said of the period following the 2012 Olympics: 'Everyone else was taking long holidays, partying, celebrating exams, while Tom had to get straight back to diving.' Daley is depicted as future oriented, driven by his aspirations, sacrificing pleasure today for future success.

The public defence of Daley by his mother is part of ongoing tensions between him and the UK sporting establishment. He was criticized by British diving coach Alexei Evangulov prior to the 2012 Olympics for his 'excessive media commitments' (Sportsbeat 2012), the most high-profile example being a YouTube video of the Team GB diving squad lip-syncing to LMFAO's hit *Sexy and I Know It*. Sparkes repeated these public criticisms following the launch of *Splash!*. Both Evangulov and Sparkes contrast Daley's actions with the commitment of the Chinese divers who dominate the sport. Daley's (2013) mother's response stresses her son's individualism: 'He was not born in Beijing. He was born in Plymouth. I saw a documentary a few years ago which showed the Chinese boot-camp style of training in sport. This is not Tom.' This echoes his autobiography:

> When the Chinese are younger, their parents make the decision whether they want them to be musicians, well educated or sportsmen or sportswomen and they keep working at it for their whole life. The diving training sounds brutal. The Chinese coaches are very forceful but are normally technically excellent. It's a very different culture; one that I'm sure I would do really badly in. (Daley 2012: 110)

Daley's success is constructed as a triumph of British individualism against the Chinese 'brutal', militaristic production line where parents 'make the decision' about their children's futures and coaches 'are very forceful'. He is also opposed to the British establishment. Daley's success is implicitly constructed as more valuable because he chooses it and motivates himself.

The final element of the entrepreneurial success discourse is impact. This is central to *Splash!*. In the second episode, Daley tells us that he is participating in the programme 'to show people that diving isn't as easy as it looks'. There are many references across the episodes to the difficulty of diving, and to the fears and dangers associated with it:

> Getting disorientated in the air is one of the most scary feelings because you don't know how you're going to hit the water or when. It hurts every time you hit the water. You hit the water at 34 miles per hour so it hurts even more if you don't get it right. The worst possible injuries are instant bruising, split skin, hitting your head on the board, breaking your back, tearing muscles. (Daley, in *Splash!*)

Daley's celebrity may rely on his media work but it is grounded in remarkable sporting achievements.

After the data collection was completed, in December 2013, Daley 'came out' about his relationship with Dustin Lance Black (whom he married in 2017). Posting a video on YouTube entitled 'There's Something I Want to Say', he explains: 'My life changed, massively, when I met someone and it made me feel so happy, so safe, and everything just feels great, and well, that someone [pause] is a guy. And it did take me by surprise a little bit.' Ken Plummer (1995) identifies a pattern to 'coming out' stories: they describe the teller as a subject who has been on some kind of journey of self-discovery, moving from isolation into a community, and doing so by taking on a new identity and revealing the 'truth' about their self. Daley's story is different in two key ways. First, he avoids all collective labels for his sexuality, even adding 'of course I still fancy girls', presumably to try to avoid being classified as gay. Second, he does not talk about a journey or a community to which he travels. Both of these reinforce the idea of him as an individual, yet again overcoming an obstacle to his success, in this case homophobia. The mode of his 'coming out' via a viral YouTube video supports the idea of him as an entrepreneurial self, using this forum rather than the mainstream media to speak on his own terms directly to the public. The video is bookended by talk of his successes at London 2012 and his ongoing training for Rio 2016 and Daley is filmed leaning on two Union Jack pillows, reminding us of his Britishness.

6

Happiness

Happiness is generally seen as a good thing. The US constitution guarantees citizens a right to 'the pursuit of happiness' (though not to happiness itself) and when advising people which path – whether educational, occupational or otherwise – to choose, we often suggest that they be guided by what makes them happy. In the Global Happiness Index, nations are ranked by their citizens' reported 'happiness levels' (Helliwell et al. 2016). Given its positioning as good, we might ask, following Will Davies (2015: 5): 'Is it possible to be against happiness?' Yet, in this chapter we show that happiness, like success (as seen in the last chapter), is neither innocent nor benevolent. Rather, we show how it works to regulate young people's aspirations within austere meritocracy by defining some aspirations as 'happy objects' to be sought, and others as 'unhappy objects' to be avoided. We are building on the ideas of Sara Ahmed, who suggests that rather than happiness being natural and authentic, society shapes what we find happy. 'If we arrive at objects with an expectation of how we will be affected by them, this affects how they affect us' (Ahmed 2010a: 29).

Overwhelmingly in our data, we find that three happy objects feature in young people's talk; things to which young people direct their own future happiness *and* that they associate with celebrity happiness, some of which we discussed in previous chapters. These objects are family relationships and friendships, financial stability, and a fulfilling career. Their accounts also reveal that some pathways and destinations are located as causing or symbolizing unhappiness. Some such unhappy objects correspond to an absence of happiness – for example, failed relationships, being unable to pay bills, or repetitive and unsatisfying work. Other unhappy objects are attached specifically to celebrity lifestyles, mainly addiction, media intrusion, inauthenticity and being a target of hate. As we saw in Chapter 2, these map on to anxieties typical of being young – 'risky' behaviour, peer pressure and bullying. Yet, in being associated with celebrity as an extreme case, they function to make fame less alluring, as we discuss further in Chapter 8. In this chapter, we focus on how celebrities become a means of circulating particular ideas of happiness (and unhappiness) and how this structures young people's aspirations, divorcing feelings of happiness from their social and economic contexts.

Happiness is perhaps the ultimate example of cruel optimism (Berlant 2011), in which something you desire is an obstacle to your flourishing. Society compels us to pursue happiness and presents it as realizable, yet attaches it to goals that few can attain in the current socioeconomic context. As we detailed in Chapter 1, austerity has seen cuts to the social supports that could make such happy objects possible for most people and enable different relationships to happiness. The state has slashed investment not just in education and employment but also in social security, community facilities and physical and mental health services. These conditions increase stress, misery and illness, as they replace socialized support for all with individualized 'relaxation' and 'well-being' for a select few. They are evidenced in declines in young people's mental health (Frith 2016). There has been a creeping influence of 'positive psychology' on education policy, with its emphasis on developing resilience, character, optimism and 'bouncebackability' in young people (Binkley 2011; Bull & Allen 2018). While business leaders and policymakers focus on happiness, by turning to positive psychology for policy solutions, the 'risk is that this science ends up blaming – and medicating – individuals for their own misery, and ignores the context that has contributed to it' (Davies 2015: 6). As we try to solve economic problems via psychology without confronting the underlying causes, we do lasting damage to people's lives.

Success and happiness, austere meritocracy's two legitimized goals, are intertwined. In the last chapter, we identified two success discourses. For those who define their goals through the stability success discourse that focuses on having enough to get by, happiness and success are aligned. For example, Archibald Brunel (SW, 16–17) reduces both success and happiness to 'just being able to get a decent job, erm like being able to get a decent income, being able to support like a family or something. That would make me happy.' Similarly, Daniella Norris (SW, 14–15) says that her happiness will come from 'being successful in what I'm doing, . . . being financially stable, erm, and then starting a family one day'.

In contrast, those young people who adopt the entrepreneurial success discourse tend to distinguish between a notion of success which involves perpetually striving for something better, and feelings of security and completeness that they associate with happiness. Thus, while our participants held two contrasting ideas of success, they held a single idea of happiness: family, stability and fulfilment. This is not surprising, for, 'We align ourselves with others by investing in the same objects as the cause of happiness' (Ahmed 2010a: 38). In the first two sections of this chapter we look at two of these shared happy objects: family relationships and fulfilling employment. We note some instances of the third happy object: financial stability (but we do not focus on it in depth here as it is discussed in Chapters 5 and 7). We then offer case studies of two young people, Sabeen and Person, who disrupt the dominant discourses of happiness. In this chapter and the last, in looking to people who break with what is normal, we are partly driven by sociologists' romantic attachment to 'rebels'. But primarily, we use those young people who, intentionally or unintentionally, break society's written and unwritten rules to explore how far it's possible for those imagining their future happiness (and success) within an austere meritocracy to resist neoliberal logics. Throughout, we track the central role of celebrity in circulating contemporary discourses of happiness.

'I think Will Smith is happy because I've seen his family': Happy families and happy celebrities

Family came up often in young people's discussions of happiness, and only rarely in relation to success. As Olivia Bolt (SW, 16–17) puts it, personal happiness is 'the sort of stuff outside' success 'like getting older, being married, having children and that sort of thing'. In these words, happiness, unlike success, appears to just happen, 'like getting older'. Yet a recurrence of talk of family and friends, marriage, and children in our data, including from Olivia, suggests the opposite: that people are already directed towards certain objects as things that will make them happy. As Ahmed (2010a: 23) argues, it 'is not that good things cause pleasure, but that the experience of pleasure is how some things become good for us over time'. Happy objects are good because we want them and we want them because they are good. They send us in the right direction, as indicated by the approval of our family and friends, their wishes for our futures, and the discourses of appropriate pathways that circulate throughout wider society, including via celebrity. Thus happiness is attached to some choices, not others.

While family and relationships can clearly be a source of unhappiness, they were almost exclusively spoken of in terms of happiness. Here are two of the many participants who talked about the role of family and friends in their future (and current) happiness:

> I wouldn't like be who I was if I didn't have my friends or my family around me, all of that. I think that's primarily what makes me happy. . . . But then there's obviously you want to be successful, be rich, but . . . I think friendship and family are worth more than money, because you could have all the money in the world but not be a happy person. You can't buy happiness can you? (Tom, SW, 16–17)

> I suppose as long as I'm with, I'm surrounded by people that you know, love me and care for me and I feel that we're happy and strong and

friends, and you know, I can support myself with whatever job I've got, I can live a happy life. . . . I'm able to support my children and I can give them the best life that I can give them that's happy. And then obviously to be happier, to have more money, to have a nicer life – that would obviously make me even happier, but to be basic happy that's just enough. (Rick, London, 16–17)

This is a profoundly relational version of both happiness and selfhood ('I wouldn't like be who I was if I didn't have my friends or my family around me'). Money is present, but there is a distancing from it as a goal, or at least an awareness that a desire for money is viewed as morally problematic (see Chapter 7). Rick, who, as we saw in the last chapter, ascribes to the entrepreneurial success discourse, distinguishes between 'basic happy' and 'happier'. It was unusual to construct wanting *more* as part of happiness, and even Rick sees basic happiness as 'enough' and, like other participants, to be found within family relationships. Some young people, particularly those aged 14 or 15, were reluctant to talk about their future family. While most imagined that marriage and parenthood would 'happen one day', it felt too distant for some to discuss in detail. Thus, celebrity talk – the abstracted discussion of others' lives – offered easier ways to express their collective commitment to such happy familial futures. Within their talk, some celebrities became happy objects precisely because of their proximity to family, and thus fulfilment. Others became unhappy objects because of their distance from family *and* their proximity to fame's unhappy objects.

Children, and to a lesser extent marriage, came up regularly in young people's rationales for why Beyoncé, Will Smith, Kim Kardashian and Kate Middleton were considered to be happy. For example,

I think Will Smith [is happy] because I've seen his family and they're all sort of doing well . . . when I've seen them on the red carpet they all interact, and he just messes about. . . . I'd say Kim as well again, because she gets along with like all of her family and stuff. I think they can have all the money in the world, but that isn't going to make you happy. And it's like Katie Price, she's got all the money but I think none of her relationships are working and she always seems to go downhill after a relationship's broke. (Kirsty, Manchester, 14–15)

Similarly, Wolfgang (Manchester, 14–15) feels Katie Price must be unhappy because of her failed marriages and states that Kim Kardashian 'must be the happiest woman in the world as well, because having a baby may be a struggle, but at the end of the day, the reward is like a gift, a diamond, a miracle'. Such statements are presented as *obvious*, something Lolita (SW, 16–17) makes explicit: 'Obviously, like [Kate Middleton] was happy because she fell in love with Prince William . . . the princess-ship . . . opened up lots of amazing opportunities . . . she seems very loveable and everyone seems to like her.' Through this obviousness a common sense of happiness circulates. 'Rather than assuming happiness is simply found in "happy persons", we can consider how claims to happiness make certain forms of personhood valuable' (Ahmed 2010a: 11). Drawing on this, attributions of happiness within celebrity talk are a key mechanism through which the social norm and ideal of family (and, arguably, a heteronormative nuclear family ideal) becomes affective, 'as if relative proximity to those norms and ideals creates happiness' (ibid.). Such celebrities simultaneously generate good feeling and act as validation for your own aspirations towards the same objects.

Occasionally participants talked about which celebrities deserve to be happy, for example, when Mariam (Manchester, 16–17) says of Kim Kardashian: 'She might be happy but she is basically just selling herself. . . . I don't think that anyone in her family has a real talent to deserve where they are now.' This discourse of celebrity deservingness is less common in participants' discussions of happiness than of success. It is part of why Kardashian's family happiness does not render her a happy object. But she is also associated with an amalgam of unhappy objects, including media intrusion, public abuse and, as we discuss in Chapters 3, 4 and 8, 'illegitimate fame'. In the individual interviews, we asked young people which of our twelve case-study celebrities they would want to befriend and which they would want to avoid if they were to attend their school. Through this exercise, they imagined patterns of friendship and avoidance which indicate desired proximity with people, and dis/alignment with their lifestyles, choices and values. They are thus orientations towards happiness and away from unhappiness. Within this, fifteen said they wanted to avoid Kardashian and only six to befriend her, with most of the others who recognized her making negative comments. The two young men who wanted to befriend her only did so through positioning her as 'hot' and 'hysterical to laugh at'. Just four young women, all from Manchester, (Aliyah, Kirsty, M9argi3, Manjula) gave positive reasons, citing their enjoyment of her television shows and her beauty, fashion knowledge, sense of humour and relationships with her sisters. As we can see in the talk about Kardashian, while there are always divergent views and counter discourses (for example, positioning her as a supportive sister or successful businesswoman), there are also dominant patterns (positioning her as an unhappy object).

Two celebrities emerge as the happiest of happy objects because of their combination of family and career fulfilment: Beyoncé and Will Smith. Smith is Chapter 3's celebrity case study and Beyoncé is this chapter's. In Beyoncé's, we show how inspiration and love circulate through her media representation, which is focused on combining family life with career success. Such evaluations of celebrity happiness were not consistently shared among all participants. For example, Alisha Ryan (London, 14–15) was sceptical about celebrity happiness, disputing its authenticity: 'I think they just act like they would be normal, like when they're at home . . . they're not really all happy.' But even she conceded that Will Smith is happy 'cos he's got everything that he – he's settled down'. Smith was the only celebrity who, if he were a student at their school, no participants wanted to avoid him. Over half wanted to befriend him and there was a striking enthusiasm for him across region, age, social class, gender and race.

In her individual interview, Orlando (Manchester, 14–15) said: 'I don't think I've ever come across someone who doesn't like Beyoncé.' While eleven distanced themselves from Beyoncé in the individual interviews (a few saying they would avoid her, others that she was too focused on popularity), in all three groups where people said something negative about Beyoncé, the dissenting participants were quickly pulled back into the 'right' direction. The 'borders of skepticism' are reached and the 'skeptic returns to the paths of common-sense' (Billig 1992: 33). For example, in a London school, Strawberry says, 'I like Jay-Z and Beyoncé as a couple', Taylor agrees, 'They're a cute couple.' But Pringles sees them as 'overrated' and then Dr Lighty says, 'I don't like Beyoncé.' This last comment provokes strong and immediate outrage, and makes Dr Lighty jokingly give in to 'peer pressure' and agree that he likes her after all:

> Pringles: What?
> George: What?
> Lewis J: What? [laughter]
> Pringles: You don't like Beyoncé?
> George: How can you not like Beyoncé?
> Pringles: That's just weird.
> Dr Lighty: Then I like her then. [laughter]
> Pringles: You can dislike her if you want.
> George: Peer pressure.
> Dr Lighty: No, it's alright, I like her. (London, 16–17)

In these group interviews we can see that people are collectively oriented towards happiness through the policing of their taste in celebrities:

> Taste is not simply a matter of chance (whether you or I might happen to like this or that) but is acquired over time. . . . When people say, 'How can you like that!' they make their judgment against another by refusing to like what another likes, by suggesting that the object in which another invests his or her happiness is unworthy. . . . We have to work on the body such that the body's immediate reaction, how we sense the world and make sense of the world, take us in the 'right' direction. (Ahmed 2010a: 33–4)

This also, of course, applies to people who say, 'How can you not like that!' It is not just Beyoncé's happy family, as a new mother in a long-term relationship, that make it 'weird' not to like her. It is also that she is seen to successfully combine this with career fulfilment and a populist feminist articulation of empowerment, as we discuss next.

'When she was pregnant, she released an album as well': Happy careers and happy celebrities

Across our dataset, young people related happiness not simply to having a job for financial security, but to having a fulfilling and rewarding career, as we showed in Chapter 4. They disavowed routine jobs, epitomized by office work. For example, Julia (SW, 16–17), who hopes to become a military police officer, sees her personal happiness as 'to get somewhere where I feel like I'm doing a job that makes me happy because I'm achieving something, and doing something positive, not just for the money' (alongside, of course, 'a proper little family'). Anonymous (Manchester, 16–17) enjoys and is excited by mathematics and physics, subjects commonly constructed as antithetical to creativity (Mendick 2006). He wants a job using these subjects: 'The best job . . . would probably be the best job that keeps me like awake. . . . I'll get a job that shows something new every day.' Similar comments also come from people seeking the 'creative' work which is commonly associated with fulfil- ment, autonomy and creative expression (Allen et al. 2013; Gill 2002). For example, Joanna (London, 14–15), who wants to act, said, 'I would be really happy if I ended up getting a role in something out there.'

As noted in Chapter 4, an absence of human flourishing within work has been a long-standing critique of capitalism. It was seen by Karl Marx (1976/1867), and those developing his ideas, as humanity's goal, in contrast to alienation under capitalism. More recently, it has been raised by those arguing that we should use automation to do less paid work and have time to follow our own interests (Srnicek and Williams 2016). However, these approaches focus on providing the social and collective structures than can enable individual fulfilment and end our dependence on paid work, includ- ing a universal basic income from the state. Within an austere meritocracy, self-realization is entirely an individual and economic responsibility, within a precarious and casualized labour market in which the chances of attaining even an 'average' secure job have dropped. To exemplify this, we can return to Ginny, who we encountered in the last chapter. She associates happiness with books and online creativity through the microblogging site, Tumblr:

If you were to lock me in the library I'd be the happiest person alive. . . . I enjoy reading and I enjoy writing, so if you were to just, just give me that for the rest of my life I'd be happy. That and my Tumblr account. (London, 14–15)

Ginny, typical of our participants, sees the run up to her 16+ examinations as a big moment as 'even people with degrees are finding it hard to find jobs': 'This is my time . . . this is my point to do what I want to do, otherwise I'm just gonna be unhappy in a job that's average, . . . it's your life and you have to make it your own.' Examination success does not guarantee happiness, which is a site of ongoing work, but the spectre of examination failure dooms her to unhappiness. Ginny presents her own efforts as critical to escaping unhappiness in 'a job that's average' rather than one she enjoys. Once again we see a relation of cruel attachment for Ginny as she hopes not only for a decently paid job but one that offers variety and pleasure in an economy which cannot even provide most young people with the first. This leaves them 'embedded in a system of desires in which desiring itself makes that which the desired object promises more difficult to access' (Stuhr-Rommereim undated: 1–2). This attachment is doubly cruel: it conceals the structural inequalities of neo-liberal capitalism and it does this by provoking feelings of desire and shame. Fulfilment has a sense of closure that appears to be the opposite of the constant striving of the entrepreneurial success discourse, but they are linked. Happiness, like success, is constructed as one's own responsibility. It should be planned and worked towards by individuals, just as unhappiness must be guarded against. Celebrity talk, as we show next, is central to this.

Boo dreams of 'being able to write my opinions down and get money for it': 'I want to be a writer so I guess the things that could make me happy in being a writer would be money, success and . . . fame.'

> At home, I like write little short stories, or poems or whatever, I enjoy doing that. I don't show them to anyone, so I guess that sort of proves that it is what I want to do, rather than, because I want to please other people. . . . I think it is important to enjoy what you are doing, and I think to a lot of people, and probably to me, it is important to, to feel like you are doing something important or making a difference. Or, or inspiring people. . . . I don't think I will ever be good in a normal job, because I would always think I know better than the people who are in charge. . . . I think I would find it difficult to just sit back and give somebody a burger. (Manchester, 16–17)

Although Boo expresses desires for both money and fame, he is careful to manage his relationship to these illegitimate goals. He offers his private writing as proof that this is an authentic aspiration, that writing 'is what I want to do' rather than borne of a desire 'to please other people'. He also talks about 'higher' motivations, such as 'inspiring people', and 'making a difference'. He constructs himself as unfit for a 'normal job' associated with a lack of autonomy. This resonates with how he presents himself elsewhere in the interview as unable to conform to school rules. He invokes serving burgers (perhaps in McDonalds) to typify this routine 'normal job', constructing it as passive – 'just sit back'.

Boo's inspiration is Bill Gates, of whom he says, 'I think he has probably gone beyond structured education, intelligence-wise.' Boo saw Gates as someone 'cleverer than the teacher. . . . You would probably find it a bit arrogant, but in another way you would admire it and want to be like that.' Similarly, Syndicate (London, 14–15), who aspires to 'stuff that entertains me and like stuff that looks cool', including football, also wants 'to know that I've made a difference' and sees recognition by others as validation. As for Boo, Gates provides his model for this form of happiness: 'Bill Gates invents, if I made something, even if it wasn't that popular or anything. I just feel like I've done something that . . . I've achieved something that I've set out.' Gates is also associated with altruistic motivations such as philanthropy and inspiring others, rather than pursuing fame and money for their own sake. We return to Boo and Syndicate's aspirations for fame in Chapter 8.

Although Gates offers inspiration to those attaching happiness to 'making a difference', he is more strongly associated with success, as we saw in the last chapter. In the individual interviews, twelve people said they would try to avoid him and fifteen that they would try to befriend him. But even many of those who wanted to befriend him were not looking for close friendships with him; instead, they sought help with homework, to satisfy their curiosity about his lifestyle or to learn more about technology. These are strategic and instrumental alignments with Gates, rather than the kind of desire for proximity found in discussions of other celebrities. Will Smith and Beyoncé are the dominant happy objects because, unlike Gates, their celebrity combines family *and* career fulfilment. Beyoncé is associated with a plethora of socially approved goods: marriage, motherhood, career success, creativity, autonomy, respectability, dedication, talent, empowerment and philanthropy. Beyoncé was often seen as a good role model and compared favourably with other female artists such as Nicki Minaj, who attracted hate. As Roman (Manchester, 14–15), who idolizes Beyoncé, explains, 'You would see [Minaj] more of as a sex symbol, whereas Beyoncé . . . she does look sexy, . . . [but] classy and sexy at the same time.' A group in a rural school agreed that 'she's the most like, stable celebrity there is':

Tom: And her like values, and what she stands for. Like she's, she's like, isn't she like best friends with Michelle Obama? I swear she is. [laughter]

Paris: I'd love to be best friends with her. . . .

Interviewer: What are her values that you like?

Tom: Like she's quite, is she a feminist? Yeah, because her, all of her, when she goes on tour, all of her da –, well, not dancers, all of her band are women.

Paris: Yeah, they all are female, aren't they?

Tom: Yeah, there's an all-female band.

Paris: She's just incred –

Joe: She's also a working mum as well. She balances like being a mum as well as like, like when she was pregnant, she released an album as well, so.

Paris: Yeah. And she waited a while to get pregnant. Like they obviously planned for when her, when she wanted to get pregnant, so she could still have a career. (SW, 16–17)

Not all working mothers were praised in our data, as other chapters in this book attest, but as a 'hard-working' woman who combines career success with planned parenthood, Beyoncé is austere meritocracy's ideal subject (Allen et al. 2015b). Beyoncé was widely praised for her girl power feminist politics by young men and women alike, as this extract shows. While feminism has long been an unhappy object (Ahmed 2010a), Rosalind Gill (2016) talks about a 'new visibility' for feminism in which it becomes happier by distancing itself from 'angrier' versions, voiding itself of political content, and relating instead to style, beauty and confidence. The talk of a friendship between Beyoncé and Michelle Obama connects these two celebrity happy objects: autonomous women who combine career and family. Next we turn to two case studies of people who reject society's happy objects, starting with Sabeen, who sees marriage and motherhood as compromising her career ambitions.

'She's strong-minded, she knows what she wants': Feminist happiness and unhappy celebrities

Sabeen's (Manchester, 14–15) mother is employed as a carer, her brother works in a call centre and she identifies as working class 'through my parents'. However, she has some access to middle-class social capital through her uncle, who has contacts working in law, the field to which she aspires. While she discusses experience of racism, sexism, classism and Islamophobia, like others in this study, she is invested in meritocracy's promise: 'If you work hard enough I think you can get past the class barrier and just have the same opportunities as everyone else.' We include her in this chapter because she was the participant who most strongly rejected family as part of her future happiness. Ahmed (2010b) discusses 'the feminist killjoy', identifying how 'becoming a feminist can be an alienation from happiness', putting you out of line with your peers and community, as 'you do not experience happiness from the right things'. Sabeen, in focusing on her autonomy as a woman, in opposition to marriage and motherhood, becomes a happiness alien. We analyse this position, its relationship to celebrity and its feminist politics.

A few young women said they did not prioritize relationships, taking up a feminist discourse of focusing on their career and following a middle-class model of delayed, planned motherhood (McRobbie 2008). For example, Orlando explains, 'Everyone says "oh I want to be with someone", but ... my priority is not to find someone, fall in love, blah blah blah. . . . I do want children but not early.' Some others also spoke of delaying mother-hood, perhaps reflecting an awareness that society no longer easily accommodates young mothers. But only Sabeen took a strong position against family:

> No, no, no. I'm not one for getting married. I hate the whole marriage thing. . . . I just think if I get married that'll hold me back. Like I can't achieve my goals, I can't do anything if I've got a boyfriend or a hus-band. . . . And kids. I don't like kids. I don't like babies, they cry a lot. ... I don't find any point in having children at all. (Manchester, 14–15)

In a society where happiness and hope for the future are symbolically linked to children, this is a bold thing to say as a young woman (Edelman 2004). In contrast, Sabeen sees a career as a lawyer as a source of happiness for herself and others: 'I would like to be a lawyer' because 'you're making sure they're happy . . . through bringing them justice. . . . Like if some-body wants a divorce, they're unhappy and you know giving them a divorce makes them, like lifts a burden off their shoulders.' Her choice of examples is telling: she locates happiness in divorce, not marriage.

Although she cites her mother's independence in bringing up her children alone as the source of her own independent disposition, she draws exten-sively on female celebrities as resources to construct herself as autonomous and strong willed. These include Judy Sheindlin, a US professional judge and star of the reality television show *Judge Judy,* and rapper and singer Nicki Minaj. Sabeen's legal aspirations are linked to her memory of watching *Judge Judy* on television: 'I was like, I want to be that. I want to be a part of, in the courts, defending people and having arguments [laughs], which you get paid for. . . . Just the control that she had over them.' It is in such power-ful female celebrities that she finds support for her anti-family position. Two of the three people she identifies as wanting to befriend are commonly labelled 'strong women' within the media: Emma Watson and Nicki Minaj (the third is the ubiquitous Will Smith). She values their strength, intelli-gence and bravery and that they represent women in the male-dominated spaces of Hogwarts and rap music. Of Emma Watson's *Harry Potter* char-acter, Hermione, she says, 'She's the only girl and she always knew what to do, she knew the facts, she was a know-it-all, which helps, she's quite brave.' Sabeen, like other academically driven young women, enjoys seeing a 'know-it-all' smart girl on screen (Paule 2013). Aligining herself with Nicki Minaj was more controversial.

Sometimes young people took different positions in the group than the individual interviews, being more likely to follow collective views in the former. Those taking minority positions in groups, often, when challenged, conceded to the collective view, as Dr Lighty did in the earlier extract on Beyoncé. But Sabeen enacts the same contested position on Nicki Minaj in her group and individual interviews, persisting in the face of opposition from the rest of the group. In the individual interview she says of Minaj, 'She's strong-minded, she knows what she wants.' In the group interview, which we quoted in Chapter 4, when participants are considering celebrities they dislike, Dave classifies Minaj as 'the worst out of all of them'. The others agree, except Sabeen who asks: 'How's she bad?' When her sexualized lyrics and outfits are cited, Sabeen counters, 'I know, but that's her style.' When Dave suggests that 'she's only famous because she doesn't wear any clothes', Sabeen elaborates on her defence: 'She's the only good rapper that's a girl.... Like she's an independent female. She's put that across through her music.... Like you don't need a man to pay for you.' Dave and Jerome laugh at this, but Sabeen insists, 'It's not funny.' This shows her aligning with different happy objects than her peers: women like Minaj, who do not temper their autonomy with marriage, motherhood and respectability, as Beyoncé does. Sabeen is aware of this difference. When comparing herself to girls of similar backgrounds and ages, she finds, 'They're not as career-committed as me. They would prefer to get married first.... Like I wouldn't ever depend on anyone.' Her position as one of society's *happiness aliens* is also reflected in her relationships to her mother and her religion. When her mother tells her, 'You'll have to have children, because in Islam it's seen as good if you get married, have quite a lot of children, you've been blessed by God', she responds, 'Oh, I don't find anything like that.' Sabeen presents herself as starkly rejecting her mother's views, in contrast to other South Asian young women who describe engaging in complex processes of 'negotiating their own ideals with commitments to their parents and communities' (Bagguley & Hussain 2016: 53). The position of happiness alien is a difficult one to occupy. We have shown how celebrity offers a resource for this, but it creates tensions too.

Despite her distinctive position, when discussing reasons for celebrity happiness, Sabeen cites family and career fulfilment along with everyone else. She judges Will Smith happy as 'he's got a family, a very stable family. He's got a very successful career and just everything has worked out for him.' Similarly, Beyoncé is happy because 'she had a miscarriage and now she's got a family, she's on a world tour'. After the discussion of celebrity happiness, the interviewer asks Sabeen about her personal happiness and her reply diverges from the extracts above: 'Definitely a successful career. ... I'm not really concentrating on family or anything, I'd prefer to get my career successful, make sure I'm happy with that and then start with a family.' Here family appears as an object to orient towards, rather than against. The commonsense discourses within celebrity, and the dominant happy objects that circulate via celebrity, shape what Sabeen can say about her own life. Black feminist scholars point to the subversiveness of women's rap to 'create new conceptions of black womanhood that challenged traditional models rooted in racist and sexist stereotypes' (Chepp 2015: 214; see also Rose 1994). Controversial figures, unhappy objects like Nicki Minaj can create spaces to articulate Sabeen's different aspirations, ones that the feminist struggle has and continues to make possible. In the next section, we meet a young woman who resists the dominant norms of happiness not by orienting away from our society's happy objects, as Sabeen does, but by refusing to orient herself to anything at all.

'It might be difficult to achieve your dreams if you don't have any': Letting (un)happiness happen

Most of the young people with whom we spoke seemed comfortable in interview situations. Interviews are a familiar part of our culture and young people are increasingly asked to speak about themselves and so usually have well-rehearsed answers. However, Person McPerson – expressing perhaps quirkiness, perhaps a desire for anonymity in her choice of pseudonym – was an exception. She was studying for post-16 qualifications in English, film and drama in London. Even at the start of the interview, describing her locality, her talk is filled with uncertainty and hesitation, saying only 'It's okay' and then offering 'I don't know', 'Maybe, I don't know' and 'I have no idea' before finally reasserting 'It's okay' when the interviewer repeatedly attempts to get her to elaborate. Person knows much more about her local area than her interviewer, yet, she professes ignorance. Although giving slightly longer answers to some later questions, it is her refusal to speak directly about society's happy (or unhappy) objects, including celebrities, that we analyse here.

During most of the interview, she persistently and insistently expresses doubt and ignorance, including when asked about her future:

Interviewer: So what do you want to do after school?
Person: Maybe go university.
Interviewer: Okay. Erm, and have you got any idea of where you would want to go?
Person: No, I have no idea.
Interviewer: Okay, do you want a chance to stay in London, would you like to leave London?
Person: [exasperated] I don't know. [both laugh]
Interviewer: Okay. Have you figured out what subject you want to do?
Person: Nope.

Interviewer: Okay.

Person: I might do English but I'm not sure.

Interviewer: Okay. So why English rather than film or drama?

Person: I don't know.

Interviewer: [laughs] Okay, and have you got people to talk to to help you make your choices?

Person: Not really. . . .

Interviewer: Okay. So what is it about university that makes you want to go there?

Person: I don't know, to kind of put off whatever I have to do with my life. (London, 16–17)

Here, Person refuses not simply to tell the interviewer her plans, but to construct herself as the future-oriented, rational subject that austere meritocracy requires: one who plans her future and carefully weighs up the options before deciding where to invest herself. Instead, Person presents her next decision – to go to university – as arising out of a desire to delay such a future. She knows there is a prescribed pathway towards the happy objects she alludes to with the phrase 'whatever I have to do with my life'. But she orients herself askew from these rather than being directed by them. We can also see this dis/orientation in her celebrity talk.

When asked which celebrities she would want to befriend or avoid, Person mentions only Emma Watson, briefly explaining, 'She seems really cool. I don't know.' When the interviewer asks is there 'anybody else you'd want to be friends with?', she responds, sounding sarcastic, 'Maybe not. I don't know? I'm sure they are all great people.' She is then asked to identify celebrities from whom she wants to distance herself: 'Is there anybody who stands out as someone you'd want to avoid?' Sounding exasperated and a little uncomfortable, she simply replies, 'No.' Given the role of celebrity talk in circulating ideas about happiness, as developed above, in not speaking about other celebrities, she also does not align with those objects her society deems the causes of happiness. Her discomfort here can be read as a discomfort with the interviewer's demand that she do this. While this is also a refusal of dominant success discourses, Person talks differently about celebrity happiness and success:

Interviewer: Do you think that there are things that would make these people happy or unhappy?

Person: Things?

Interviewer: Yeah.

Person: Erm. What type of things?

Interviewer: Well I'm asking like do you think there's things which, you know I think 'oh I think Justin Bieber, this would make Justin happy or this would make him unhappy'?

Person: Erm, er [pause, slight laugh] I don't know.

Interviewer: You don't have any sense of what makes any of them happy or unhappy? Okay. [slight laugh] And what do you think makes them successful or not?

Person: [voice more assured now] Maybe the publicity they get.

Interviewer: Okay.

Person: And the followers.

Interviewer: So people who have more followers are more successful?

Person: Or I don't know it depends sometimes people that, are quite hated are quite successful as well. Like Katie Price I guess. She just gets a lot of publicity.

Interviewer: Yes, so why do you think she's hated?

Person: Erm, I don't know people seem to think she's, I don't know a bit attention seeking maybe.

Interviewer: Okay. Erm, any other things which make people successful?

Person: Erm, their attractiveness. And their, the things that they offer like their music or talent or acting I guess.

Person is visibly uncomfortable talking about happiness, unwilling to offer the conventional happy objects of family and fulfilment that appear to come easily to other young people. She is more comfortable discussing success and offers specific examples of publicity, hate and talent, in what, for her, are relatively long and certain answers. This suggests that acknowledging dominant ideas of happiness is more challenging to her way of being than acknowledging dominant ideas of success.

People, particularly her teachers (and her interviewer), may find Person's apparent inability to choose anything – from her future to her favourite celebrities – frustrating or annoying. But Person's silences and brief responses can be read as a form of resistance (Parpart 2010), specifically resistance to the invitation to account for herself as aspirational and to plan for her future happiness. Towards the end of the interview, she is asked, 'Do you think there are things which make it difficult for young people to achieve their dreams?' After asking for an example, she offers, 'Er, erm. [pause] I'm not sure, it might be difficult to achieve your dreams if you don't have any. But I don't know, maybe.' The interviewer, thinking aloud, begins to conceptualize Person's position, commenting that the question 'assumes that you have something you want to end up doing, but if you haven't got that then actually, if you just let things happen, as they happen, which is kind of what you do isn't it'? Person's relatively assertive 'yeah' in response suggests we can read her refusal to dream as a way of being in the moment and letting things happen. Rather than planning happiness around 'whatever I have to do with my life', she deliberately postpones this so that she can find happiness in whatever happens to happen. 'When we are estranged from happiness, things happen' (Ahmed 2010a: 218), happiness becomes one possibility among others. Within our austere meritocracy, this appears as unhappiness. But refusing the dominant version of happiness may carry new possibilities for happiness for Person and Sabeen, and a partial escape from the social relations of cruel optimism.

Conclusion

Happiness, the thing which carries the illusion of being deeply personal and individual, shows the most uniformity in our data. Happiness, like success, takes on legitimate (and illegitimate) forms within austere meritocracy. Individual goals – of family, security and career – are prioritized over collective ones, such as justice, equity and solidarity. Although the focus on family and friends is relational, it is privatized, not collectivized, recalling former UK Prime Minister Margaret Thatcher's famous words: 'There's no such thing as society. There are individual men and women and there are families.' (in Keay 1987). Happiness has become an individual responsibility, rather than a human right. Happiness must be strived towards through self-work, and as such, it is positioned in the future: 'Happiness is weighty not because of its point, as if it simply had a point, but because happiness evokes a point that lies elsewhere, just over the horizon, in the very mode of aspiring for something' (Ahmed 2010a: 204). Happiness is therefore central to the operation of austere meritocracy – its promise via 'happy objects' creates a space in which growing inequalities and poverty can persist without overturning the dominant narrative of social mobility. Happiness is perhaps the book's clearest example of cruel optimism, given how distant its 'objects' are for most young people.

Happiness, like success, must be achieved through work and authenticity, as discussed in Chapters 3 and 4. When it is perceived to have been achieved through other means, as in the case of Kim Kardashian, her happiness cannot convert her from an unhappy to a happy object. She – like the other celebrity unhappy objects of Justin Bieber, Katie Price and Nicki Minaj – is aligned with the illegitimate goals of austere meritocracy: gratuitous wealth and talentless fame. We examine these in the next two chapters. But before that, it is worth reflecting on our two case studies of happiness aliens, who point to what might happen if you remove the 'goals' of happiness. 'If we do not assume that happiness is what we must defend, if we start questioning the happiness we are defending, then we can ask other questions about life, about what we want from life, or what we want life to become' (Ahmed 2010a: 218). As noted above, this letting go might allow other, more bearable ways of being, something to which we return in the conclusion.

CELEBRITY CASE STUDY: BEYONCÉ

FIGURE 6.1 *Beyoncé, photograph by Kristopher Harris, no changes made. Licence https://creativecommons.org/licenses/by/2.0/.*

Given the value attached to happiness, many celebrities project an image of themselves as having a fulfilling career that they combine with rewarding family relationships and friendships. In this case study we exemplify this through African-American singer and actor Beyoncé. Beyoncé became famous as part of the girl group Destiny's Child, managed by her father, Matthew Knowles. After a series of hit singles and albums, she launched a solo career, often cowriting and coproducing her output, and has developed a parallel acting career. She is well known for combining her career with marriage to rapper Jay-Z (Shawn Carter). Their daughter, Blue Ivy Carter, was born in 2012. We largely discuss her image as it was when we collected the interview data, commenting briefly at the end on recent shifts in her celebrity.

Beyoncé's marriage to Jay-Z is central to her public profile, with regular stories in the press about everything from a cinema trip to a family holiday. The 2013 autobiographical documentary *Life Is But a Dream* includes many 'private' moments, perhaps the most intimate of which is home video footage showing Beyoncé and Jay-Z, at the end of his birthday celebration, her arm around him, singing Coldplay's song *Yellow* as they look into each other's eyes. As the footage rolls, the audio is lowered and replaced by Beyoncé's voice:

> I just pray that Jay and I stay a team cos right now we are really connected and really are communicating well and completely understand each other, support each other and need each other. This baby has made me love him more than I ever thought I could love another human being. It's just I love him so much, like, we almost feel like one.

The audio then replaces the voice-over and switches again as the scene ends with Beyoncé's words: 'I hope I remember this when the baby comes and it gets tough cos it's going to be an adjustment cos this feeling is so beautiful. It's every woman's dream to feel this way about someone.' This moment, widely shared on social media, locates happiness in a loving relationship. The film covers Beyoncé's pain after she miscarried, and her happiness at her second pregnancy and motherhood. Its penultimate image shows her holding Blue Ivy. Its final image is Beyoncé on stage. These two images depict family and career, the happy objects her celebrity representation combines.

Beyoncé presents herself as 'living the dream' not just through her family but also through her career. In the image where she stands on stage at the end of the documentary, she declares herself 'the luckiest girl in the world' because 'I get to stand up on this stage and entertain all y'all. And for two hours, y'all are not thinking about your break-ups, your money, your problems. Y'all are just having a good old time.' Beyoncé provides escape from the toxic cruelties of the present, the stifled dreams and fraying fantasies of the good life. But she also drives reattachment to these fantasies: if you work hard like Beyoncé, you too can achieve the good life. Hard work saturates Andrew Vaughn's (2012) biography, with recurring references to Beyoncé's 'remarkable work ethic' (p. 8), 'tireless determination' (p. 32) and identity as 'a self-confessed workaholic' (p. 156). Memes circulating online contain quotes from the star, such as 'whenever I feel bad, I use that feeling to motivate me to work harder'.

But Beyoncé's image shows how, despite being a 'workaholic', she displays a carefully balanced commitment to family *and* career. It is this that enables her to align with feminism without sharing its associations with unhappiness that we discussed earlier. It is typified by this quote from her: 'After giving birth, there's a moment of rediscovering who you are. … I wanted to make sure I still was this strong woman with my business and also making time for my child and balancing the two' (in Asi 2013). In *Life Is But a Dream,* a dual assertion of career independence and motherhood is manifest in her commitment to working throughout her pregnancy. Over footage of her Billboard music awards performance, Beyoncé explains, 'Nobody knew I was pregnant during that performance and I'm cool with that. I'm not interested in a free ride. But it absolutely proved to me that women have to work much harder to make it in this world.' Tellingly, this performance is of 'Run the World (Girls)', one of her many anthems to female power. However, she carefully negotiates this position. Beyoncé uses parody to distance herself from the more risqué characters she performs on stage or film, and from her 'alter ego' Sasha Fierce, 'the fun, more sensual, more aggressive, more outspoken side and more glamorous side that comes out when I'm on stage' (in Vaughn 2012: 131). Beyoncé foregrounded her identity as a wife by using her 'married name' on her 2013 'Mrs Carter' tour. Reports of the tour asserted conservative gender relations, noting that it was 'named in honour of the man who wears the trousers in her house' (Smart 2013). She frequently credits Jay-Z with shaping who she is as an artist.

Following Angela McRobbie (2008), we could understand Beyoncé's feminism as a popular version within which feminism is 'taken into account' so as to negate the need for a deeper social critique. This girl power variant focuses on women's actions as barriers to their success, deflecting attention from the social and economic forces that produce gender and intersecting inequalities. Given the decimation of state-supported childcare, Beyoncé's do-it-all working mother is perfectly in sync with austere meritocracy's demand that women take responsibility for their success, pursuing their professional ambitions without abandoning desires for family life. However, this reading of Beyoncé ignores the intersections of race and gender in the United States. As Patricia Hill Collins (2012: 132) identifies, 'the strong-black-woman/weak-black-man thesis' shapes what is possible for African-American celebrity couples. Beyoncé, as a black woman, has to be careful to negotiate her public (and private) position in relation to her husband. Her talk about the difficulties of being a working mum softens the stereotypes of the strong black (emasculating) woman and fulfils the social obligation to 'simultaneously show that her career harms neither her marriage nor her family life' (Collins 2012: 138).

Since we collected data, there have been rumours of Jay-Z's infidelity. It is unclear how this will impact her alignment with happiness (although her latest pregnancy announced in February 2017 will reaffirm this). More significantly, Beyoncé has engaged with US race politics. She has attended protests with Jay-Z and posted bail for fellow protesters. 2016's hit 'Formation' visually referenced the Blank Panther and Black Lives Matter movements. Despite this, her celebrity still draws strongly on discourses of individual responsibility and success through entrepreneurship. 'Formation''s lyrics advocate wealth and consumerism, speaking of a 'Black Bill Gates'. However, it – and other songs on her *Lemonade* album – also contains discourses of collective struggle against sexism and racism. The song's racial politics shocked white America. When she performed it at the Superbowl, her black anger was seen as disturbing white people's viewing pleasure. US comedy show *Saturday Night Live* captured this shock in a trailer for a fake horror film entitled 'The Day Beyoncé Turned Black'. This suggests that she may be puncturing austere meritocracy and offering a critical voice on race, raising questions about whether her status as a happy object can survive this. Her celebrity suggests the possibilities that emerge from fracturing the dominant discourse of happiness that silences discussions of justice and solidarity.

7

Money

Individually, man is thrifty; collectively he tends to be spendthrift, and Governments in general, and Labour Governments in particular, simply love spending other people's money. When they talk about government giving subsidies to this, that, and the other it really sticks in my gullet. Government hasn't got any subsidies to give! They can only get their subsidies by taxing the chap who works hard, by taxing the chap who has acquired extra skill, by taxing the manager, by taxing the professional person, by taxing the small businessman, by taxing even some of the pensioners if they've got a bit of savings of their own.

(THATCHER 1979)

Money is at the heart of a fundamental contradiction of austere meritocracy. Our conversations with young people show that the contemporary discourse of 'responsible citizenship' requires them to be both financially secure through paid work ('striving' not 'scrounging') and thrifty. Money was thus framed as an implicit requirement to be a successful subject of austere meritocracy. But desiring too much money or focusing on wealth or conspicuous consumption as a goal were derided as illegitimate or inauthentic aspirations. The moral othering of overt materialism seems at first glance to contradict the wider requirements of global neoliberal capitalism – which needs steady markets for its goods, particularly during an economic downturn. Indeed, as we argued in Chapter 1, the 'customer' was the ideal enterprising subject of 1980s social mobility. Our data show that Margaret Thatcher's connection of consumption to citizenship remains in contemporary neoliberal rhetoric. However, within our austere meritocracy, the consumer-citizen has been reframed through moral discourses of waste and thrift.

A central feature of the narrative of austerity has been the problematizing of waste and wastefulness – both in terms of the previous Labour government's budgets and 'overgenerous' welfare programme, and 'irresponsible' and 'excessive' spending by individuals, namely the poor (Cameron et al. 2016). In austerity, practices of thrift and fiscal restraint become privileged solutions to the crisis at national and individual levels (Allen et al. 2015b; Jensen 2013), alongside entrepreneurship and resilience in the pursuit of the legitimized aspirations of success and happiness, as discussed in the previous two chapters. Moral discourses of waste and thrift not only crystallize in speeches about the government's economic plan, but also in responses to events such as the 2011 riots and through reality television (see Chapter 1). These framings were evident in our conversations with participants, who presented money as a symbol of responsibility and stability, but also potentially of irresponsibility and deviance (when not spent wisely).

Government privatization since the global financial crash represents the biggest shift of money from public to private wealth, 'of all time, higher than the previous record in 1987', as the Chancellor boasted in 2015 (Williams-Grut 2015). Austerity rhetoric has had to find a way to reconcile the call for everyone to 'tighten their belts' at the same time as there is visible and escalating wealth among the richest in society (Dorling 2014a; Sayer 2014). As we show in this chapter, celebrity talk is a way that young people make sense of this economic inequality. Evaluating the behaviours and motivations of the rich and famous provides a space to negotiate the contradictions and tensions surrounding wealth within austere meritocracy. Analysing their talk helps us untangle the position of money in their own lives.

In the context of requirements for financial stability and thrift, there were two main ways that wealth was rendered legitimate in young people's talk: via discourses of entrepreneurship and philanthropy. In this chapter, we tease apart these discourses. We begin by analysing how young people talked about money in their own lives, looking at those who wanted 'enough to get by' and the small number of participants who wanted to be rich. Then we turn to exploring participants' evaluations of celebrity consumption – examining how conspicuous consumption and thrift were presented as evidence of 'undeserving' and 'deserving' wealth respectively. Finally we examine the justifications young people made to account for extreme wealth – looking at how entrepreneurship and philanthropy figured to inoculate celebrities from criticism of greed or excess.

'I think no matter how much I don't want to say, money is a big part of it': Managing the contradictions of money in austere meritocracy

Contrary to the dominant narrative that young people want to get rich quick, becoming wealthy was rarely stated as an explicit aspiration by our participants. However, talk of money threaded through the group and individual interviews and played an important role in many young people's imagined futures, with thirty-nine of the fifty-one individual interviewees aspiring to have enough to get by. For example,

> Having enough money to support myself so like for a house and paying bills and stuff. Erm, well yeah, get a job. . . . Obviously just keep having enough to feed your family and stuff. That's all you need really I think. I don't, and any added extras would be a bonus but they're not essential. (Herbert, SW, 14–15)

Money was mostly presented as a resource that could be used to achieve success or happiness – austere meritocracy's legitimized goals. But becoming rich rarely appeared as an objective in and of itself. Herbert's comment above and Rick's (London 16–17) desire for a 'happy life' discussed in Chapter 6 show how talk of money was often accompanied by, and couched within, aspirations for family, security and career fulfilment. This serves to distance participants from the 'illegitimate' desire for 'excessive' wealth, while nonetheless signalling the need for financial security. As we showed in our analysis of the stability success discourse in Chapter 5, young people had to grapple with this tension as they talked about their futures:

> I think no matter how much I don't want to say, money is a big part of it, and I think that does make people, it allows people to achieve what they need to become successful. And also, yeah, I've kind of covered it, money second, like just general like being happy in yourself, achieving what you want to achieve, having a family. . . . Like having a job, I want to like constantly be learning and doing something I enjoy, and yeah, getting some money for it as well, preferably [laughs]. But if I didn't, but everything was still fine, then like, yeah, money doesn't have to matter if everything still runs smoothly. (Lolita, SW, 16–17)

Lolita's account illustrates the fundamental tension between the necessity and illegitimacy of money in austerity. She '[doesn't] want to say' that money plays a big role in her imagined future. She even tempers her need to be paid to work as something that would be 'preferable' rather than essential. However, for many young people, finding paid work was an important part of having a secure future. The need to be able to make 'next month's payments' (Rick, London, 16–17) surfaced regularly across our interviews, as the requirement for money was largely articulated in terms of the risks of its potential absence, rather than a desire to amass wealth. A lack of money was therefore presented as a potential barrier to achieving dreams, both in terms of accessing resources now and in the future:

> If you have money you've got a better chance. I mean you can get into greater colleges, you can like you're kind of cushioned if things don't go quite right for you, so you can fall back on that and like pick yourself up. Whereas if you're in a lower class, it's either get it right first time or die trying. (Archibald, SW, 16–17)

> I think money is a huge thing, a huge, huge thing. Everything, anywhere you want to go, anything you want to do, anything you want to achieve, has become really expensive. Going to uni[versity] for any amount of time is extortionate now and there's not as much help as there used to be. (Julia, SW, 16–17)

As discussed in Chapter 2, while few participants explicitly mobilized a language of austerity, its marks can be seen across the interviews. Many oriented themselves towards a potentially insecure future in which they would need to ensure that they could support themselves and their families. Thus, as in Archibald's comment above, money appears as a resource, but also as a safety net in times of uncertainty. Both Julia and Archibald indicate that not everyone has access to the same level of financial security. However, while these accounts of inequality can be found in the interviews, young people overwhelmingly presented financial security as an individual responsibility. The discourse of earning enough to get by is expressed in the everyday language of bill payment, but its implications are stark. Not getting by means being unable to 'feed my family' and 'support myself', failing to meet 'basic' needs such as housing and utilities.

There was little discussion of the possibility of social support to meet everyday needs. Talk about the welfare state was conspicuous in its absence. Social security was rarely mentioned, except for one young person who was critical of stereotypes of benefit claimants. Wider cuts to public spending were mentioned slightly more regularly – largely through reference to rising university tuition fees and cuts to the Education Maintenance Allowance (EMA) to support post-16 study. This framing of everyday security as an issue of individual rather than collective responsibility has been a cornerstone of neoliberal political rhetoric since the late 1970s. As in the quotation from Margaret Thatcher's speech that opens this chapter, the dismantling of the welfare state under her government was presented as a responsible solution to Labour's spendthrift approach. This narrative of debt caused by irresponsible public spending has reappeared with the current Conservative government's austerity policies. Previous Labour governments are criticized for creating a broken benefit system which trapped the poor in a state of 'welfare dependency' (Cameron et al. 2016). Austerity is framed as a 'necessary evil' to 'balance the books' after the global financial crisis (Afoko & Vockins 2013; Clarke & Newman 2012).

However, while both Thatcher and Reagan positioned the rollback of the state as responsible spending, under them becoming wealthy was presented as a legitimate goal of the enterprising neoliberal subject. Acquiring property and luxury consumer goods were presented as symbols of social mobility through entrepreneurship (Littler 2013). This new 'self-made' middle class was sometimes derided in stereotypes of yuppies with tasteless desires for loadsamoney (Biressi & Nunn 2013b). Despite this, the accumulation of wealth and consumer goods remained a central aspirational discourse in the early years of neoliberalism – evidence of graft and enterprise (Littler 2013). In contrast to this narrative of consumerist meritocracy, as we have seen, in our data young people were critical of desiring too much money or being motivated by money alone. This was particularly apparent in participants' discussions of celebrity wealth, in which excessive money and conspicuous consumption usually met with disapproval, as we show below.

It is important to note that while some forms of conspicuous consumption and wealth were framed as problematic, eleven out of fifty-one participants explicitly mentioned wealth in their aspirations. This aspiration, however, was generally framed within a discourse of social mobility and the possibility of buying things for their families. For example, in Chapter 5 we explored Homer's (London, 14–15) aspirations to become a plasterer, plumber, electrician or welder. In Homer's narrative, money was a marker of both success and happiness, enabling him to access 'a nice estate' and other consumer items for his family. Homer talks about wanting to 'get to upper class' and be 'posh' like his uncle, who 'always dresses well, he's got everything he wants. He's got a big house. Yeah, that would be good if I could have that'. His aspiration to buy things for his family, live in a nice house and 'get to upper class' reflect a wider meritocratic discourse in which hard work leads to social mobility. However, the cracks in this cruel optimism are clear in Homer's prediction that he would not become rich – an avenue he felt was only open to 'clever' people.

Aspirations to acquire wealth manifest in a different way in Manjula's account. Manjula wants to work in finance, which she sees as a well-paid career path that would allow her to get 'stuff I can't get at the moment, like I want to get a pair of Louis Vuitton's' shoes. She describes herself as 'upper middle class' in relation to her father's job as a dentist, and that she has 'enough money for university and [does not] have to worry about the bills and everything'. Although Manjula occupies a different class position to Homer, her aspirations for money and designer goods are also infused by discourses of social mobility. Despite her father's professional occupation,

Manjula's class position is complicated. She discusses her mother's geographical and social mobility from a tiny village on the border between Pakistan and Afghanistan (a 'very quiet and a not very wealthy area'). She explains that her mother

> didn't come from a very wealthy family, like she didn't get a lot of clothes, she didn't get a lot of good, nice things . . . [her] lifestyle was different from mine . . . because like when she was a little kid she told me she always imagined that, what it's like having a lot of money and stuff. (Manchester, 16–17)

In this light, Manjula's aspirations for wealth and consumer goods are not simply signs of materialism, but of desire for symbols of upward class mobility, what Carolyn Steedman (1986: 38) refers to as the 'goods of the world of privilege and possession'. Manjula's aspirations to work hard and earn money are thus embedded within family histories of migration and desires for class mobility.

The moral discourse that surrounds money can make it tricky to navigate, particularly when talking about personal aspirations. Talk about other people, like celebrities, provides a less risky space to explore such difficult topics. Unlike young people's talk about themselves, when they were asked what made celebrities happy and successful, money was often discussed. However, the relationship between money, success and happiness needed to be carefully managed. Much of the talk about celebrity wealth focused on their practices of consumption, framed by the distinction between wasteful conspicuous consumption and responsible thrift, as we explore in the next two sections.

'I think money destroys them really': Celebrity consumption and illegitimate wealth

Young people did not uncritically accept celebrity wealth and status. Talk about celebrity wealth was often accompanied by explicit or implicit criticisms and justifications, as participants grappled with inequalities between their own lives and those of celebrities. Celebrities whom they considered to be motivated purely by money, and engaging in excessive consumption, were criticized:

Interviewer: Any thoughts on [the] perfect celebrity, their lifestyle?
Saafi: Um not someone that spends way too much on stuff they don't need. . . . If they've got money, fine, they can buy a few things, but then like, I think it was Beyoncé and Jay-Z's baby [All: yeah] they bought it a like, a solid gold rocking horse, or something.

Interviewer: [laughs] Okay.

Saafi: And I was just thinking, what kind of a baby's going to need that, like.

Kirsty: They won't even know what it is at that age.

Saafi: Yeah, like you shouldn't spend too much on something that you know is not really a necessity. (Manchester, 14–15)

The wealth of celebrity couple Beyoncé and Jay-Z is presented as almost impossible to imagine. There is an implicit reference to the inheritance of wealth, in which their baby is bought a 'solid gold rocking horse' – presented as an ostentatious display of money which cannot even be appreciated by the (young) recipient. Describing the toy as 'solid gold' serves to reinforce its otherworldly status as 'not really a necessity'. Money here is constructed as something that should not be splashed around.

The tension between the right to spend earned money ('if they've got money, fine, they can buy a few things'), and not taking too much could also be seen in the disagreements between participants:

Interviewer: What else makes them an ideal celebrity? What kind of life do they have?

Ryan: Someone who doesn't go out and buy a big twenty-bedroom mansion.

Alisha: Yeah. But everyone would want that wouldn't they?

Homer: Everyone wants it.

Alisha: If you deserve it, you owned it, you should deserve it. Exactly.

Homer: No. I'd have a big house but not something that cost like a million pounds.

Alisha: Well if they can afford it they should get it.

Ryan: Yeah, but depending on the cost.

Homer: Everyone wants to be a cut above.

Lise: Like everything luxury and then they forget that there is other people that need help as well.

Alisha: Yeah but they can help people if they have the money too, and plus like give them something.

Lise: Some people they just waste their money on themselves.

Jack: Some people don't need. (London, 14–15)

In the extract above, the participants do not initially agree upon whether it is acceptable to buy an expensive mansion. Their disagreement provokes the need for the different speakers to provide further explanations and justifications for their points. Michael Billig (1996) has argued that the presence of such argumentation reveals the different versions of common sense circulating at a given moment. He argues that common sense is inherently contradictory, and that in thought and talk, its 'various elements . . . are seen to collide in a way which on occasions necessitates difficult decisions'

(Billig et al. 1988: 16). As participants seek to resolve the disagreement, or persuade each other of their position, they draw on other forms of shared common sense – highlighting which ideas are most widely shared.

Thus in the extracts above, two versions of common sense about money collide and require resolution. First, that people should not 'waste' money on unnecessarily ostentatious items, such as a twenty-bedroom mansion (or a solid gold rocking horse), particularly when other people have less money or need help. Second, if you have earned your wealth, you should be able to spend it on what you want. The criticism of conspicuous consumption here is rooted in questions of inequality: Why take something that you 'don't need' when someone else 'needs help'? Homer's own desires to consume and become 'posh' are not articulated as explicitly in this group interview as in his individual interview. This suggests such aspirations are less accept-able in a peer group situation. While social class is not explicitly articulated, Homer's comment that such purchases reflect a desire to be 'a cut above' point to consumption's role as a marker of social difference: to be 'above' points to someone being 'below'.

Wealth inequality is not immediately accepted by participants, but has to be justified as legitimate. It is not enough to simply 'want' a mansion; it must be 'deserved'. And even if it is deserved, purchasing luxury items can only be acceptable if the wealthy individual *also* gives to others. We return to the justificatory function of philanthropy later in this chapter. Here we want to explore this relationship between conspicuous consumption and 'deserved' wealth. In the following extract a different group of young people discuss footballers' salaries:

Julia: They should not earn five million pounds for kicking a ball around a field, it is wrong.
Jinny: They don't do what doctors do, it's ridiculous.
Dumbledore: I wouldn't –
Julia: They don't deserve it.
Dumbledore: Yeah.
Steve: There are footballers who do give their wages away to charity, they give like a lot away.
Jinny: They do that because they're in the press though.
Dumbledore: I wouldn't care if they got paid that much.
Steve: They don't want too much hate from people but they still – the fact that they get this money, they're not just keeping it for them-selves, they know that footballers don't need that much.
Julia: But they've got it to throw around, haven't they really?
Dumbledore: The trouble is I really don't care how much a person earns, I wouldn't use that to judge them, it's just the fact that a great many of the most famous footballers shall we say, oh each time I talk I just sound more stupid and up myself, that's not what I'm trying to do. [laughter] Who was the guy a couple of weeks ago

who went around, for no reason whatsoever, other than the fact his girlfriend suggested it, and he had a big sack of um money and stuff, and he distributed it to people, to homeless people? . . . You get a footballer like that, who did, because his girlfriend suggested it, and someone who contributes absolutely nothing, clearly because he hasn't got any press coverage on his back at that particular time. (SW, 16–17)

The exchange above is characteristic of the disagreements young people had about footballers' pay (introduced in Chapter 4). As with the twenty-bedroom mansion, here participants are grappling with questions of extreme wealth and inequality. Footballers' salaries were commonly contrasted with those of other workers – particularly in the armed forces and the health service. Much like the conversations above, some of the young people are critical of wealth that seems 'too much'. While they do not necessarily agree about how much footballers should be paid, there is consensus that money should not be 'thrown around'. Dumbledore's story is about footballer Mario Balotelli. What is important for us is not whether the story itself is true, but how it constructs a particular image of wealth and consumption. The narrative is one of the 'wrong' kind of wealth: flashy, self-oriented and irresponsible. There is a performative aspect to Dumbledore's talk, expressing views that are likely to be shared by the group. As we saw in Chapter 5, in his individual interview, he speaks of Balotelli's stunt as something he would like to be able to do. This talk resonates with the discourse of immaturity that was often evident in young people's discussions of Balotelli. Portraying him as someone who does not spend his money wisely, has not yet grown up and is still 'playing'. This image of Balotelli's stupidity aligns with deeply-rooted racist discourses of intelligence in which black people figure at a lower stage of 'development' (Gillborn 2016).

Although charitable donations could be used to justify wealth, as we show below, Balotelli's mythical gift is constructed as inauthentic, in a way that many formal charity donations, such as those made by Bill Gates, were not. We discussed this difference between real and fake philanthropy in Chapter 4. It stems partly from the relationship between the notion of 'deserved' wealth and the ideas about hard work and entrepreneurship discussed in Chapters 3 and 5. Julia's comment about the level of payment some footballers receive for 'kicking a ball around' highlights a sense of injustice, with discomfort levelled at the prospect of receiving higher salaries for less effort than those working in other jobs. It was sometimes possible for footballers to be described as hard working through reference to their training. However, the comparisons between footballers and public sector workers set the latter up as heroic figures who sacrifice themselves in order to 'do good' for wider society. These celebrities are symbolic of the 'hard-working families' that circulate within the government rhetoric of deservingness that is used to justify welfare reform (see Chapter 3). Dumbledore's irritation with Balotelli's mythical 'big sack of money' is grounded in a feeling that this was a cynical publicity stunt from 'someone who contributes absolutely nothing'. Steve's comments above, that footballers give to charity to show that they are 'not keeping it all for themselves', point to a commonsense position that the wealthy should contribute to society. The discourses surrounding wealth in austere meritocracy are therefore moral ones. While extreme riches could be justified in some cases, having vast sums of money was largely positioned as potentially dangerous and wasteful in the wrong hands:

> I don't think [footballers are] someone to look up to. Like, young boys, or whatever, they expect like, they're interested in football, and they think like 'Oh, I'm gonna become a footballer', but footballers don't really work as hard as some other people, and they get paid extreme amounts of money. And I just think they flunk it on wrong things, and they act like idiots with it. And they end up sleeping with other people, when they're like married. And I think money destroys them really. (Luigi, London, 16–17)

Luigi criticises and infantilizes footballers for acting like 'idiots' with their money. Historically, footballers are a classed and racialized category associated with stupidity and immaturity, along with other working-class and black celebrities. As the other to middle-class responsibilized spending, 'working-class people are not primarily marked as lacking and disgusting through their poverty, but through their assumed lack of knowledge and taste . . . which would, presumably, enable them to "see through" consumerism' (Lawler 2005: 800). Positioning footballers' spending habits as immoral is compounded by locating these spending habits as leading to other bad behaviour, such as extramarital affairs. Money in this narrative is itself the cause of other problems. It is money that 'destroys them'. Having extreme wealth is therefore presented not just as potentially unfair, but risky: causing celebrities to 'go off the rails' (Harvey et al. 2015).

Not all celebrities were considered at risk from the dangers of extreme wealth however. The following exchange followed Luigi's comment about footballers:

> **David:** But doesn't every celebrity do that if they get loads of money, they just waste it?
> **Luigi:** No.
> **Mavie:** No, not Alan Sugar. [laughter] Sorry, but he's like –
> **Ally:** He's a good role model.
> **David:** Yeah.
> **Ally:** Cos he only got one GCSE at school, and he could still, that gives other young people who are maybe not as clever as others a

lot of hope, because if he only got one GCSE at school, and he still becomes a multi-millionaire.

David: Basically an entrepreneur. They're good role models, and they're celebrities. (London, 16–17)

It is significant that the counterpoint to the wasteful wealth of footballers here is Alan Sugar – entrepreneur and star of the UK reality television series *The Apprentice*. In contrast to footballers, Sugar's wealth is presented as acceptable given his status as a business 'role model'. David's closing statement illustrates how the form of wealth which was most legitimized across the study was that gained through business and enterprise. We discuss this in more detail below.

Aspirations for wealth require justification in order to be considered legitimate. The existence of extreme wealth inequality was implicit in much of participants' talk – both through discussions about the need to build a safety net for themselves, and in their evaluations of high-earning celebrities. Distinctions between those who 'deserve' their wealth and those who do not are rooted in young people's evaluations of hard work. As we showed in Chapter 3, business celebrities were more readily able to legitimately claim a status as hard working. Austerity's counterpoint to this discourse of waste is the thrifty and responsible consumer, which we explore next.

'She doesn't flaunt her money around': Thrift, ordinariness and legitimate wealth

Across our data, celebrities seen to be flaunting their wealth were evaluated negatively in contrast to those whose consumption was seen as less conspicuous. Royal Kate Middleton was often spoken of as deserving her wealth, as in this extract:

> Before that [her marriage to Prince William], even though she wasn't royalty she seemed like a cool person anyway, so that's fine. . . . She doesn't flaunt her money around, which is the main thing. Like if you are rich and you flaunt money around in the wrong places, to me you're like, what are you doing? Because like these people, all of them: bleugh. (Dave, Manchester, 14–15)

Dave draws a distinction between being rich and being ostentatiously wealthy – it is inappropriate spending rather than wealth inequality that he sees as an issue. He lists Justin Bieber, Katie Price, Kim Kardashian and Nicki Minaj as celebrities who 'flaunt' their money, presenting them as disgusting ('bleugh') in comparison to Middleton whose 'coolness' he attributes to her moderation.

Like many young people, Dave does not identify strongly as a particular social class, settling on 'middle class' rather than 'lower class':

> because every time I ask for say a new game, it's like 'I haven't got the money because that game is £40 and I've got other stuff to buy, like food.' . . . But like at Christmas there's piles of stuff, on my birthday there's piles of stuff, and I get them then so yeah, . . . it's fine.

Dave reflects on his own access to consumer goods when thinking through his class position, highlighting the long-standing relationship between consumption, status and class (Archer et al. 2010; Veblen 1994). Dave's valuing of Middleton's spending habits reflects a dominant cultural narrative in austere meritocracy. As we discussed in Chapter 1 and in the opening of this chapter, responsible spending and fiscal restraint have become central features of austerity's discursive register. They figure as both solutions to the crisis and the means to classify those who are wasteful in their spending as deviant others. Returning from national economic ruin requires collective sacrifice and a 'stiff upper lip' (Biressi & Nunn 2013b).

There is a nostalgic echo of wartime austerity, refracted through the colourful kitsch of bunting, 1950s fashion, cupcakes and the slogan 'keep calm and carry on' (Bramall 2013; Jensen 2013). Contemporary austerity recasts post-war poverty as a time of simpler pleasures and self-sufficiency. Having to 'make do and mend' thus becomes a moral imperative for the nation – set in opposition to the wasteful excesses of the more recent past. This discourse of restraint circulates at the level of the nation and the individual; wrapping up cuts to public services and existing on the breadline into a neat ration package with a cheerful bow. It is not the experience of surviving in poverty that carries value, but the visible performance of a particular kind of aesthetic and relationship to the self through one's consumption practices (Jensen 2013). Thriftiness is framed as a cheerful, resourceful disposition that does not make a fuss (or riot in the streets). This paradoxically enables middle-class and elite groups to claim value from their performance of thriftiness, set in contrast to austerity's working-class others – presented as drains on the nation who must learn to live within their means.

Against this backdrop the Duchess of Cambridge, Kate Middleton, has been widely represented as a frugal royal (Allen et al. 2015b). There has long been a public fascination with the lives of the royal family, whether through high-profile events like coronations, weddings and jubilees or in the reporting of the everyday lives of its members (Billig 1992). Although the British monarchy is an institution of immense wealth and inherited privilege, Kate Middleton and Prince Harry were often described as 'ordinary' and 'down-to-earth' (discussed in Chapter 4). As detailed in the celebrity case study for this chapter, Middleton's representation – like that of Princess Diana before her – is built around a mythic rags-to-riches fairy tale, despite having been born into a wealthy family and being privately educated. Diana's representation as more like us than other royals positioned her as a modernizing influence on the royal family, thereby legitimizing the continuation of inherited power (Couldry 2001a). Middleton's 'ordinariness' performs a similar role, repackaged in the wistful tones of 'austerity chic'.

On the whole, participants talked about Middleton in positive terms, as 'genuine' (Tom, SW, 16–17) and 'down-to-earth . . . not like all the other princesses' (Sasha, London, 16–17). Through the discourse of thriftiness, Middleton embodies a fantasy of social mobility into an elite world, in which she is valued as authentic and 'like us' by virtue of not 'flaunting' her money. This tale of social 'progression' is illustrated in Ginny's account of Middleton's rise to fame:

> She started off from, well, her parents started off from Southall which was where I was from, and they eventually progressed to become like entrepreneurs and made, sort of created their own business. And then she went through that whole progression of school like most of us are going to do, and then she went to university and that's where she obviously met Prince William, and it progressed for her. And she just seems so genuine throughout all of the interviews she did, and all the appearances she does like she's just, even though she's meant to act like a princess, but she's just, she looks like she's happy, like genuinely happy to interact with kids and loads of different people. (London, 14–15)

Ginny identifies with Middleton through a geographical connection to her home, but also through her aspirational story about education that we explored in Chapters 3 and 5. Middleton's thriftiness and ordinariness are valued precisely because she is a member of the social elite. It is her positioning as socially mobile yet restrained, authentic yet happy that signal her as an ideal of austere meritocracy. The positioning of Middleton as ordinary despite her wealth and privilege relies on the discursive contrast between those who flaunt their wealth and those who do not. Young people's evaluations about wealthy celebrities being 'deserving' or 'undeserving' serve a dual purpose. They enable wealth inequality to be criticized, while simultaneously reinforcing the position of some elites as natural and just.

These differentiations were connected to criticisms of wealth inequality, combined with ideas around the responsibility not to waste resources while others are struggling to get by. Therefore, while extreme wealth required justification and provoked disagreement, some of the richest celebrities did not attract criticism or judgement for their wealth. The framing of economics in terms of individual responsibility or household budgeting enables the mechanics of capitalism to be obscured (Cameron et al. 2016) – in particular the increasing concentration of capital in the hands of the richest. In the next section we move from thrift to other discourses that were drawn upon to make sense of and justify wealth inequality.

'Every year he gives like a 100 million to charity': Legitimate wealth, entrepreneurship and philanthropy

Not all rich celebrities were positioned as ordinary or thrifty. Some were seen as successful because of their status as high earners. There were two main strategies that young people used to defend such celebrities against criticisms of greed or excessive wealth: that the celebrities had earned their money through entrepreneurship, and that they were giving back via philanthropy.

Only two of the celebrities discussed in our interviews made it onto the top twenty of the *Forbes* or *Sunday Times* rich lists at the time of writing: Richard Branson and Bill Gates (Blankfeld 2016). However, even though they were the richest celebrities discussed, participants did not criticize them for their relationship to money as they did footballers or other celebrities, such as Katie Price and Kim Kardashian. One reason for this is the positive value given to business and entrepreneurship by many young people. We showed in Chapters 3 and 5 how enterprise and effort are presented as desirable attributes in celebrities – legitimate ways of achieving success. In this discourse of entrepreneurial success, money could be positioned as a reward for hard work often attached to celebrities associated with technology. Here are two groups of young people discussing their ideal celebrities:

> **Edward:** Sir Alan Sugar. . . . Because he knows that it's all about the money.
> **Makavelli:** And um, he seems like a pretty much hard worker. So like if he thinks, if he, I mean if he thinks he deserves respect then I think that most of the time he's probably right. (London, 16–17)
> **Bob12:** Richard Branson, who's like really rich, and he like he has a big business, so you can like improve someone's ideas and make better – better business as well. He owns a private island, that is pretty cool as well.
> **Bob:** I would say Bill Gates because he's really rich and yeah. I just like his lifestyle. (London, 14–15)

Entrepreneurial celebrities' status as 'ideal' often served to shield them from the kinds of negative judgements about wealth directed towards the conspicuous consumers discussed above. Entrepreneurship was used as evidence that a celebrity deserved their wealthy lifestyle and was worthy of respect rather than criticism.

It was clear from the disagreements that young people had during the group interviews that being 'really rich' occupies a contested position in the context of austere meritocracy. Wealth could be justified on the basis of merit resulting from hard work and enterprise. But there was nonetheless discomfort about the unequal division of resources and power in society. The solution many young people put forward for this was individualized – it was the responsibility of those who had more resources to 'give back' via philanthropy. This was particularly apparent in discussion of Gates, whose wealth was often discussed alongside his philanthropy, as this excerpt shows:

> **Interviewer:** If you were going to design a perfect celebrity?
> **Homer:** Oh what's his name, the guy who made the computers, [laughter] Bill Gates. . . .
> **Ryan:** Oh he's like a beast. He's got loads of money.
> **Jack:** He's good as well.
> **Homer:** He gives it away for free. (London, 14–15)

While Gates is able to claim value from having 'loads of money', this is qualified by Jack and Homer: it is important for Gates to be 'good' as well as rich, evidenced by him giving his money away. Similarly, Tim (London, 14–15) explains how 'every year he gives like a 100 million to charity'. The participants present Gates's wealth in extreme terms to strengthen their claims (Pomerantz 1986; Potter 1996). It is hard in this conversational moment for anyone to argue with the worth of giving away the unimaginable amount of '100 million'. Thus, he is positioned as someone who does good with his money rather than spending it all on himself or wasting it on 'wrong things'.

Such calculations were not reserved for businesspeople. Both charitable giving and hard work could be used as a counterclaim against criticisms of unfairness in footballers' pay. This is evident in Bruno's talk about footballer David Beckham, whom he identifies as an 'ideal' celebrity:

> You can't argue with him. . . . Like he wasn't born with talent, there are so many people that are born with something, he had to work for it, like every day, day in, day out. And he would be playing at the time when he would get like £10, and now, £10 a week, and now people get 100k a week. And since then, even now he's giving, three like three, three million pounds to charity for five months, and he's playing for a Paris club, but he's not taking the money, he's going to give it to charity straight away. I don't think he's a wrong person, something you can tell like, he's done nothing wrong. (London, 16–17)

Beckham is presented as having worked tirelessly 'day in, day out' in order to progress from £10 a week to £100k a week. The emphasis on hard work combines here with philanthropy in order to justify Beckham's wealth and status. Bruno's almost defensive comment that Beckham has 'done nothing wrong' suggests that without evidence of hard work and philanthropy – if he were seen to be just 'taking the money' – he would be considered a 'wrong person'.

Much like the contrast between conspicuous consumption and thrift, some participants juxtaposed philanthropic giving with the spending habits of other celebrities:

Bill Gates . . . he's probably richer than anyone here but he gives away like 80 per cent of all his money but he's still like a billionaire [laughing slightly] so, whereas like those lot they just keep it all and live in huge mansions which they don't need, but Bill Gates he just gives it all to charity which is yeah, that's good. (Herbert, SW, 14–15)

He points to images of Bieber, Kardashian, Minaj and Price as 'those lot'. Like Dave earlier, Herbert draws on distinctions between celebrities within his evaluations of celebrity wealth. Herbert compares those who 'keep it all and live in huge mansions' to Gates, who 'gives away like 80 per cent of all his money'. His criticisms point to a sense of unfairness about the wealth of certain celebrities – with the group above seen in the following way:

They grew up rich, like most of their parents are rich and they're just spoilt and don't socialize really and I think they're just crazed on money and fame and stuff like that. And they don't care about like their fans or anything like that, just as long as they keep buying their albums or books or whatever, that's all that they care about. (Herbert, SW, 14–15)

Herbert's characterization of these celebrities as extravagant, selfish and materialistic contrasts starkly with the way he talked about his own aspirations to have 'enough to feed your family and stuff'. Herbert lives at home on a farm in the rural South West. He describes himself as middle class on the basis that his family 'can afford everything that's essential which is all that you need really. We haven't got any added luxuries.' Like many other participants, Herbert talks about inequalities between poor people and 'rich people [who have] got it all made up for them already'. Herbert's anger about the celebrities who keep all their money (in contrast with those who 'give it all to charity') shows how individualized discourses of money and financial security position philanthropy as a response to wealth inequality.

The use of entrepreneurship and philanthropy as justifications for celebrity wealth reflect the central position of privatization in the neoliberal project. In austerity politics, enterprise and the farming off of previously publicly funded services to the private or third sectors have been endorsed as solutions to the crisis and to 'wasteful' spending. In the UK, this manifest in the language of the Big Society, which uses rhetorics of collective social action and individual responsibility to justify the rolling back of state support. Under austerity, the redistribution of wealth is presented as something that must be left to individual decisions, rather than something for which the state has a responsibility (Sayer 2014). It is not surprising then that inequality appears quite static in the young people's accounts: it is unfair – but that is the way it is. Discourses of philanthropy enable criticism of extreme wealth inequality to exist, without disrupting the principle of capitalist accumulation as the foundation of the contemporary economy. This is particularly apparent in the combination of philanthropy and entrepreneurship embodied by Gates. The growing 'charitable industrial complex' (Harvey 2014: 211) applies the logic of markets and entrepreneurship to problems of poverty via this 'philanthrocapitalism' (Dutta 2015). Such an approach speaks the language of social justice, but reinforces the position of global capital – finding new markets and new ways for corporations to influence policy across the world, without challenging the underlying causes of poverty.

Conclusion

In this chapter we have explored the contradictory position that money has in austere meritocracy. Young people were grappling with this contradiction in their conversations about their own aspirations. We have shown how many young people experience a profound sense of personal responsibility for mitigating the risks of an insecure labour market and receding social safety net. The stability success discourse explored in Chapter 5, and the desire to have 'enough to get by', must be understood in the context of precarious employment, stagnating wages and the decimation and stigmatization of collective social provision. The aspiration for self-reliance can also be understood as a defence against the escalating stigma directed at those in poverty. The strength of this discourse of self-sufficiency among our participants reflects the cruel optimism of austere meritocracy. At the same time as young people are urged to create a secure future, the aspiration for a modest secure income has become increasingly out of reach, as growing numbers of young people experience in-work poverty.

Our data show that discussions about wealth inequality reflect the central but fraught place that consumption occupies in austere meritocracy. From the outset, the political rhetoric of neoliberal capitalism has had to find ways to justify the transfer of collective resources and support from public into private hands (Harvey 2005). The discourse of individual liberty that has helped secure public consent for this transfer is often expressed in terms of the freedom to choose – whether as a 'customer' of public services or the local corner shop. In the first decades of neoliberalism, 'acquisitive consumerism' was held up as a sign of meritocratic success – a reward for the graft and enterprise needed to rise up the social ladder (Littler 2013). In this chapter, we have shown that money and consumption remain important components of the neoliberal idea of meritocracy, but that these have been reframed in the context of austerity. The construction of the 'responsible consumer' is unstable, played out in the disagreements and justifications in young people's celebrity talk. Some forms of consumption are seen as excessive and irresponsible – particularly those judged flashy and ostenta-tious. These moral evaluations reproduce earlier ridicule of the 'nouveau riche' – never quite passing in their new social position (exemplified in the celebrity case study of Kim Kardashian in Chapter 4). The discourses of austere meritocracy combine enduring anxieties about class boundaries and nostalgic ideas of self-reliance and thrift. Consequently, anger about inequalities and unfairness can be expressed in relation to visible excess while the structure of resource inequality built into capitalism sits quietly in the background.

Tracy Jensen (2013) argues that moral judgements about greed and excess have tended to be directed towards 'underclass others' (benefit claim-ants, urban youth) rather than wealthy elites. They are classed judgements – about wanting the 'wrong things' – as evidence of failures to be resilient and restrained. Our data show that these judgements are also directed at *some* wealthy celebrities. While these celebrities' lives are markedly different to those in poverty, who are regularly stigmatized within dominant discourses, the ways that they are evaluated are deeply connected. The othering of par-ticular celebrities (footballers, reality television stars) and their consumption practices reinforce the classed (and gendered and racialized) politics of taste and consumption operating more broadly within austerity. The investment portfolios and luxury goods of the elite global classes escape unscathed in our data. They do not come under the same microscope of celebrity as foot-ballers and pop stars (the media give less attention to Gates's mansion than Beyoncé's golden rocking horse). The wealth of those business elites who did surface in the interviews was generally celebrated and made acceptable through discourses of deservedness, entrepreneurship and philanthropy. The resentment directed at *some* wealthy celebrities therefore serves a dual pur-pose. It enables the expression of anger at the unfairness of inequality, while simultaneously naturalizing that inequality by categorizing *some* forms of wealth as more legitimate than others.

CELEBRITY CASE STUDY: KATE MIDDLETON

Catherine Middleton, the Duchess of Cambridge, is often referred to by her nickname 'Kate Middleton' rather than her more formal royal title. Middleton rose to fame through her relationship and subsequent marriage in 2011 to Prince William – the heir to the British throne. As noted above, she is often presented as a fairy tale princess with humble roots, despite having been privately educated and having grown up in a wealthy family. During our research, she became pregnant and gave birth in 2013 to her first child, George Alexander Louis, an event that cemented her status as a 'thrifty housewife' through discourses of domestic happi-ness in motherhood (Allen et al. 2015b). Two years later she had a second

FIGURE 7.1 *Kate Middleton, photograph by Sebastián Freire, no changes made. Licence https:// creativecommons.org/licenses/by-sa/2.0/.*

child, Charlotte Elizabeth Diana. In this case study, we show how nostalgic discourses of 'austerity chic' can counteract judgements attached to extreme wealth and privilege – exploring her celebrity representation as 'the princess of thrift'.

At the foundation of Middleton's representation as a thrifty royal is a rags-to-riches story of upward social mobility. In this narrative, her entry into the monarchy is framed as evidence of social transformation and meritocracy – focused in particular on the entrepreneurship of her parents, as this extract from one online biography attests:

> Kate's ancestry on her father's side is Leeds-based woollen cloth merchants and manufacturers, while on her mother's side she is descended from working-class labourers and miners from Sunderland and County Durham. Carole [Middleton's mother] herself was raised in a council flat. . . . We live in a world in which those with ambition and talent can move far more fluidly between classes, where money often speaks louder than titles. . . . The Middletons . . . are aspirational achievers,

and self-made New Money . . . the acme of middle-class success, forged through energy, enterprise and sheer hard work. (Thornton 2013)

The TV documentary *When Kate Met William: A Tale of Two Lives* provides a fascinating example of the media's crafting of Middleton as ordinary. Telling the story of 'the girl who rose from "humble beginnings" to become one of the world's most famous women', it deploys visual and narrative tropes to generate a sense of the ordinary and familiar. Montage footage of the garden of a semi-detached suburban house with a child's climbing frame and framed pictures of a young Middleton in school uniform provide a visual backdrop. Over this, the narrator and talking heads emphasize the Middleton's 'Victorian semi', her parents' 'regular' jobs as an air hostess and flight dispatcher and their modest income. Through the crafting of this Cinderella story of a normal girl catapulted into the world of wealth and privilege, Middleton's celebrity, like Princess Diana's before her, represents a 'curious variant of the myth of success' (Couldry 2001a).

This narrative of meritocracy is one in which Middleton does not forget her humble roots – rejecting a 'lavish lifestyle' (Twomey 2013) in favour of frugality. Newspapers regularly report on Middleton's tendency to wear the same dress twice with her 'modest' choice of high-street brands such as TK Maxx framed as evidence of her 'careful approach to shopping' (Graafland 2013). Other stories focus on Middleton preparing a 'humble nursery' in a 'modest' two-bedroom house (Hello Magazine 2013), and buying inexpensive baby products from high-street shops. In July 2013, television presenter and figure of 'new thrift' culture Kirsty Allsopp publicly endorsed Middleton and Prince William on daytime television as 'the most frugal . . . the poster boys and girls for the "make do and mend" generation'. Here we see how Middleton's positioning as a 'humble' royal is achieved in part through a nostalgic nationalist discourse which looks back to the post–second world war years of austerity as a time of self-reliance, hard graft and restraint. The fact that she has married, rather than been born into royalty enables her celebrity to carry both notions of stability and tradition that call on the nation to 'keep calm and carry on' while tempering accusations of unjustified privilege and wealth (Billig 1992; Harvey et al. 2015). Thus, through her image as a thrifty royal, Middleton functions as a key cultural figure of austere meritocracy, defusing resentment at the growing inequalities unleashed since 2008.

8

Fame

Celebrities are often used as role models and a global industry is dedicated to sustaining the idea of celebrity as desirable. Despite this, fame is usually viewed as an illegitimate and immoral aspiration. Publicly, fame is associated with narcissism, materialism and undeserved wealth. Those who seek it are positioned as the epitome of a something-for-nothing culture. Young people are seen as especially susceptible to celebrity, as commentators frequently bemoan a generation of youth who reject hard work and seek fame in and of itself. Such sentiments are captured in politician Iain Duncan-Smith's claim that appeared in the opening chapter of this book, that the 2011 English riots were caused by celebrity-fuelled moral delinquency. Similarly, former Education Minister Nicky Morgan (Gurney-Read 2016) stated, 'I think sometimes people will look at the *X-Factor* winners or they will look at reality TV shows and they will think you can have instant success, fame, money overnight.' This discursive construction of young people as holding unrealistic and damaging desires for fame harbours much public anxiety. Opinion polls reveal widespread adult concern about the harmful effects of celebrity on young people (YouGov UK 2014). Small-scale surveys citing 'evidence' that young people would rather become glamour models and reality television stars than doctors and lawyers are frequently taken up with relish by the press (see Allen & Mendick 2012).

In this chapter, we explore how young people negotiate these dominant discourses. Building on previous chapters, we show how participants enact distinctions between 'deserved' and 'undeserved' fame in their celebrity talk. We show how fame must be legitimized through evidence of skill, hard work and authenticity, and enjoyed only as a by-product of these things. We then examine how these discourses police participants' imagined futures, with them dissociating themselves from aspirations for fame as an end in itself, and articulating aspirations for recognition based on determination, authentic self-realization and giving back. In the final section, we discuss YouTubers: a relatively new subcategory of microcelebrity. We describe how, through the YouTuber, fame is rescued from its denigrated status. We also argue that their popularity is revealing of the worker subjectivities idealized within austere meritocracy as (individualized) solutions to uncertain youth transitions.

'If you've done something amazing, you have the right to be there': Deserved success and the right kind of fame

As we demonstrate throughout this book, participants' celebrity talk is structured by distinctions between 'deserving' and 'undeserving' fame, with hard work and authenticity central to these evaluations. These distinctions are tied to broader moral imperatives that govern individuals' aspirations within austere meritocracy. Fame – as a reward or goal – must be earned through skill and determination, with young people seeking out evidence for this as they attribute value to both individual celebrities and celebrity types. We have provided many examples of such evaluations throughout this book. However, the following quotations serve as reminders:

> Chris Hoy, for instance, like, he's like the world's best sprint cyclist, so he's immediately up there cos he's like the world's best. So, if you've done something amazing you kind of have the right to be there. (John, SW, 14–15)

> I absolutely adore the lead singer of the Macabees, Orlando Weeks. Erm, not many people know who he is, because he's not really famous for being who he is, he's actually got famous for creating music. . . . And he just seems really down-to-earth. . . . He's just doing what he enjoys and because of that he's become famous. (Orlando, Manchester, 14–15)

John and Orlando praise Chris Hoy and Orlando Weeks (Orlando even chose the latter's name as her pseudonym). They locate them as legitimate celebrities because of their achievements and authenticity. Rather than courting the media and seeking fame in and of itself, their celebrity is constructed as a consequence of pursuing their passions and being talented.

As we show in this chapter's celebrity case study, actor Emma Watson typifies the 'deserving' celebrity who shuns fame. In Chapter 4 we saw Lolita (SW, 16–17) praise Watson for staying 'true to herself'. The following quotations further illustrate this interlinking of authenticity and 'deserving' celebrity:

> **Anna:** Emma Watson manages to stay out of the like, she's never in the magazines cos she wore a really short dress and everyone saw her underwear. Whereas you can kind of imagine Katy Perry doing.
> **Jane:** Rihanna is always in the magazines.

Poppy: Rihanna's just gone crazy, but Emma Watson's like really cool. [laughter] (SW, 16–17)

Similarly, Amelia (Manchester, 14–15) said of Watson, 'She's just amazing. . . . In interviews she just seems like a really down-to-earth person. She doesn't seem really sucked in by the fame.' In contrast, those seen as seeking fame without the requisite evidence of talent or hard work are derided:

There's people who work really hard to become someone . . . like a really famous actress, she's had to work to be famous. . . . Whereas the Kardashians are just famous for being who they are: being a Kardashian. (Naomi, Manchester, 14–15)

Kim Kardashian, she's famous for being a socialite, and a socialite is at the bottom of the celebrity pit. It's like, there's the really rich businessmen, then there's the singers, there's the actresses, then there's the socialites who are famous for knowing people, and knowing people makes them famous, they use that fame to know more people and the cycle continues. (Dave, Manchester, 14–15)

Naomi and Dave's comments echo the discussions of 'undeserving' celebrities throughout this book which typically included Kardashian and Katie Price, and reality television celebrities. In the extract below, participants discuss reality television fame, as embodied in scripted docusoap *The Only Way Is Essex*. Often abbreviated to *TOWIE*, the show focuses on the lives of a group of friends in Essex in southern England:

Alison: People off these reality shows, they aren't talented. The only reason they're famous is because they've just been put on a TV show.
Schmidt: And now they've got millions of –
Shane: Yeah. And the thing is they're all ridiculously stupid.
Rick: That's the annoying thing.
Shane: That's the only reason they manage to make a TV show out of it.
Rick: That's why people watch it. And then you get people who want to live like that, and the circle goes on.
Shane: Yeah, like, *The Only Way Is Essex*, you've got quite a lot of dumb people on that, and you –
Rick: [laughing] That's an understatement.
Shane: Yeah, okay. And like some people I know aspire to be like them, I don't know why, but they just think, 'Oh, they're famous because they're like that', so they wanna be like them. Everyone wants to be famous, so they'll copy what famous people are doing. If you're putting them in the limelight then everyone will act like them. (London, 16–17)

Essex has long functioned as a condensed class signifier (Skeggs 2004). In the 1980s under Thatcher, the 'Essex girl' and 'Essex man' were 'rhetorically linked to new right conservative political values' of aspiration, entrepreneurialism and flashy consumption (Biressi & Nunn 2013c: 273). While always occupying a fragile relation to notions of respectability, the Essex girl has increasingly appeared as a derogatory figure of the working class, associated with vulgarity, immorality, hypersexuality and stupidity. In *TOWIE*, its stars playfully perform these stereotypes in 'hyperbolic cartoon fashion' (Biressi & Nunn 2013c: 273), provoking accusations of narcissism, poor taste and stupidity. Our participants criticize the show for making celebrities out of 'dumb people', and fuelling desires for fame. Their discussion is performative. While Rick states that 'everyone wants to be famous', he and his peers exclude themselves. In criticizing reality television fame, they distance themselves from those who aspire to fame per se.

As illustrated throughout this book, the means through which celebrities attain fame is central to assessments of their worth. However, simply having talent or working hard did not shield celebrities from criticism. This discussion about Somalian-born British athlete and Olympic medallist Mo Farah and his sponsorship deal with Virgin Media illuminates this:

Syndicate: I hate Mo Farah.
OrangeJuice: Why would you hate Mo Farah?
Syndicate: He's such a publicity-hungry person. I give it to him that he won, that's good, but why do so much publicity? . . . He's a sell-out.
OrangeJuice: No he's not. Think about it, he came from Somalia.
Babatunde: Yeah, but Syndicate, you need to think about it this way: this is his only job. He's not getting paid for anything else but the publicity.
Syndicate: Yeah, but he – he has been a sell-out, he –
OrangeJuice: He donates it to charity. That's why he did the Virgin advert.
Syndicate: Yeah, but you see him everywhere, everywhere you look you see him.
Babatunde: Yeah, because that's where he's getting his money from.
OrangeJuice: Yes. And he donates most of it to charity.
Syndicate: No. It is my opinion. (London, 14–15)

Farah's athletic talent is undeniable. However, for Syndicate, Farah courting the media for money is evidence of 'selling out'. OrangeJuice and Babatunde defend Farah. First, they construct his promotional work as necessary to earn a living (suggesting that his primary talent in athletics does not directly generate income). Second, they position Farah's charity as giving back, drawing on the discursive strategies discussed in Chapter 7. Finally, they evoke Farah's meritocratic journey from poverty to sporting success. Farah's celebrity representation rehearses a well-worn, albeit globally inflected, rags-to-riches backstory (Littler 2003) in which he escapes a childhood in the 'tin-roofed shacks' of war-torn Somalia through drive and determination (Cox 2016).

In these extracts, fame is rescued from illegitimacy through qualifying discourses of hard work, charity and authenticity. Such patterns within young people's talk closely resemble the policy and media discourse of fame that opened this chapter. In these, celebrity is positioned as both cause and consequence of society's moral decline, and young people's desires for fame are troublesome. These distinctions also map closely onto some academic scholarship on celebrity. For example, in the early 1960s, historian Daniel Boorstin (1963: 11) argued that celebrity represents the superficiality of consumer culture: a celebration of individuals who 'lack greatness, worthy endeavours or talent'. Building on this, Chris Rojek (2001) distinguishes three types of celebrity: 'achieved celebrity', where success and visibility are based on accomplishments (such as athletes, film stars and musicians); 'ascribed celebrity', where status is given through lineage (such as royalty); and 'attributed celebrity', where status is a product of manufactured media representation rather than talent or skill (such as reality television stars and those linked to 'kiss-and-tell' scandals) – those 'famous for being famous'. Rojek's distinctions resonate with our participants' discussions of varieties of fame and their legitimacy. Cyclist Chris Hoy, singer Orlando Weeks and athlete Mo Farah occupy the revered status of achieved celebrity. But others (Kardashian and the *TOWIE* cast) resemble Rojek's (2001) attributed celebrity: the 'famously unworthy', who, in Dave's words, sit at the bottom of the 'celebrity pit'.

These categories involve judgements about who can legitimately occupy the position of celebrity, premised on commonsense ideas of value. This 'classification process operates unequally along the lines of gender' as well as class and race (Tyler & Bennett 2010: 377). As a symbolic figure of the 'famous for being famous', the working-class female celebrity operates as the 'constitutive moral limit of propriety' (Skeggs 2005: 970). In both celebrity and wider society, she symbolizes excess, immorality, a lack of accomplishment and – as discussed in Chapter 4 – inauthenticity. In doing so, she plays a key role in sustaining wider social hierarchies and classed, gendered and racialized forms of othering (Allen & Mendick 2013; Williamson 2010). In this way Rojek and Boorstin's theories feed into a broader value system 'that is punitively middle-class, policing the appropriateness of its players and shaming those who fall short' (Yelin 2016: 190). Throughout this book we have shown how young people's talk was infused with these hierarchies and distinctions. We have also shown how some participants challenged these, albeit with limited success. In the next section we demonstrate the ambivalent and fraught place that fame occupies within their imagined futures.

'I wouldn't like to be overly famous, like just if people knew who I was that's just enough': Young people aspiring to fame

Contrary to claims that all young people seek fame, the majority of participants stated that they would not like to be famous. Participants frequently highlighted the downsides of celebrity (including media intrusion and addiction), and emphasized the pleasures of ordinary over celebrity life (Harvey et al. 2015). Few claimed the label of celebrity fan, instead articulating relationships to celebrity that ranged from disinterest, through ambivalence, to hostility. As we argue elsewhere (Allen et al. 2015a), this sometimes involved distancing oneself from celebrity through performances of humour and disgust. As discussed in Chapter 2, participants often spoke about celebrity influencing *other* people rather than themselves and as something that they had outgrown, becoming less vulnerable to media influence and developing more mature tastes. In these ways celebrity fandom was feminized and infantilized.

Claims that young people possess unbridled desires for fame draw upon notions of youth as naïve, shallow and pathological. The assumptions underlying these debates resonate with the psychological concept of 'parasocial interactions'. This theory understands audiences' relationships to individuals and texts within the media as one-sided, futile and illusory 'bonds of intimacy' and associates these with the 'socially and psychologically isolated' (Horton & Wohl 1956: 222). The concept has been widely critiqued for constructing (celebrity) consumers as irrational others, and ignores the active dynamics of fan relations (Jensen 1992; Jenkins 2006). It is gendered, reproducing dominant constructions of girls and young women as irrational and hysterical consumers (McRobbie & Garber 1977). Yet it continues to haunt both academic work and public debates around young people's celebrity consumption.

Given this, it is not surprising that participants largely rejected desires for fame when articulating their aspirations within group settings. In the individual interviews, however, a slightly different picture emerged. Away from the policing gaze of their peers, aspirations for fame were more readily discussed. In this section, we draw on accounts of some of those who discussed the prospect of fame within their futures. Contrary to dominant discourses, of the fifty-one participants, only nine discussed fame in their imagined futures (seven male, two female). Almost exclusively, these participants aspired to creative or sporting careers in which fame is a possible (though not inevitable) by-product. All mentioned other career paths as back ups. As we show, aspiring towards celebrity is risky and the threat of being judged as holding illegitimate aspirations looms large.

Perhaps more than any other participant, Boo (Manchester, 16–17) distanced himself from celebrity: 'I don't really engage with celebrity culture'. In both the group and individual interviews, he adopted the position of distanced celebrity critic, voicing disdain, particularly for manufactured celebrity. He had little interest in our case study celebrities – other than expressing respect for Bill Gates and Will Smith – and was particularly critical of famous-for-being-famous celebrities such as Katie Price and Kim Kardashian. Boo's interview was replete with instances of cultural distinction (Bourdieu 1984), expressed in his educational orientations (including applying to Oxbridge) and his cultural tastes. He discussed admiring a selection of authors, journalists and musicians, including the Arctic Monkeys and Bob Dylan. His parents have professional careers in education and the creative industries, and Boo's tastes are likely to be informed by the stocks of middle-class cultural capital available to him (Bourdieu 1984). In distancing himself from manufactured celebrity and aligning with legitimized cultural forms, taste operates as a mechanism of social distinction in his account. Orientations towards celebrity – both as cultural object and way of being – are part of these practices of differentiation.

Despite his vehement criticism of celebrity, Boo expresses aspirations to fame. He writes poetry, short stories and articles for his school newspaper, and wants a career writing crime fiction or in investigative journalism.

> The things that could make me happy in being a writer would be money, success and . . . fame, yes. . . . What's difficult about the arts in general is [you could be] financially successful now and massively popular now, like Justin Bieber, or less financially successful, but remembered in years to come. If you look at Van Gogh for instance, he wasn't looked at highly in his time at all, and it wasn't until after he died that he is remembered and considered to be hugely influential and important, and an incredible artist. But it is balancing, which is more important? It is difficult really because you think is it worth a lifetime of unhappiness and struggling to get by with little money, to be remembered and revered in the future?

Boo navigates the moral discourses surrounding aspirations for fame through mobilizing his middle-class cultural capital. He articulates his aspirations by dissociating himself from manufactured popular culture (Justin Bieber) and aligning with nineteenth century art (Van Gogh), demonstrating his knowledge of 'high culture' in the process. Alluding to the precariousness of creative professions, he draws on the romantic image of the struggling (male) artist who sacrifices immediate popularity and financial success to be 'remembered and revered in the future'.

As discussed in Chapter 6, Boo qualifies his aspirations for fame through constructing his imagined future as a writer as a form of authentic self-realization that is driven by his inner self rather than external pressures.

These echo the discourses of work as a site of self-realization and fulfilment discussed in Chapter 4. Boo aligns himself with the position of legitimate celebrity, for whom fame is a by-product of pursuing their passions ('it is what I want to do'), rather than an end in itself or 'because I want to please other people'. He emphasizes the value of 'inspiring people' and 'making a difference', key mechanisms throughout our study by which celebrities gain value. We see this when he explains, 'A lot of the time fame gives people something to aspire to, and it gives them an inspiration', but adds, 'I think it's exploited in the wrong way, particularly with people like Kim Kadashian and Katie Price. . . . They don't do anything. That's where fame becomes a negative thing.'

Aspirations for fame were not the preserve of middle-class participants like Boo. Syndicate (London, 16–17) defines himself as working class and lives with his 'stay-at-home mum' and his stepfather, who is a vehicle engineer. He has played football since he was a child and wants a career in it. Like Boo – and those discussed in Chapter 4 – Syndicate constructs his aspirations within a discourse of authentic self-realization:

It was my [fourth] birthday and I got these football nets and we stayed out [all day] just playing football. And then I knew I wanted to play football for like –, because when I play football I feel happy. You get that adrenaline rush. . . . It's just something I feel like I want to do, . . . represent my country at sport, . . . I think that feeling is probably better than any other feeling. The fans and everything just cheering for you, and knowing that you have like the weight of the country on your shoulders, it's sort of like lifting you up. (London, 16–17)

Syndicate's aspirations – expressed in his child self and imagined future self – are infused by powerful emotions: the adrenaline rush of playing, and the uplifting cheers of fans as he enters the pitch. Fame enters the frame. Asked to define success, Syndicate explains:

People knowing me maybe. Erm, like say Bill Gates invent – if I made something, even if it wasn't that popular or anything, just [to] feel like I've done something. . . . To know that I've made a difference. Like I think I wouldn't mind if people didn't recognize me, but like if I've made a difference to someone, made something, helped someone with my work. You'd get that sort of feeling that helps you in your life that [you're] gonna, have a good future. And if I had a fan base I think it would be even better. . . . I wouldn't like to be overly famous, just if people knew who I was that's just enough, like if people knew my name. (London, 16–17)

Here, as with Boo's account, fame – being known – symbolizes the validation of Syndicate's achievements – a recognition that he has 'done something' (like Bill Gates). Also like Boo, he qualifies this through drawing on a discourse of giving back, contributing to the public good by 'helping some-one with my work'. Being able to help others through your celebrity pro-duces positive emotions – in Syndicate's words, a 'good feeling that helps you in life'.

Boo and Syndicate have different social positions, resources available to them and aspirations. Yet they use similar strategies to defend against accu-sations of illegitimate desires for fame. Both draw on discourses that pos-ition fame as a by-product of hard work and self-realization, and so distance themselves (and their future selves) from 'valueless' forms of celebrity. They reproduce a dominant narrative in which fame is legitimate if it is used to benefit others – through charitable giving, representing the nation or inspir-ing people. The image of 'deserving' celebrity that emerges is in line with the ideal subject of austere meritocracy: responsible and self-reliant, yet willing to contribute to the public good.

The final participant in this section is Roman (Manchester, 14–15). He is British Asian and his father works for a fast-food restaurant and his mother is a seamstress. As we discussed briefly in Chapter 4, Roman spoke of being bullied at school for being 'different'. He did not specify the nature of this difference, however, his gender performance did not resemble the dominant forms of masculinity typically privileged within schooling's heteronormative environment (Epstein & Johnson 1998). We argue that Roman's nonnorma-tive gender identity (Butler 1990) is significant for how he relates to celeb-rity and his aspirations.

Roman aspires to become a singer and plans to study music at college alongside biology and chemistry 'as a fall back'. Echoing the distinctions discussed earlier, Roman distances himself from reality television singing contests: 'I wouldn't do *X-Factor*. . . . I don't want to be just known as some-one who's just won a competition. I want to be known as someone who, from my own struggle, has built up my career.' Like Boo and Syndicate, Roman narrates this aspiration as a form of self-realization, recalling a childhood memory as he describes the moment he 'knew' that this was the path he wanted to take:

The first time I ever performed like in front of a few people was probably in primary school and it was like just in front of my family and every-thing, and I felt at home on the stage. I felt really like comfortable singing in front of everyone, so then that's when I like knew that I wanted to do that. . . . It felt good to just let all my emotions out. I could let everything out in my music without hurting anyone. (Manchester, 14–15)

Below, Roman describes why a music career appeals:

Just being on stage, and getting that rush, and having all these scream-ing fans in front you would just make me very happy, make me feel like I've actually helped all these people throughout their hard times. And like when I watch Beyoncé's concerts, I see everyone screaming for her, screaming her name, saying like, and then she obviously got really emotional feeling like I've helped these people through something that no one else could have helped them through, . . . being able to like change someone's whole view of their own life and the view of the whole, like the world that they're living in and make them feel better about themselves and make their confidence rise, make them feel good about who they are. (Manchester, 14–15)

Roman's description of his past and imagined (ideal) future self is remarkably similar to Syndicate's: the feeling of belonging on stage, the 'rush' of screaming fans and the pleasure of inspiring others and making them 'feel good'. Their accounts demonstrate how celebrity carries an emotional intensity that shapes how young people think about their futures. As Gavin Brown (2011) argues, aspirations are deeply entangled with young people's emotions, including, fear, hope, excitement and guilt. Policy interventions to 'raise' aspirations are designed to operate on this level, seeking to increase young people's confidence or provoke 'wow' moments that inspire action towards 'happy' futures. However, as we demonstrated in Chapter 6, happiness is not innocent. It regulates and polices young people's dreams, classifying some aspirations as happy objects to be sought, and others as unhappy objects to be avoided. Interventions to raise aspirations 'seldom engage holistically with the full range of emotions that young people experience in relation to their imagined adult lives' (Brown 2011: 1). Particular emotions are not only overlooked by the dismissal of fame as illegitimate, but constructed as pathological – feminized, delusional and immoral.

Roman's desire for a career that inspires and helps people 'feel better about themselves' is entangled with his investments in celebrity. Roman is a self-defined Beyoncé fan. In the individual interview he elaborates on the role she plays in his life:

She's got a fierce personality and she'll always give it back if anyone gives it to her. . . . She's quite strong and independent. . . . Listening to her music made my self-esteem rise, made me more confident [to take] more risks in life to do the things that I love. . . . I think if Beyoncé's music wasn't there I don't think I would have come on as far as I have with myself and my confidence. (Manchester, 14–15)

As we have discussed, Nicki Minaj was subject to much derision, including from Roman in the group interview. However, in the individual interview, he praised Minaj for her 'self-belief'. Imagining her as a fellow pupil in his school he explained that 'she wouldn't be popular, because she's different and everyone at this school, if you're different you get bullied . . . people judge her . . . saying that she's a bad person but they don't really know what's behind that person, they shouldn't judge'. This resembles his defence of the Kardashians in Chapter 4, where he emphasized their self-belief and perseverance in the face of criticism.

Richard Dyer's (1986: 155) early work on US film star Judy Garland illustrated how her stardom was appropriated by US gay men, providing an emotionally intense cultural resource through her suffering, strength and survival, and signifying 'difference within ordinariness'. This allowed her to capture the attention of marginalized groups, offering identification with their struggles for acceptance, but also a promise of escape from the constraints of gender and sexuality through the imaginary realm of stardom. We can read Roman's identification with these female celebrities and his desire for fame as similar cultural strategies through which he negotiates his difference, managing, and perhaps resisting, the heteronormative discourses that position him.

This symbolic function extends beyond gender and sexuality. For the working class, celebrity may offer recognition and validation within contexts of disempowerment – providing a promise of the chance to accrue symbolic and economic capital through media attention and the (potential) profits from this (Couldry 2001b; Littler 2003). This is especially important for individuals who have few other opportunities for gaining value and recognition (Allen & Mendick 2012). Borrowing from Valerie Walkerdine (1990: 92), celebrity offers 'solutions and escapes, ways out, in fantasy and in practice, by the proffering of what and who one might be'. Such visibility and power through celebrity may be injurious, fleeting and minimal. However, young people's connections with celebrity and their aspirations for fame must not be dismissed as delusions or pathologies. Attending to the biographical and socioeconomic conditions in which individuals invest in celebrity raises different possibilities for what fame represents. In her work on scripted docusoap *Geordie Shore*, Helen Wood (2016) suggests that seeking fame – even in precarious and derided forms of celebrity – may be an increasingly pragmatic choice for some young people. In the context of downward social mobility and insecurity, media visibility offers one of the few (temporary) escapes from the crisis of possibility facing working-class youth under austere meritocracy. In the rest of this chapter, we explore this by turning to YouTube celebrity.

'They're self-made . . . they've done it all themselves': YouTubers, new worker subjectivities and contemporary capitalism

YouTubers are a relatively new genre of microcelebrity produced by changes in the mediascape, namely the rise of digital platforms such as YouTube and Instagram. YouTubers gain their fame not through mainstream media but internet-enabled visibility. As Alice Marwick (2015) argues, the growth of digital and participatory media has ushered in a new era of celebrity that has transformed the celebrity-audience relationship and altered who can inhabit the subject position of celebrity. It has broken down distinctions between consumers and producers – celebrities and fans – by enabling fans/consumers to become cultural producers and celebrities themselves. For young people, for whom digital media are part of their everyday practices (Livingstone & Sefton Green 2016), these changes have had significant effects on their relationship to celebrity, as our data attest. Being a YouTuber not only garnered respect and affirmation among participants. It was also discussed as a viable and attractive career route. We demonstrate how YouTubers represent austere meritocracy's ideal celebrity and quintessential subject, and consider what young people's talk about YouTubers can tell us about contemporary worker subjectivities.

YouTube appears to offer a more democratic and meritocratic space than traditional celebrity, as the position of celebrity is not restricted to those within the industry but can be occupied by 'anyone with a tablet, mobile device or laptop' (Marwick 2015). As Daniel Smith (2014: 262) notes, 'YouTube celebrity is an ordinary person turned extra-ordinary as they gather fame on-line.' It is an extension of what Graeme Turner (2010) labels the 'demotic turn' in celebrity – introduced in Chapter 4 – in which 'ordinary' people and 'everyday' acts have become more visible in the media sphere. But YouTube celebrity offers more than visibility to so-called ordinary people; it can also offer possibilities for commercial success. Popular YouTubers – such as Jenna Marbles, PewDiePie and Charlieissocoollike – have leveraged their online following to gain sponsorship deals from large brands, and to move into other fields, including publishing, cosmetics and video games. Media commentary on the rise of YouTubers positions the social media platform as a utopia of upward mobility, where 'nobodies' can become 'somebodies' by 'carving out careers from their bedrooms' (Doran 2015): 'YouTube "geek" one day, millionaire celeb the next . . . British teenage boys in their bedrooms – anyone can now become a global internet sensation and a millionaire in the process' (This Is Money 2010).

Such celebratory narratives were present in young people's talk as they discussed comedians, animators and gamers who had found fame on the global video-sharing site. YouTubers were largely – though not exclusively – very popular. Those liked by participants were praised for their relatability and intimacy with their followers – attributes that were intertwined with their perceived authenticity and ordinariness. As discussed in Chapter 4, authenticity is highly valued within celebrity, however, it is particularly significant to YouTubers' credibility, and key to their distinction from mainstream celebrities (Marwick 2015). Participants in this study distinguished YouTubers from traditional celebrities, who were seen as more manufactured. YouTubers figure as a new category of celebrity that appears more accessible to young people like themselves. For example, Arial (Manchester, 14–15) explains, 'They're normal and they're doing what we could be doing, . . . just buy a camera', and Bob (SW, 14–15) states, 'They're self-made . . . they've done it all themselves, well most of them have.'

Despite this positioning of YouTube as a space where anyone can become famous, participants still distinguished between 'undeserving' and 'deserving' YouTubers: between overnight sensations and those who had achieved success through hard work, skill and determination. This extract discussing gamer Syndicate illustrates these distinctions:

> **Jerome:** Syndicate is really successful on YouTube, because you know, he's sponsored by Lucozade, and everything, yeah. But that's because he's setting goals for himself. . . . And he's really worked his way up in life.
>
> **Interviewer:** Do you mean, are they quite talented then?
>
> **Jerome:** Yeah.
>
> **Dave:** Syndicate is.
>
> **Jerome:** For what they do they're talented.
>
> **Maajida:** Who's Syndicate?
>
> **Dave:** Some guy on YouTube, he's not that good, but he's good.
>
> **Maajida:** What do they do?
>
> **Jerome:** Play games.
>
> **Dave:** Play games.
>
> **Sabeen:** I've never. . . . Is that all they do, is just play games?
>
> **Dave:** Yeah. And there's other people, like scientists.
>
> **Jerome:** Yeah, he's [Michael Stevens] got, he's made like how much the internet weighs.
>
> **Dave:** Yeah, he answers a load of really odd questions. Like he knows how much the internet weighs now, it weighs eighteen grams. (14–15 Manchester)

YouTuber Syndicate's legitimacy is constructed by reference to his financial viability through sponsorship. Yet his and other gamers' skill cannot be straightforwardly asserted. Sabeen and Maajida question their celebrity status, prompting Dave and Jerome to defend them through mobilizing discourses of skill, talent and hard work and by aligning them with the high-status subject of science. In this way YouTube celebrity is constructed through many of the discourses discussed throughout this book.

Some participants discussed becoming a YouTuber as a potential career option, and similar qualifying discourses were present in their accounts. Working-class Sarah (London, 16–17) describes aspiring to a creative career, unlike her parents, who work at the local airport. Her favourite subject is film studies and she explains how participating in a school filmmaking project has influenced her future plans: 'It gave me a chance to like express myself and express my creativity . . . having like ideas and then just putting them on film and showing them to everyone.' Sarah posted the film and three video-blogs on her YouTube channel and attracted fifteen subscribers and two comments: 'Somebody posted a video response and that was really good, because that was the first thing I put on YouTube. I was like "Ooh!" [both laugh] "My god, what is this?"' YouTube offers a space for external recognition of her talents. Asked what would make her happy in the future, her response includes the two happy objects discussed in Chapter 6 – relationships with family and friends and career fulfilment:

> Family and friends and like maybe even like doing something knowing that people like what I'm doing. Like say I could do something like paint a picture or take a picture and then like put it out there, and then people might be like 'Oh that's nice. She sounds cool.' I, then yeah, I think that'd make me really happy. (London, 16–17)

Like Sarah, middle-class John P (SW, 16–17) describes YouTube as a space to gain recognition and as a viable career path:

> I am a big gamer, I enjoy playing video games a lot, like a lot of people do these days, because I find them a new form of art which can pull you into the game stories and such. So a career doing that on YouTube would be pretty good.

Like Sarah, John has his own YouTube channel, and demonstrates in-depth knowledge of how YouTube fame can be achieved, where media visibility (and popularity with followers) lead to sponsorship and ultimately a career:

> Well you start off, get a little camera and just play video games. If you get noticed, people start following you, people can subscribe to you, and then they'll talk about this person and you'll get more subscribers. And very soon you can get partnered by either YouTube or Machinima, where you get money from the amount of views you get and that can lead to a career. Like PewDiePie, he started 2012 with about 7,000 which was still quite good back then. Now he has almost 8 million. . . . I have a capture card to record video games, and a microphone set-up. I'm going to try that and if I become successful I'll go from there and see how far I can go. (SW, 16–17)

YouTube appears as a space of discovery and community, where fame is organic and bottom up, led by creators and users rather than by commercial interests. This narrative is enthusiastically reproduced by YouTube: In 2016, it launched a viral campaign with the hashtag #MadeForYou. Celebrating YouTubers and their fans, it stated: 'There's no one story that can sum up YouTube – we're what users and creators make us.' Yet the construction of YouTube as an accessible and democratic space of DIY celebrity needs troubling. As Marwick (2015: 15) notes, 'Opportunities are typically limited, fleeting, and unaccompanied by the financial resources available to the traditionally famous. . . . While in theory anyone could become a microcelebrity . . . not all can convert this attention into financial capital.' Of the millions like Sarah and John who upload content to YouTube, very few are able to translate this into a viable career and profit from their visibility. Celebratory narratives of YouTube as a meritocratic space enabling ordinary people to achieve success through their skills, charisma and entrepreneurialism also obscure the encroachment of corporate interests within online spaces. Belying the seemingly ad hoc and accidental nature of the platform, advertisers and large corporations (including YouTube's owner Google) have considerable power to manipulate what goes viral and who profits from this (Ashton 2013).

Not only is this form of microcelebrity unlikely to bring financial rewards for the majority who pursue it, YouTube fame can also attract negative attention, from overt criticism to online trolling. In our study, some YouTubers were vehemently criticized as inauthentic, fame seeking and 'undeserving'. Most were young women, including teen singer Rebecca Black and viral sensation 'Tampon Girl' (Giovani Plowman):

Babatunde: Giovani Plowman.
Hanna Marin: Oh my God.
OrangeJuice: Ooh!
Eleanor-Marie: Oh Jesus Christ.
Babatunde: We dislike her a lot.
Eleanor-Marie: She's the Tampon Girl.
Babatunde: She ate a tampon.
Hanna Marin: Oh my God.
Syndicate: Oh! Oh that was disgusting.
OrangeJuice: Yeah, she ate a tampon.
Babatunde: She's famous for like the wrong reasons.
OrangeJuice: Yeah.
Eleanor-Marie: And she takes advantage of it. (14–15, London)
Ann: We have a classic example of an overnight celebrity quite recently, Tampon Girl.
Bob: Urgh. . . . Don't! Don't! You can't. [laughs]
Ann: Yeah. She um ate her used tampon. [laughter in group]
Dory: Well apparently it's fake.
Mat: She sucked it.
Ann: Yeah it is, it's fake, you can see the red dye in the corner. . . . She became an overnight celebrity just by putting that video up. (SW, 14–15)

Tampon Girl generates disgust through her associations with the leaky, fleshy corporeality of the female body – signalled by ingesting her own menstrual blood. She is also associated with the wrong type of celebrity, gaining attention and notoriety 'overnight' via illegitimate means, rather than through demonstrable skill or enduring hard work. Furthermore, we see Dory and Ann question the truth of her YouTube performance, declaring it 'fake'. As such, she falls short of the authenticity required to gain value within celebrity generally, and YouTube celebrity in particular. Like Kardashian and Price, Tampon Girl is mocked and relegated to the position of 'undeserving' celebrity. While producing new opportunities for 'ordinary people' to achieve media visibility and, with this, symbolic and economic capital, YouTube is structured by the gendered, classed and racialized hierarchies and distinctions that we have traced throughout this book. We must therefore trouble optimistic appraisals of YouTube's democratic potential for their implication within 'neoliberal ideologies of market meritocracy, which use the rhetoric of equality of opportunity to disguise and sustain massive inequality' (Tyler & Bennett 2010: 379).

It is not surprising that YouTubers are idealized, as they embody austere meritocracy's dominant discourses of aspiration: entrepreneurial success and career fulfilment gained through hard work and authenticity. This has wider implications for the worker subjectivities that young people in particular are invoked to enact. Strategic intimacy is key to YouTube celebrity. YouTubers must invest time and effort in maintaining their connectivity with followers (Marwick & boyd 2011; Senft 2013). This relies on techniques of self-commodification: a self-conscious crafting of persona or brand. Such practices are not only prominent within celebrity but infiltrate an increasing range of areas of social life, including job seeking (Gershon 2016). Self-branding is now widely promoted by 'recruitment gurus', employers, and university career services as appropriate responses to a competitive labour market (Ingram & Allen 2016). Job seekers are encouraged to use social media to build networks and create a 'personal brand', projecting a bundle of skills, experiences and competencies that will attract and impress potential employers. These endorsed practices for enhancing one's employability, and the neoliberal conceptions of the ideal-worker self that they promote, echo those defining YouTube celebrity: editing yourself and collating your experiences and qualities in attractive ways; building networks and visibility across multiple platforms; crafting your brand as an expression of an authentic and coherent self; and measuring and tracking your brand's success through metrics (including likes, hits, followers, subscribers).

It is not just young job seekers who are subject to these imperatives. These have become compulsory practices for even the most marginalized individuals. In Ken Loach's film *I, Daniel Blake* (2016) the protagonist Daniel – declared unfit for work by his doctor and subject to punitive benefit sanctions – attends a mandatory 'CV workshop' where the instructor explains to the unemployed attendees how the local coffee shop had 1,300 applicants for eight available jobs. 'You have to get yourself noticed', he tells them, enthusiastically suggesting they create videos on their smartphones to 'sell themselves' to employers. Within even the harshest economic context of declining job opportunities, entrepreneurialism and self-commodification – as well as positivity – have become significant features of welfare conditionality (Friedli & Stearn 2015).

It is important then to locate YouTubers in the current socioeconomic context. Analysis of austerity and recessionary media culture documents the proliferation of worker subjectivities across popular culture oriented around entrepreneurialism, self-commodification and the monetization of one's personal pursuits, from reality television to fashion blogging (Biressi 2011; Negra & Tasker 2014). Like these texts, YouTube celebrity promotes the turn *inwards* to the self as an idealized response to precarious employment and decimated social security. The endorsement of self-commodification as an idealized response to an uncertain labour market generates a multitude of dilemmas for job seekers. Techniques of self-branding are often premised on the notion – discussed in Chapter 4 – that we possess an authentic self that can (and should) be fulfilled through work (Gershon 2016). One's personal brand should reflect this inner core, and this authentic projection of the self is deemed a crucial factor in one's employability. This presupposes that such an inner self exists, that we can know it and that our career decisions should be informed by this self-knowledge. This demand for authenticity can conflict with the neoliberal imperative to demonstrate one's flexibility and adaptability to the needs of different employers and working environments (especially within a highly precarious and competitive labour market). These tensions are thrown into sharp relief within YouTube celebrity. As Marwick argues,

> While viewers crave the authentic, the messiness that comes with it can be off-putting. Selectively editing oneself into a palatable product, remaining consistent, and dealing with potentially belligerent audience members are difficult tasks that prioritize performativity over any true sense of self. (2015: 19)

The task of presenting oneself in ways that are attractive to multiple and different publics – be that employers or subscribers – while ensuring that this self appears consistent and coherent, is fraught and, ultimately, unsustainable. When microcelebrities fail to present a palatable and authentic product, the costs can be great – as revealed in the discussions of Tampon Girl above and of Kardashian, Minaj and Price in Chapter 4. However, these 'failings' also expose the internal contradictions of neoliberal logics (Gershon 2016) that govern young people under austere meritocracy. In this way, studying them can help us to crack open the fault lines of neoliberalism out of which alternatives can emerge.

Conclusion

In this chapter we have suggested that young people's talk about fame provides a productive site for analysing the many tensions and contradictions of growing up in an austere meritocracy that are discussed throughout the book. We began by troubling simplistic constructions of young people as fame hungry, exposing the ambivalent and complex place that fame occupies in their imagined futures. We showed how dominant discourses, which position fame as an immoral and illegitimate aspiration, infused and policed both their celebrity talk and their aspirations. We argued that young people use fame in attempts to gain value within conditions that have created a crisis of possibility for many, but that such attempts are perilous.

Even as fame is derided, new ideal forms of celebrity emerge, illustrated in the final section of this chapter. The place of YouTuber celebrity within our participants' talk, and its idealization, generate new questions about celebrity's function in the current moment. YouTubers are emblematic of worker identities within contemporary capitalism, where entrepreneurialism and self-commodification are increasingly upheld as the only (or at least the best) responses to economic uncertainty and precarity. Their popularity shows how broader economic transformations are registering in new genres of celebrity. We have also troubled optimistic framings of YouTube as a meritocratic space by exposing its hierarchies and exclusions. As such, even in its legitimate form of YouTube celebrity, fame becomes another object of cruel optimism. Holding onto it as a possibility is vital to being hopeful, yet it is unattainable for the overwhelming majority.

CELEBRITY CASE STUDY: EMMA WATSON

Given the powerful discourse of aspirations for fame as immoral, it is not surprising that we see this come into play within the representations of celebrities. Celebrities are aware of their positioning within the taxonomies of celebrity – from A-list to Z-list – and they too are implicated in reproducing distinctions between legitimate and illegitimate fame. In this case study of British actor Emma Watson, we show how the distinctions discussed in this chapter are constitutive of her on-screen roles and 'private' off-screen persona, as constructed through interviews, social media and newspaper reports. We suggest that Watson's middle-class femininity plays a crucial role in enabling her to occupy the position of 'achieved' and 'deserving' celebrity.

The child of Oxford-educated lawyers, Watson is best known for playing Hermione in the Harry Potter film franchise, starring in all eight films, the first of which she appeared in aged 11. Watson is frequently conflated with Hermione – both are aligned with elite education and high achievement. Watson attended private school, completed a degree in English at Brown University in America and attended Oxford University as a visiting student. (Hermione, of course, attended selective boarding school Hogwarts.) Her biography (Nolan 2011) makes much of her commitment to her education, including achieving high grades and her love of learning.

FIGURE 8.1 *Emma Watson, photograph by sophe5400, no changes made. Licence https://creativecommons.org/licenses/by-nd/2.0/.*

It quotes Watson saying of herself, 'I was a proper, proper nerd' (p. 163) and 'it sounds so geeky, but I really *do* like studying and reading' (p. 180, original emphasis). Watson represents the high-achieving 'smart girls' or 'can-do' girl (Harris 2004; Paule 2013), the female equivalent of Tom Daley's exceptional youth, discussed in Chapter 2.

Watson is aligned not only with cleverness, but also with hard work. She is described throughout her media representation as a 'workaholic' (McCormack 2014) and 'high achiever', not only through her educational success and film career but also through her determination to move into other artistic fields. Her Facebook page includes inspirational quotes which refer to her constant striving to improve and achieve, such as 'I'm my own worst critic. I always want to do better. I'm always striving towards the next thing.' While the character of Hermione is central to Watson's celebrity representation, the actor has also taken on other roles in film, theatre and fashion. Most notably, Watson was the face of the British high-fashion label Burberry, a brand associated with heritage, luxury and the social elite, including royalty. Watson's middle classness plays a central role here. In her biography, David Nolan (2011: 177) describes how Watson rescued the brand from its appropriation by the working class:

> The distinctive check design had been hijacked by the chav culture associated with football hooligans and vulgar soap opera stars dressed top to toe in brown check. The 150-year-old brand needed someone who was a world away from the image described by one commentator as 'council-house chic' to front their new campaign.

Juxtaposed with signifiers of 'low culture' associated with the working class – 'football hooligans', 'vulgar soap opera stars' and 'council house chic' – Watson is constructed as the embodiment of propriety and good taste (Skeggs 2005).

A central theme running throughout Watson's celebrity representation is that of her ambivalent relationship to fame, and desire for anonymity and normality: 'Ignoring fame was my rebellion, in a funny way. I was insistent on being normal and doing normal things' (Schwartz 2013). In the following quote, Watson's disinterest in fame and alignment with valued forms of cultural capital recalls Boo, discussed earlier:

> Fame never attracted me. Actually, I'm quite shy, I've never liked attention and money. . . . In my house, nobody watches movies, they are academic-oriented, they are just not interested in this. My being an actress is not their dream made true. They just want to watch me happy [sic]. Their main focus is not my stardom. (Watson in Nolan 2011: 263–4)

Watson's aspirations are constituted through precisely the moral discourses that have been discussed throughout this chapter, whereby the pursuit of fame in and of itself, and desires for attention and money, are constructed as immoral. Fame can be legitimized only as an incidental by-product of one's passions and authentic pursuit of happiness.

Watson's distancing from fame is reproduced intertextually. Notable here is her role in art-house film director Sophia Coppola's *The Bling Ring* (2013), a text which offers a critique of celebrity. Based on a true story, the film is a cautionary tale about a group of 'fame-obsessed' teens (Nixon 2013) who broke into the houses of Hollywood celebrities, including Paris Hilton and Lindsay Lohan, to steal their designer goods. The film criticizes the celebrity industry and the unbridled materialism it is seen to encourage, thus enacting the very moral panic around celebrity's damaging effects that opened this chapter. Much of the publicity for the film focuses on Watson's dissociation from celebrity. The *Daily Mail* newspaper report how Watson 'condemns extravagant celebrity lifestyles', stating that she only owns eight pairs of shoes and criticizes the dissociation of 'celebrity' from 'craft': 'There's a whole new definition to celebrity now. And I think that's why you see a lot of actors blanching at being associated with that word "celebrity" because it's become something that isn't really associated with having a craft' (Daily Mail Reporter 2013).

Watson described preparing for her role in *The Bling Ring* by watching *Keeping Up with the Kardashians* and studying Paris Hilton (Reife 2013). Watson is thus positioned – and positions herself – through categories of 'deserving' and 'undeserving' celebrity, and distances herself from the desires for fame and excessive consumerism represented by both the film's protagonists and the celebrities that the real-life protagonists targeted. These distinctions embodied in Watson's 'respectable' femininity (constructed through classed euphemisms of her 'low-key', 'natural' beauty and 'elegance') are contrasted with the excessive and tasteless femininity of both her on-screen character and 'white trash' celebrities, such as Kim Kardashian, Lindsay Lohan and Paris Hilton.

9

Conclusions

Our concept of austere meritocracy captures the tensions in inciting young people to aspire against a backdrop of escalating inequalities unleashed by neoliberalism and accelerated by post-crash austerity. As we outlined in Chapter 1, these transformations have had a disproportionate impact on young people in the UK and globally. While uncertainty and precariousness have long characterized the transitions of working-class youth, these experiences are becoming the new normal for more and more young people, including middle-class graduates. Despite this bleak and punishing landscape, discourses of social mobility thrive and the vigorous assertion of the meritocratic ideal has even intensified, solidified in narratives of 'hard-working families' and 'strivers' vs 'scroungers'. We argued that these tensions are a powerful instance of what Lauren Berlant (2011) calls cruel optimism. Young people under austerity must continue to invest in the meritocratic ideal, at a time that opportunities for achieving their aspirations – however modest – are being drastically eroded. In this book, we have shown how young people negotiate these relations of cruel optimism. In this concluding chapter we begin by summarizing our key arguments and reflecting on the original questions that framed our study. We then offer suggestions for how others might engage with our findings. We end by considering some of the dramatic transformations that have taken place since we completed the research, discussing their relationship to our work and their implications for those of us seeking progressive social change.

What have we have learned from this study?

In Chapter 1, we set out our three research questions: What kind of futures do young people imagine for themselves? What is required of young people in achieving these futures? How are social class and gender inequalities embedded and reproduced within these futures? By framing our investigation in this way, we sought to uncover austere meritocracy's distinct logics, rationalities and subject positions, exploring how it governs young people's aspirations and maintains inequalities. Uniquely, we used celebrity as a lens through which to do this, locating it as a key site for austerity's cultural politics. Celebrity is both a disciplinary technology that circulates austere meritocracy's dominant discourses and subjectivities and a sense-making resource though which young people negotiate these discourses and subjectivities.

In the detail of our participants' conversations about their own and celebrity lives, we examined how austere meritocracy is lived – threaded through their hopes and fears for the future. Young people are both in the vanguard of austere meritocracy and its site of greatest vulnerability. As society's dreamers, they personify the cruel attachments that hold austerity's contradictions in place. Discourses of hard work, thrift, entrepreneurship, authenticity and happiness run through their aspirations. These ideas echo through history. Decades of research show how these operate as neoliberal modes of governance, shaping young people's imagined futures and translating structural inequalities into individual problems. Yet, as we have identified, these discourses take on specific forms in sync with the requirements of a post-crash landscape. These include emphases on optimism, resilience and self-realization, and the moral policing of relationships to consumption and wealth through discourses of thrift and deservingness. Hard work has become pivotal to evaluations of success. Effort has always been part of the meritocratic equation, but now it occupies prime position as *the* way that success must be achieved, evidenced and legitimized. Hard work is endowed with a moral status. If you are not striving for social mobility, you are failing in relation to society's expectations and above all, failing yourself. We saw this in our participants' accounts as they drew on individualized frameworks which position future success as dependent on their individual effort, determination and entrepreneurialism: as though the 'world is in your hands'. We demonstrated how the meritocratic ideal is embedded within celebrity representations, from rags-to-riches backstories to Will Smith's instruction that 'your success originates from your attitude'. And we showed how it manifests within young people's celebrity talk, structuring distinctions between 'deserving' and 'undeserving' celebrities.

In the context of austerity, now set to continue into the next decade, the goals that young people are encouraged to seek are unattainable for an ever-increasing majority. Our attachments to the goals of happiness and success, and to the belief that the primary means to achieve these are effort and authenticity, are cruel. This current configuration of attachments makes up austere meritocracy and is circulated through celebrity representations. Our analysis reveals that the second question that framed this book is a trap. In asking what is required of young people in realizing their aspirations, we assume that young people can realize these through their own actions. Attachments to the cluster of promises represented by happiness and success are cruelly optimistic in the sense that young people (like all of us) are continually drawn back towards them even though these attachments are toxic. It is the very persistence of our investments in them that, ironically, makes the happiness and success they promise less achievable. They wear us down, they obscure the injustices produced by the system and they stop us from seeking alternative ways of being. For young people, their optimistic commitment to meritocracy is damaging: meritocracy's assertion of the power of the individual naturalizes inequalities, recasting structural constraints as personal failures and collective responsibilities as private struggles. The persistence of these cruel attachments is evident in how we structured them into the second question.

While cruel attachments subdue criticisms of and alternatives to austerity, they do not – as we have seen – completely silence them. Within participants' talk we find moments where these attachments fail, the contradictions of austere meritocracy are exposed, and alternative value systems and ways of being are tentatively imagined. These cracks occurred within young people's accounts of their futures. They sometimes appeared as fleeting fractures within their stories when neoliberal logics became irreconcilable, momentarily revealing themselves before being smoothed over and brought back into the groove of neoliberal common sense. There were also participants who mobilized alternative ideas of success and happiness, such as Dumbledore's hedonistic desires and Sabeen's rejection of family, and those who refused the demand to aspire to anything at all, like Person McPerson.

These fractures appeared in struggles over the meaning of different celebrities. Through our analysis of young people's celebrity talk and in the celebrity case studies, we showed how celebrity is inscribed with austere meritocracy's values, rationalities and ideal subjectivities, circulating powerful 'fantasies of success . . . and utopias of self-sufficiency' (Hall et al. 2013: 19). However, we also highlighted how celebrity provides a space in which young people negotiate and at times reject and rework these. Discourses have to be inhabited and they have to inhabit us. But in so doing, contradictions and tensions appear, and with them the possibility of something else (Butler 1990, 1997). In particular, we analysed instances where participants took up distinctive and alternative positions, defending Katie Price or Nicki Minaj against accusations of laziness, immorality and inauthenticity or choosing Tupac Shakur as a role model, and so challenging dominant value systems. These divergent readings of celebrity provide insights into the messiness of neoliberalism as young people tussle with, and at times resist, the discourses that seek to position them in particular – and often injurious – ways. Of course, resistance is never pure: 'Even while resisting power, individuals or groups may simultaneously support the structures of domination that necessitate resistance in the first place. . . . A single activity [will] constitute both resistance and accommodation to different aspects of power and authority' (Hollander & Einwhoner 2004: 549). While fleeting, often shut down by other participants or drawn back by the speaker themselves into familiar commonsense discourses, these utterances remain important. They reveal the discursive contingency of our subjectivities which, rather than absolute or fixed, are 'formed at the unstable point where the "unspeakable" stories of subjectivity meet the narratives of history, of a culture' (Hall 1987: 44). The next section considers the implications of these findings for research and practice.

How can we use this book?

We hope that people will not just read this book but find that they can use it in their work. Our research study and analysis have been informed by scholarship from a range of fields. We begin this section by reflecting on some of these fields and identifying how this book might encourage new ways of thinking about – and researching – young people, celebrity and aspiration. We then briefly consider how it might inform policy and practice with young people.

Our work builds on a body of work in sociology of education concerned with young people's aspirations and educational experiences and how these relate to broader social divisions. This includes research that problematizes the individualized policy discourses of aspiration (for example, Abrahams 2017; Roberts & Evans 2012; St Clair et al. 2013). Like this work, our study shows that young people hold a range of aspirations for their futures – most of which would be constructed as high within the hierarchy that dominates in policy documents. We too identify how the politics of aspiration obscures deep-rooted structural inequalities that shape young people's opportunity structures, and provides an individualizing framework through which young people must narrate their future transitions.

We also contribute to work in sociology of education on how young people negotiate and are positioned by dominant versions of success, and how social class, gender and race inform the possibilities for occupying successful school subjectivities (for example, Archer & Francis 2007; Stahl 2016; Walkerdine et al. 2001). Notably, we showed that austere meritocracy has brought a growing focus on effort and determination within young people's accounts of success. A key argument made within this book is that celebrity is central to how these practices operate: as a site that circulates dominant discourses of success, work, achievement and social mobility, and as a sense-making practice that young people 'can "talk with" and "think with"' (Kehily & Nayak 2008: 330). Studying young people's celebrity talk provides a productive and alternative approach to exploring young people's imagined futures, offering a way of speaking about yourself without appearing to do so. We hope that more sociologists of education will join us in bringing celebrity back from the 'margins of classroom life' (Marsh et al. 2005: 12) to examine how it mediates young people's aspirations and sense-making practices. We also hope they will look at work and success in relation to other key discourses, including those identified in this book of happiness, authenticity, money and fame.

Youth researchers have, like us, shown that attending to young people's lives can offer insights into processes of social and cultural change. Being 'in between' – moving through institutions such as education, work and the family, and being in the process of making sense of themselves and the world around them – young people's experiences illuminate the wider world (Roberts 2003). We have demonstrated that studying the conditions of youth is vital to critical enquires into the operation of power and inequality within austere meritocracy. Throughout recent history young people have carried a particular burden of representation, holding together society's hopes and fears. In times of social change and economic crisis, this contradictory positioning of youth intensifies as they become both the cause of society's problems and the stakes upon which the nation's future depends. In Chapter 2 we demonstrated how young people experience being one of the main bearers of the crisis –held responsibile for spearheading the nation's economic recovery *and* imagined as a lost generation without hope. In exploring young people's aspirations and transitions within austerity through the lens of celebrity, our study responds to three agendas within the field of youth studies.

First, we explore the operation of both structure and agency in young people's aspirations. Such a focus is challenging in the context of austere meritocracy, which offers an agentive promise that constraints can be overcome by hard work and determination. This is a story that, as we have seen, was often recounted by participants. We have foregrounded young people's accounts and analysis based in 'critical respect', which 'involves attentive, respectful listening' while also attending to questions of power in order to 'capture the complexities' of young people's growing up in a deeply unequal society (Gill 2007: 78). This book illustrates the significance of young people's engagement with celebrity as reflecting broader social processes. This brings us to our second contribution to youth studies. Rather than treat the two traditions of youth research – 'youth cultures' and 'youth transitions' – separately, we concur with Robert MacDonald (2011: 438) that studies of youth are enhanced by a holistic engagement with 'how youth cultural identities shape and are shaped by the transitions people make'. Contextualizing young people's celebrity talk within both their individual biographies and the socioeconomic landscape, we follow others who have connected young people's leisure, style and consumption to their education and employment transitions (Archer et al. 2010; Hollingworth 2015; Shildrick & Macdonald 2006). This work, like ours, demonstrates the ongoing role of social class, gender and race in structuring young people's cultural practices and trajectories. We have argued that young people's engagement with celebrity can be analysed for both what it expresses about young people's current circumstances and for how it mediates their sense of possible and desirable futures.

Our book also responds to recent calls to attend to the 'missing middle' of youth research (Roberts & MacDonald 2013). Paralleling the focus on fans within celebrity and media studies (discussed below), youth researchers have tended to focus on the spectacular over the ordinary. Work exploring youth transitions has concentrated on those who are remarkably success-ful or disadvantaged, and youth cultural work has paid great attention to exotic subcultures (Brown 1987; Shildrick & MacDonald 2006). This ten-dency to attend to the spectacular has meant that the diversity of young people's lives has been hidden. There is an urgent need to take a wider view. As MacDonald (2011) notes, given the expansion of higher education and rising youth underemployment, youth transitions can no longer be neatly demarcated along class lines. We need a 'more panoramic view', allowing 'for greater critical interrogation of "slow-track transitions" through col-lege, university and the graduate labour market, understanding their new insecurities and risks and that such transitions are no longer solely the preserve of middle-class young people' (MacDonald 2011: 437). Our par-ticipants are 'ordinary' both in their position within the education system – enrolled in state schools and neither especially problematic nor exceptional in their achievements – and in their cultural practices. While some were highly invested in particular celebrities, the vast majority rejected the pos-ition of fan. We hope that it indicates how attending to the ordinary can provide rich insights into young people's lives.

Finally, this book contributes to the field of celebrity studies. Most sig-nificantly, we address the lack of empirical investigations into celebrity audiences as compared to the vast array of textual analyses (Holmes 2004; Turner 2010). While significant empirical work does exist and remains influ-ential on the field, 'such work has often tended to be sporadic or small scale' (Barker et al. 2015: 1). This project was in part motivated by a desire to address this absence, and in doing so to challenge assumptions about who the audiences of celebrity are and how celebrity operates in all of our lives. We have been influenced by earlier feminist work on stardom and on girls' and women's other cultural practices (for example, Ang 1996; Duits 2010; Hermes 1995; McRobbie & Garber 1977; Radway 1984; Stacey 1994). As this suggests, work on celebrity audiences tends to focus on women rather than men (Barker et al. 2015, though see Cann 2014). The absence of men as participants limits our understanding of the relationship between gender and celebrity. The default position of the celebrity audience as female plays into the historical trivialization both of celebrity consumers and of celebrity studies as a 'glossy topic' rather than a 'serious' scholarly pursuit (Beer & Penfold-Mounce 2009). By including young men as well as young women, we have opened up questions about the role of everyday celebrity in the construction of gender (see also Allen et al. 2015a).

There is a considerable amount of work within fan studies that has facili-tated a more active conceptualization of audience-celebrity relationships. However, a focus on celebrity fans can overlook more mundane and even hostile engagements with celebrity. Just as we emphasize the importance of attending to the experience of 'ordinary kids' in youth studies, we see our book as arguing for the value of studying ordinary celebrity consumption. We have demonstrated that even for those who dismiss celebrity, their celebrity talk is significant. Indeed, distancing from celebrity is performative and constitutive of their and others' social positions. As such, we contribute to recent analysis of people's engagement with celebrity within digital spaces – that is often characterized by ambivalence, hostility and disgust (Jensen & Ringrose 2014; Tyler & Bennett 2010). We have shown that these (collective) performances reproduce social hierarchies.

Exploring celebrity through its audiences is vital to how we understand its social function in times of change. Young people's everyday consumption challenges scholarly assumptions. As Ien Ang (1996: 514–15) states, a focus on 'the unruly and heterogeneous practices and accounts of real historical [people] . . . forces the researcher to come to terms with perspectives that may not be easily integrated in a smooth, finished and coherent Theory'. Talking to people about their uses of celebrity also brings to light how the powerful discourses that circulate within celebrity – such as of aspiration, social mobility and work – are resisted and reworked. This has epistemological implications. The textual celebrity case studies in Chapters 2 to 8 take on different meanings in relation to the empirical data and vice versa. We hope other researchers will develop this project, and the recent special issue of *Celebrity Studies* on celebrity audiences is an encouraging sign that more academics are returning to questions of the empirical audience (Barker et al. 2015).

While we anticipate that this book will contribute to these fields, we also hope it will have life and meaning outside academia. In the course of the project, we engaged with teachers, youth workers, careers educators, parents, young people and activists who told us that they connect with our data and our interpretations. Their insights have fed into our analysis. We hope our book can support those who work professionally with young people. Accompanying it, there are resources for practitioners on our myth-busting website (www.celebyouth.org/mythbusting). In particular, we hope that this work can help to facilitate forms of critical pedagogy (Friere 1973; hooks 1994) that challenge – and transgress – the individualizing narratives of aspiration and meritocracy that infuse the sites of policy, education and youth work.

Despite decades of research disproving the claims of an aspiration deficit among young people made by successive governments, policymakers continue to present this as the cause of educational inequalities and declining social mobility. Under the current government, young people are increasingly constructed through the lens of neuroscience and behavioural psychology (Brooks 2013). This is captured in the Coalition and now Conservative government's preoccupation with building children and young people's 'character' and 'resilience'. These moves reflect an intensifying political rhetoric that explains poverty and inequality as resulting from behavioural and moral deficiencies rather than the structural inequalities unleashed by neoliberal austerity (Bull & Allen 2018). Our research attempts to challenge such constructions of youth and trouble their epistemological effects – that is how they make available certain ways of understanding young people's transitions and opportunities while silencing others.

As we have discussed, the Conservatives have slashed UK spending on youth services. Their only new youth work provision is the National Citizen Service, a summer programme for young people. Before and after completing this programme, participants are asked to complete a survey. One item asked them to agree or disagree with the statement, 'If someone is not a success in life it's their own fault.' As Tania de St Croix (2016: 23) reports, the 'proportion of young people agreeing with this statement increased after they had taken part in the 2011 programme, a result the evaluators saw as "encouraging" evidence of young people's feelings of control over their own lives'. St Croix goes on to point out that this ignores the role of society in determining who is successful, and even what success looks like. Critical practitioners 'aim to challenge the idea that individuals are entirely responsible for their own circumstances' (St Croix 2016: 23). We hope our participants' stories, and our celebrity case studies offer resources for youth practitioners to engage in critical dialogues with young people about their futures in ways that help them to think differently about success and failure and to challenge the forces of oppression.

Young people's desires for happiness, success, fame and money work through cruel optimism, as do our own desires for these things. Disengaging from such investments is difficult and emotional work. Teachers, including those in universities, are part of sustaining these attachments. And indeed, as academics – who currently or previously worked in universities – we recognize our own complicity in this regime. The 'success' of institutions and individual academics is assessed by metrics of student satisfaction and employability. These measures are tied to – and reproduce – the myth of meritocracy. When we have used this research with undergraduates, critiquing neoliberal discourses of aspiration, work and success, they have often responded that it is okay for us to be critical of dominant discourses from a position of success and security but that they do not have this luxury and so must conform to them. In opening up a discussion about the presence and significance of class and other inequalities in shaping young people's opportunities, we may therefore find ourselves within our attempts to be critical pedagogues, 'affect aliens' and killjoys (Ahmed 2010a), killing their optimism, often in ways that stifle rather than liberate. Indeed, we as youth researchers have a tendency to project our own anger at the present and hopes for the future – for revolution and progressive change – onto those we research. We can be guilty of seeking out and romanticizing young people's 'resistance' in ways that obscure the costs – material and psychological – incurred if young people do not invest in these cruel attachments and produce themselves as aspirational. This suggests that we need collective, not individual, strategies if we are to transform the damaging conditions outlined in this book. We reflect on the possibilities and challenges of this in the final section.

Where are we right now?

The concept of austere meritocracy that we have developed in this book attempts to capture the most recent articulation of a much longer neoliberal story in – and about – the lives of young people. We do not know what mutations this story will take next, and the wider social, political and economic climate in which we have been writing only reinforces our sense of uncertainty and our caution about providing conclusive answers or predictions for the future.

Since we collected our data, a series of significant events have occurred and are still unravelling. We are writing this concluding chapter in February 2017 in a country bracing itself for Brexit after the UK's vote to leave the European Union (EU). Last month, reality television star and entrepreneur Donald Trump was inaugurated as the 45th president of the United States. We do not know how events will unfold in the year it will take this book to reach publication. It has been challenging writing during this time, torn between attending to the details of the situation in 2012–13, when we collected these data, while being overtaken by current developments. Some commentators linked the tumultuous political events of 2016 to the year's toll of celebrity deaths. For example, the UK's most widely read tabloid newspaper, *The Sun* (Ferrett 2016), headlined a review of the year, 'Trump, Brexit and ALL those celebrity deaths – is 2016 the most bizarre year in history?' This death toll included Carrie Fisher, David Bowie, George Michael, Muhammad Ali, Prince and Victoria Wood. Although there was only a small increase in celebrity deaths in 2016, easily attributable to chance combined with an ongoing expansion of the category of celebrity, this statistical 'truth' is irrelevant (McDonald 2016). Again we see celebrity's function to express public feeling as, for those on the liberal left in particular, these celebrity deaths came to symbolize other losses and anxieties.

The Brexit and Trump victories are supporting a rise in white supremacism and the far right and a return of social class to political rhetoric. A disenfranchised white working class have been blamed for Trump and Brexit, ignoring the role of privileged white people, including political and media elites, in both events (Greenwald 2016). We now hear politicians discuss the working class as victims of global capitalism, in ways that, at first glance, *appear* to unsettle and even critique the pervasive meritocratic narrative. Notably, in October 2016, incoming Conservative Prime Minister Theresa May (2016) talked of her 'government stepping up. Righting wrongs. Challenging vested interests. . . . To stand up for the weak and stand up to the strong', adopting Trump's economic populist message. She continued:

No vision ever changed a country on its own. You need to put the hours in and the effort too. But if you do, great things can happen. Great changes can occur. And be in no doubt, that's what Britain needs today. Because in June people voted for change. (May 2016)

In May's incorporation of a critique of elite politics, we see the flexibility of the intertwined rhetorics of austerity and meritocracy, as she doubles down on the discourses of effort and individual responsibility we have identified throughout this book. The everyday nationalist nostalgia of thrift is being reshaped through a discourse of post-Brexit self-sufficiency, even as banks and corporations are handed billions in taxpayers' money via quantitative easing.

With the benefit of hindsight, we can use patterns in our data to understand these political shifts. Trump was able to use his position as a business-*man* as the basis for his presidential campaign. Our analysis demonstrates that entrepreneurship is central to austere meritocracy, with celebrities, such as Bill Gates, viewed as more deserving of wealth and status than other celebrities because they are seen to have impact, be innovative and show initiative. These discourses construct their own truths independent of the role of familial economic and social capital in Trump's success, or that his enterprises consist mainly of towers that he did not build but carry his brand, a television series and a range of failed ventures of dubious legality, such as Trump University. His white middle-class masculinity is crucial here; Hillary Clinton's entrepreneurialism was either ignored or linked to corruption. As part of a group who are seen to have earned their wealth, Trump can tap into an 'anti-elite' discourse that dismisses expert knowledge, as could the privileged UK politicians who campaigned to leave the EU, such as Boris Johnson. Trump and Johnson ward off criticism by producing themselves as authentic. Johnson's gaff-prone, man-of-the-people persona parallels Trump's, as does Nigel Farage's, the UK's leading proponent of Brexit. Their racism, sexism and homophobia are presented as part of their authenticity: 'telling it like it is' rather than conceding to 'political correctness'. Johnson and Farage are often photographed holding a pint of beer, a classic British symbol of ordinariness. Their so-called authenticity enables them to rail against globalization for leaving behind working-class people, while promoting further deregulation and cuts that will punish and marginalize these groups. Their victories are part of a post-crisis reshaping of capitalism, rather than a challenge to it. In the United States, Trump has appointed the wealthiest cabinet in US history and in the post-Brexit UK, quantitative easing by the Bank of England has pumped an additional seventy billion pounds into the financial markets, increasing wealth inequality (Positive Money 2016).

The UK's opposition party, Labour, is, at the time of writing, led by socialist Jeremy Corbyn. The movement that swept him to power in 2015 and got him reelected in 2016 parallels the Bernie Sanders movement in the

United States and the rise of new left-wing parties and leaders across Europe (notably in France, Greece, Spain and Iceland) who are challenging free-market rhetoric. Whether these will filter down into genuine and progressive change in the lives of young people is not clear. However, the different ideas that are coming through the left present challenges to the common sense of austerity where there were previously none. They attack the wealthiest '1 per cent' who do not play by the rules but, in expressing a desire for fairness, they perhaps reinforce an underlying attachment to the possibility of an authentic meritocracy. Corbyn's Labour Party, like Ken Loach's Cannes award-winning film *I, Daniel Blake*, rejects the scrounger image of benefits claimants, instead emphasizing an understanding of people in need of support and trapped in an abusive system. Many have dismissed the rise of Corbyn and Sanders as part of a celebrification of politics or even a personality cult, no different from Trump and Farage. They point to the number of people queuing for selfies, and a range of fandom dedicated to them (Mendick 2015). These can certainly be seen as a distraction from politics. But as this book attests, celebrity is now inseparable from how we relate to the world, to ideas and to each other and therefore must be taken seriously. Corbyn's ascendancy can be seen as expressing a desire for political authenticity, a reaction to growing inequality and disaffection with mainstream politicians. It can also be understood as a response to the failure of the highly individualized discourses of aspiration we have examined in this book. For after the 2015 General Election, mainstream Labour politicians 'launched a concerted and apparently coordinated push to establish a new orthodoxy around a single word: "aspiration"', insisting that it was the loss of aspirational middle-class voters that had led to the party's defeat (Nunns 2016: 49). If aspiration, as it is currently figured, sustains cruel attachments to toxic promises that cannot be fulfilled, rather than throw out aspiration, we could follow Corbyn and Sanders in reframing aspiration in ways that make lives more liveable (Butler 2006). We could articulate alternative conceptualizations of aspiration, rooted not in a personal project of competitive individualism and acquisitive self-advancement, but in collective commitments to a more equitable and sustainable future for all (Blower 2015; Levitas 2012).

We can also find hope outside of mainstream politics. Over the past few years, social movements have grown and become more and more visible: Black Lives Matter, Native American actions against the destruction of land, anti-austerity movements, environmental activism, and all of their intersections. These have been supported by independent media finding new audiences via YouTube and other social media and by some of the celebrities mentioned in this book (Democracy Now 2016; Novara Media 2016). These protests have intensified since Trump's inauguration, including the global Women's March and the series of mass demonstrations against fascism and racism that followed Trump's 'Muslim ban' in February 2017. Many involved in these movements have stressed the importance of intersectional politics. Angela Davis (in Matthews 2017), at the global Women's March, called on protestors to

> dedicate ourselves to collective resistance. Resistance to the billionaire mortgage profiteers and gentrifiers. Resistance to the health care privateers. Resistance to the attacks on Muslims and on immigrants. Resistance to attacks on disabled people. Resistance to state violence perpetrated by the police and through the prison industrial complex. Resistance to institutional and intimate gender violence, especially against trans women of color.

It is not surprising that young people have figured in these events and the commentary around them. They are at the sharp end of university debt, housing shortages and rising unemployment and will be hit hardest by the consequences of Britain leaving the EU. Carrying the burden of representation as both our hope for the future and the cause of our downfall, young people have featured in contradictory ways. They are 'low-information voters' and non-voters, whose political apathy contributed to Brexit and Trump – despite those young people who did vote overwhelmingly opposing both (Purtill 2016). They are 'snowflakes' whose vulnerability or narcissism is blocking collective action towards more progressive futures. Correspondingly, they have also been constructed as highly engaged, and at the centre of the insurgencies and social movements cited above. Given these forces on the young, and the different political possibilities of this moment, we cannot be sure where we are now. But we are sure that we need to be producing different knowledge and struggling to transform the world in ways that make lives more liveable. We hope our book can be a resource in this struggle.

Postscript

The uncertain landscape that we have sketched in this book has continued. The UK had a snap general election in June 2017. Contrary to predictions of a Conservative landslide, they are now a precarious minority government. During the election and its aftermath there have been shifts in the public framing of austerity. The Left populism and grassroots politics we pointed to in our Conclusions played a pivotal role in the mass mobilization of Labour activists campaigning for an anti-austerity programme of wealth redistribution, re-nationalization and investment, including free higher education. More young people voted in the election than in any for twenty-five years (Burn-Murdoch 2017). The British Attitudes Survey (Harding 2017) reported that the balance of opinion had tipped towards higher taxes and public spending for the first time since the financial crash.

A week after the election, the inequality at the heart of austerity was exposed when a fire destroyed the homes and lives of hundreds living in Grenfell Tower in Kensington and Chelsea – one of London's most economically unequal boroughs. The mainly working-class and multi-ethnic residents had long campaigned for safer homes but could not take legal action due to a combination of weak housing law and cuts to legal aid (Davies 2017). Many – led by the local community – see the tragedy as the result of neoliberalism valuing profit over people, with Labour's John McDonnell calling the deaths 'social murders' as they result from political decisions. So while austerity's material effects continue to cut deep, its discursive supports are beginning to fall away.

BIBLIOGRAPHY

Abrahams, J. (2017), *Schooling inequality: Aspirations, institutional practices and social class reproduction*, PhD Thesis, Cardiff University, UK.

Afoko, C. and Vockins, D. (2013), 'Framing the economy: The austerity story', *New Economics Foundation*, 11 September. Available online: http://neweconomics.org/2013/09/framing-the-economy/ (accessed 12 September 2013).

After Earth (2013), [Film] Dir. M. Night Shyamalan, USA: Columbia Pictures.

Agence France-Presse in Los Angeles (2016), 'Kim Kardashian to sue website over "fake robbery" allegations', *The Guardian*, 12 October 2016. Available online: https://www.theguardian.com/lifeandstyle/2016/oct/12/kim-kardashian-sue-website-fake-paris-jewellery-robbery-allegations (accessed 2 February 2017).

Ahmed, S. (2014), 'Selfcare as warfare', Feminist Killjoys, 25 August. Available online: https://feministkilljoys.com/2014/08/25/selfcare-as-warfare/ (accessed 23 November 2016).

Ahmed, S. (2010a), *The promise of happiness*, London: Duke University Press.

Ahmed, S. (2010b), 'Feminist killjoys (and other willful subjects)', *S&F Online*, 8 (3). Available online: http://sfonline.barnard.edu/polyphonic/print_ahmed.htm (accessed 10 December 2016).

Ahmed, S. (2004), *The cultural politics of emotion*, Edinburgh, UK: Edinburgh University Press.

Alexander, M. (2012), *The new Jim Crow*, New York: New Press.

Alexander, P. (2017), *Reframing black or ethnic minority teachers as role models*, PhD Thesis, Goldsmiths, University of London, UK.

Allen, K. (2016), 'Top girls navigating austere times: Interrogating youth transitions since the "crisis"', *Journal of Youth Studies*, 19 (6): 805–820.

Allen, K. (2013), '"Blair's children": Young women as "aspirational subjects" in the psychic landscape of class', *The Sociological Review*, 62 (4): 760–779.

Allen, K. and Hollingworth, S. (2013), 'Social class, place and urban young people's aspirations for work in the knowledge economy: "Sticky subjects" or "cosmopolitan creative"?' *Urban Studies*, 50 (3): 499–517.

Allen, K. and Mendick, H. (2013), 'Making it and faking it? Social class, young people and authenticity', *Sociology*, 47 (3): 460–476.

Allen, K. and Mendick, H. (2012), 'Young people's uses of celebrity: Class, gender and "improper" celebrity', *Discourse: Studies in the Cultural Politics of Education*, 34 (1): 77–93.

Allen, K., Harvey, L. and Mendick, H. (2015a), '"Justin Bieber sounds girlie": Young people's celebrity talk and contemporary masculinities', *Sociological Research Online*, 20 (3). Available online: http://www.socresonline.org.uk/20/3/12.html (accessed 28 July 2017).

Allen, K., Mendick, H., Harvey, L. and Ahmad, A. (2015b), 'Welfare queens, thrifty housewives, and do-it-all mums: Celebrity motherhood and the cultural politics of austerity', *Feminist Media Studies*, 15 (6): 907–925.

Allen, K., Quinn, J., Hollingworth, S. and Rose, A. (2013), 'Becoming employable students and "ideal" creative workers: Exclusion and inequality in higher education work placements', *British Journal of Sociology of Education*, 3 (34): 431–452.

Ang, I. (1996), 'Feminist desire and female pleasure', in J. Storey (ed.), *Cultural studies and the study of the popular: Theories and methods,* 513–522, Edinburgh, UK: Edinburgh University Press.

Antonucci, L. (2016), *Student lives in crisis: Deepening inequality in times of austerity*, Bristol, UK: Policy Press.

Archer, L. and Francis, B. (2007), *Understanding minority ethnic achievement: Race, gender, class and 'success'*, Abingdon, UK: Routledge.

Archer, L., Hollingworth, S. and Mendick, H. (2010), *Urban youth and schooling*, Maidenhead, UK: Open University Press.

Ashton, K. (2013), 'The Harlem make: You didn't make the Harlem Shake go viral – corporations did!', qz.com, 28 March. Available online: https://qz.com/67991/you-didnt-make-the-harlem-shake-go-viral-corporations-did/ (accessed 30 March 2016).

Asi, H. S. (2013), 'Beyonce: I am just a girl – interview', *UK Screen*, 7 May. Available online: http://ukscreen.com/articles/interviews/beyonce-i-am-just-a-girl-interview/ (accessed 10 December 2016).

Bagguley, P. and Hussain, Y. (2016), 'Negotiating mobility: South Asian women and higher education', *Sociology*, 50 (1): 43–59.

Ball, S. J., Maguire, M. and Macrae, S. (2000), *Choice, pathways, and transitions post-16: New youth, new economies in the global city*, London: RoutledgeFalmer.

Barker, M., Holmes, S. and Ralph, S. (2015), 'Celebrity audiences', *Journal of Celebrity Studies*, 6 (1): 1–5.

Bathmaker, A-M., Ingram, N., Abrahams, J., Hoare, A., Waller, R. and Bradley, H. (2016), *Social class, higher education and social mobility: The degree generation*, London: Palgrave Macmillan.

Bauman, Z. (1998), *Work, Consumerism and the new poor*, Buckingham, UK: Open University Press.

BBC (2011), 'London riots: Looting and violence continues', *BBC Online*, 8 August. Available online: http://www.bbc.co.uk/news/uk-england-london-14439970 (accessed 23 December 2012).

Beauvais, C. and Higham, R. (2016), 'A reappraisal of children's "potential"', *Studies in Philosophy and Education,* 35 (6): 573–587.

Beer, D. and Penfold-Mounce, R. (2009), 'Celebrity gossip and the new melodramatic imagination', *Sociological Research Online,* 14 (2). Available online: http://socresonline.org.uk/14/2/2.html (accessed 28 July 2018).

Benedictus, L. (2013), 'Celebrities on Instagram: Who to follow and why', *The Guardian*, February 25. Available online: https://www.theguardian.com/technology/shortcuts/2013/feb/25/celebrities-on-instagram-madonna-kardashian (accessed 2 February 2017).

Bennett, P. and McDougall, J. (eds) (2016), *Popular culture and the austerity myth: Hard times today*. New York: Routledge.

Berlant, L. (2011), *Cruel optimism*, Durham, NC: Duke University Press.

Berlant, L. (2006), 'Cruel optimism', *Differences: A Journal of Feminist Cultural Studies*, 17 (3): 20–36.

Bhattacharyya, G. (2015), *Crisis, austerity and everyday life: Living in a time of diminishing expectations*, Basingstoke, UK: Palgrave Macmillan.

Billig, M. (1996), *Arguing and thinking: A rhetorical approach to social psychology* (2nd edition), New York: Cambridge University Press.

Billig, M. (1992), *Talking of the royal family*, London: Routledge.

Billig, M., Condor, S., Edwards, D., Gane, M., Middleton, D. and Radley, A. (1988), *Ideological Dilemmas: A social psychology of everyday thinking*, London: Sage.

Binkley, S. (2011), 'Happiness, positive psychology and the program of neoliberal governmentality', *Subjectivity*, 4 (4): 371–394.

Biressi, A. (2011) 'The virtuous circle: Social entrepreneurship and welfare programming in the UK', in H. Wood and B. Skeggs (eds), *Reality Television and Class*, 144–145, London: British Film Institute.

Biressi, A. and Nunn, H. (2013a), 'Young entrepreneurs money making for the nations benefit', *CelebYouth*, 22 May. Available online: http://www.celebyouth. org/young-entrepreneurs-money-making-for-the-nations-benefit/ (accessed 10 December 2016).

Biressi, A. and Nunn, H. (2013b), *Class and contemporary British culture*, Basingstoke, UK: Palgrave Macmillan.

Biressi, A. and Nunn, H. (2013c), 'Class, gender and the docusoap: The only way is Essex', in C. Carter, L. Steiner and L. McLaughlin (eds), *The Routledge companion to media and gender*, 269–279, London: Routledge.

Biressi, A. and Nunn, H. (2008), 'Bad citizens: The class politics of lifestyle television', in G. Palmer (ed.), *Exposing lifestyle television: The big reveal*, 15–23, Aldershot, UK: Ashgate.

Biressi, A. and Nunn, H. (2004), 'The especially remarkable: Celebrity and social mobility in Reality TV', *Mediactive* 2: 44–58.

Blankfeld, K. (2016), 'Forbes billionaires: Full list of the 500 richest people in the world 2016', *Forbes*, 1 March. Available online: http://www.forbes.com/ sites/kerenblankfeld/2016/03/01/forbes-billionaires-full-list-of-the-500-richest-people-in-the-world-2016/#6d2a2ba46c24 (accessed 27 January 2017).

The Bling Ring (2013), [Film] Dir. Sofia Coppola, USA: American Zoetrope.

Bloodworth, J. (2016), *The myth of meritocracy: Why working-class kids still get working-class jobs*, London: Biteback Publishing.

Blower, C. (2015), 'Teaching aspiration', in The Centre for Labour and Social Studies (ed.), *What is aspiration? And how should progressives respond*, 9–12, London: Class.

Boltanski, L. and Chiapello, E. (2002), 'The new spirit of capitalism', paper presented to the Conference of Europeanists, 14–16 March, Chicago. Available online: http://www.darkmatterarchives.net/wp-content/uploads/2011/11/ boltanskiSPIRITofCapitalism.pdf (accessed 12 February 2017).

Boorstin, D. (1963), *The image*, London: Weidenfeld and Nicolson.

Bourdieu, P. (1984), *Distinction*, trans. R. Nice, London: Routledge.

Bramall, R. (2013), *The cultural politics of austerity: Past and present in austere times*, New York: Palgrave Macmillan.

Bramall, R., Gilbert, J. and Meadway, J. (2016), 'What is austerity?', *New Formations*, 87: 119–140.

Brooks, R. (2013), 'The social construction of young people within education policy: Evidence from the UK's Coalition government', *Journal of Youth Studies*, 16 (3): 318–333.

Brown, G. (2011), 'Emotional geographies of young people's aspirations for adult life', *Children's Geographies*, 9 (1): 7–22.

Brown, G. (2007), 'Speech on education', University of Greenwich, 31 October. Available online: http://www.ukpol.co.uk/2015/10/02/gordon-brown-2007-speech-on-education/ (accessed 8 April 2015).

Brown, M. (2013), 'We were all Justin Bieber fans and now we hate him', *The Guardian*, 5 March. Available online: https://www.theguardian.com/music/2013/mar/05/justin-bieber-fans-now-hate-him (accessed 31 July 2017).

Brown, P. (2003), 'The opportunityt: Education and employment in a global economy', *European Educational Research Journal*, 2 (1): 142–180.

Brown, P. (1987), *Schooling ordinary kids*, London: Tavistock.

Brown, P., Lauder, H. and Ashton, D. (2011), *Global auction: The broken promises of education, jobs and incomes,* Oxford, UK: Oxford University Press.

Brown, W. (2005), *Edgework: Critical essays on knowledge and power*, Princeton, NJ: Princeton University Press.

Buckingham, D. (1991), 'What are words worth? Interpreting children's talk about television', *Cultural Studies*, 5 (2): 228–245.

Buckingham, D. and Bragg, S. (2004), *Young people, sex and the media: The facts of life?*, Basingstoke, UK: Palgrave Macmillan.

Bull, A. and Allen, K. (forthcoming, 2018), 'Editors' introduction to "grit", "resilience" and the erasure of inequality? A sociological critique of the character education agenda', *Sociological Research Online*, 1.

Burn-Murdoch, J. (2017), 'Youth turnout at general election highest in 25 years, data show', *The Financial Times*, 20 June. Available online: https://www.ft.com/content/6734cdde-550b-11e7-9fed-c19e2700005f (accessed 31 July 2017).

Butler, J. (2006), *Precarious life* (2nd edition), New York: Routledge.

Butler, J. (1997), *The psychic life of power*, Stanford, CA: Stanford University Press.

Butler, J. (1990), *Gender trouble*, London: Routledge.

Cabinet Office (2011), *Social mobility strategy: Opening doors: Breaking barriers*, London: Cabinet Office.

Cameron, A., Smith, N. and Tepe-Belfrage, D. (2016), 'Household wastes: Disciplining the family in the name of austerity', *British Politics*, 11 (4): 396–417.

Cameron, D. (2015), 'The Conservatives have become the party of equality', *The Guardian*, 26 October. Available online: https://www.theguardian.com/commentisfree/2015/oct/26/david-cameron-conservatives-party-of-equality (accessed 10 December 2016).

Cameron, D. (2013), 'David Cameron admits ministers must "do far more" to increase social mobility', *The Guardian*, 14 November. Available online:

https://www.theguardian.com/society/2013/nov/14/david-cameron-social-mobility-major (accessed 10 December 2016).

Cameron, D. (2012), 'Conservative Party Conference speech', *The Telegraph*, 10 October. Available online: www.telegraph.co.uk/news/politics/conservative/9598534/David-Camerons-Conservative-Party-Conference-speech-in-full.html (accessed 16 March 2016).

Cameron, D. (2010), 'People will not get away with fraud', *The Sun*, 12 August.

Cann, V. (2014), 'The limits of masculinity: Boys, taste and cultural consumption', in S. Roberts (ed.), *Debating modern masculinities: Change, continuity, crisis?*, 17–34, Basingstoke, UK: Palgrave Macmillan.

Chepp, V. (2015), 'Black feminist theory and the politics of irreverence: The case of women's rap', *Feminist Theory*, 16 (2): 207–226.

Chetty, R., Grusky, D., Hell, M., Hendren, N., Manduca, R. and Narang, J. (2016), 'The fading American dream: Trends in absolute income since 1940', Equality of Opportunity Project. Available online: http://www.equality-of-opportunity.org/assets/documents/abs_mobility_summary.pdf (accessed 2 February 2017).

Chun, E. (2011), 'Reading race beyond black and white', *Discourse & Society*, 22 (4): 403–421.

Clark, S. (2013), 'Justin Bieber needs a therapist – expert says', *Hollywood Life*, 14 March. Available online: http://hollywoodlife.com/2013/03/14/justin-bieber-therapy-meltdown/ (accessed 10 December 2016).

Clarke, S. (2009), 'A good education: Girls' extracurricular pursuits and school choice', *Gender and Education*, 21 (5): 601–615.

Clarke, J. and Newman, J. (2012), 'The alchemy of austerity', *Critical Social Policy*, 32 (3): 299–319.

Cohen, P. (2003), 'Mods and shockers: Youth cultural studies in Britain', in A. Bennett, M. Cieslik and S. Miles (eds), *Researching Youth*, 29–54, New York: Palgrave Macmillan.

Cohen, S. (1972), *Folk devils and moral panics: The creation of the mods and rockers*, London: Routledge.

Comaroff, J. and Comaroff, J. (2005), 'Reflections ony: From the past to the postcolony', in A. Honwana and P. De Boeck (eds), *Makers and breakers: Children and youth in postcolonial Africa*, 19–30, Asmara, ER: World Press.

Conn, D. (2015), 'Olympic legacy failure: Sports centres under assault by thousand council cuts', *The Guardian,* 5 July. Available online: https://www.theguardian.com/sport/2015/jul/05/olympic-legacy-failure-sports-centres-council-cuts (accessed 2 February 2017).

Corlett, A. and Clarke, S. (2017), *Living standards 2017: The past, present and possible future of UK incomes*, London: Resolution Foundation.

Couldry, N. (2011), 'Class and contemporary forms of "reality" production or, hidden injuries of class', in H. Wood and B. Skeggs (eds), *Reality television and class*, 33–44, London: BFI Publishing.

Couldry, N. (2004), 'Theorising media as practice', *Social Semiotics*, 14 (2): 115–132.

Couldry, N. (2001a), 'Everyday royal celebrity', in D. Morley and K. Robins (eds), *British cultural studies*, 221–223, Oxford, UK: Oxford University Press.

Couldry, N. (2001b), 'The hidden injuries of media power', *Journal of Consumer Culture*, 1 (2): 155–177.

Coward, R. (1998), 'Yobs ahead. Tally ho!', *The Guardian*, 29 September. Available online: https://www.theguardian.com/world/1998/sep/29/guardiancolumnists. jackstraw (accessed 31 July 2017).

Cox, E. (2016), 'Mo Farah on fame, family and why he stuck by his coach through doping allegations', *The Telegraph*, 1 August. Available online: http://www. telegraph.co.uk/men/thinking-man/mo-farah-on-fame-family-and-why-he-stuck-by-his-coach-through-do/ (accessed 29 January 2017).

Cubarrubia, R. J. (2013), 'Justin Bieber: Don't compare me to Lindsay Lohan', *Rolling Stone*, 14 March. Available online: http://www.rollingstone.com/music/ news/justin-bieber-dont-compare-me-to-lindsay-lohan-20130314 (accessed 2 February 2017).

Daily Mail Reporter (2013), '"I only have eight pairs of shoes": Bling ring star Emma Watson condemns Paris Hilton's extravagant lifestyle after taking a look inside heiress' wardrobe', *The Mail Online*, 26 June. Available online: http:// www.dailymail.co.uk/tvshowbiz/article-2348624/Emma-Watson-condemns-extravagant-celebrity-lifestyles-I-8-pairs-shoes.html#ixzz4ZT1asg5y (accessed 23 February 2017).

Daily Mail Reporter (2013), '"One Kardashian is enough!" How Anna Wintour "banned" Kim's mom Kris Jenner from the Met Ball', *The Mail Online*, 13 May. Available online: http://www.dailymail.co.uk/femail/article-2323892/One-Kardashian-How-Anna-Wintour-banned-Kims-mom-Kris-Jenner-Met-Ball-Real-Housewives-werent-welcome-either.html (accessed 29 January 2017).

Daley, D. (2013), 'Tom's Olympic medal probably kept you in your job. He turned down his friends and holidays to keep diving after the Games. Isn't it time you left my son alone?', *Daily Mail*, 9 January. Available online: http://www.dailymail. co.uk/sport/othersports/article-2259777/Tom-Daleys-mum-Debbie-hits-David-Sparkes-Splash-criticism--EXCLUSIVE.html (accessed 10 December 2016).

Daley, T. (2013), 'Something I want to say . . .', YouTube, 2 December. Available online: https://www.youtube.com/watch?v=OJwJnoB9EKw (accessed 10 December 2016).

Daley, T. (2012), *My story*, London: Michael Joseph.

Davidson, E. (2011), *The burdens of aspiration: Schools, youth, and success in the divided social worlds of Silicon Valley*, New York and London: New York University Press.

Davies, L. (2017), 'The consequences of wealth fefore homes', *The Morning Star*, 26 July. Available online: https://www.morningstaronline.co.uk/a-d953-The-consequences-of-wealth-before-homes#.WX8YfYjyvIU (accessed 31 July 2017).

Davies, W. (2015), *The Happiness industry: How the government and big business sold us well-being*, London: Verso.

Dean, J. (2009), *Democracy and other neoliberal fantasies: Communicative capitalism and left politics*, Durham, NC: Duke University Press.

De Benedictis, S. and Gill, R. (2016), 'Austerity neoliberalism: A new discursive formation', *Open Democracy*, 15 July. Available online: https://www. opendemocracy.net/uk/austerity-media/sara-de-benedictis-rosalind-gill/ austerity-neoliberalism-new-discursive-formation (accessed 15 October 2016).

Democracy Now (2016), 'Dakota access pipeline: Playlist', YouTube, various dates. Available online: https://www.youtube.com/watch?v=nFwE9Itzzes&lis t=PLneypbodq-jYslQRTB-_ZUyMzQz7Fj6L5 (accessed 23 February 2017).

Department for Work and Pensions and Department for Education (2011), *A new approach to child poverty*, London: The Stationery Office.

The diver and his dad (2010), [TV programme] BBC1, 24 October, 22.55.

Doran, S. (2015), 'Zoella and the top 10 UK YouTubers finding fame and fortune online', Radio Times, 20 February. Available online: http://www.radiotimes. com/news/2015-02-20/zoella-and-the-top-10-uk-youtubers-finding-fame-and-fortune-online (accessed 29 January 2017).

Dorling, D. (2014a), *Inequality and the 1%*, London: Verso Books.

Dorling, D. (2014b), *All that is solid: How the great housing disaster defines our times, and what we can do about it*, London: Penguin.

Dowling, E. and Harvie, D. (2014), 'Harnessing the social: State crises and (big) society', *Sociology*, 48 (5): 869–886.

du Gay, P. (1996), *Consumption and identity at work*, London: Sage.

Duits, L. (2010), 'The importance of popular media in everyday girl culture', *European Journal of Communication*, 25 (3): 243–257.

Dutta, M. (2015), *Neoliberal health organizing: Communication, meaning, and politics*, New York: Routledge.

Dyer, R. (1986), *Heavenly bodies: Film stars and society* (2nd edition), New York: Routledge.

Dyer, R. (1979), *Stars*, London: BFI Publishing.

Edelman, L. (2004), *No future: Queer theory and the death drive*, Durham, NC: Duke University Press.

Ekman, S. (2013), 'Authenticity at work: Questioning the new spirit of capitalism from a micro-sociological perspective', in P. D. Gay and G. Morgan (eds), *New spirits of capitalism: Crises, justifications, and dynamics*, 294–315, Oxford, UK: Oxford University Press.

Elias, P. and Jones, P. (2006), *Representation of ethnic groups in chemistry and physics*, London: Institute of Physics and Royal Society of Chemistry.

Ellis, M. (forthcoming), *TBC*, PhD Thesis, Goldsmiths, University of London, UK.

Epstein, D. and Johnson, R. (1998), *Schooling sexualities*, Buckingham, UK: Open University Press.

Emmerson, C., Johnson, P. and Joyce, R. (eds), (2017), *IFS green budget 2017 (report R124)*, London: Institute for Fiscal Studies.

Fekadu, M. (2013), 'Justin Bieber: Is he the latest child star on the verge of a meltdown?', *Independent*, 22 March. Available online: http://www. independent.co.uk/arts-entertainment/music/features/justin-bieber-is-he-the-latest-child-star-on-the-verge-of-a-meltdown-8544631.html (accessed 2 February 2017).

Ferrett, H. (2016), 'Trump, Brexit and all those celebrity deaths – is 2016 the most bizarre year in history', *The Sun*, 9 November. Available online: https://www. thesun.co.uk/living/2148025/trump-brexit-and-all-those-celebrity-deaths-is-2016-the-most-bizarre-year-in-history/ (accessed 23 February 2017).

Friedli, L. and Stearn, R. (2015), 'Positive affect as coercive strategy: Conditionality, activation and the role of psychology in UK government workfare programmes', *Medical Humanities*, 41 (1): 40–47.

Fiske, J. (1992), 'Audiencing: A cultural studies approach to watching television',
    Poetics, 21 (4): 345–359.
Foucault, M. (1976), *The history of sexuality (volume 1): The will to knowledge,*
    trans. R. Hurley, London: Penguin.
France, A. and Roberts, S. (2015), 'The problem of social generations: A critique
    of the new emerging orthodoxy in youth studies', *Journal of Youth Studies,* 18
    (2): 215–230.
Francis, B. (2006), 'Heroes or zeroes? The discursive positioning of "underachieving
    boys" in English neo-liberal education policy', *Journal of Education Policy,* 21
    (2): 187–200.
Frith, E. (2016), *CentreForum Commission on children and young people's mental
    health: State of the nation,* London: CentreForum.
Furlong, A. and Cartmel, F. (2007), *Young people and social change: New
    perspectives.* Maidenhead, UK: Open University Press.
Furtado, M. (2013), 'Selena Gomez says F-U to "toxic toddler" Justin Bieber',
    The Province, 6 March. Available online: http://www.theprovince.com/
    entertainment/Selena+Gomez+says+toxic+toddler+Justin+Bieber/8062937/story.
    html (accessed 2 February 2017).
Gamson, J. (1994), *Claims to fame: Celebrity in contemporary America,* Berkeley:
    University of California Press.
Gardiner, L. (2016), *Stagnation generation: The case for renewing the
    Intergenerational contract.* The Intergenerational Commission and
    the Resolution Foundation, 18 July. Available online: http://www.
    intergencommission.org/publications/stagnation-generation-the-case-for-
    renewing-the-intergenerational-contract/ (accessed 26 July 2017).
Gershon, I. (2016), '"I'm not a businessman, I'm a business, man": Typing the
    neoliberal self into a branded existence', *Journal of Ethnographic Theory,* 6 (3):
    223–246.
Gill, R. (2016), 'Post-postfeminism? New feminist visibilities in postfeminist times',
    Feminist Media Studies, 16 (4): 610–630.
Gill, R. (2007), 'Critical respect: The difficulties and dilemmas of agency and
    "choice" for feminism – A reply to Duits and van Zoonen', *European Journal of
    Women's Studies,* 14 (1): 69–80.
Gill, R. (2002), 'Cool, creative and egalitarian? Exploring gender in project-based
    new media work in Europe', *Information, communication and society,* 5 (1):
    70–89.
Gillborn, D. (2016), 'Softly, softly: Genetics, intelligence and the hidden racism of
    the new geneism', *Journal of Education Policy,* 31 (4): 365–388.
Gillborn, D. (2010), 'The white working class, racism and respectability: Victims,
    degenerates and interest-convergence', *British Journal of Educational Studies,*
    58 (1): 3–25.
Gladwell, M. (2008), *Outliers: The story of success,* London: Penguin.
Glaude Jr, E. S. (2016), *Democracy in black: How race still enslaves the American
    soul,* New York: Crown Publishers.
Glaude Jr, E. S. (2015), 'Too many black churches preach the gospel of greed',
    New York Times, 19 March. Available online: http://www.nytimes.com/
    roomfordebate/2014/06/25/has-capitalism-become-incompatible-with-christianity/
    too-many-black-churches-preach-the-gospel-of-greed (accessed 26 July 2016).

Graafland, A. (2013), 'Kate Middleton isn't the only thrifty Royal in town'. *The Mirror*, 25 May. Available online: http://www.mirror.co.uk/news/uk-news/kate-middleton-isnt-only-thrifty-1909965 (accessed 27 January 2017).

Graham, C. and Gould, L. (2013), 'Unbeliebable! The behind-the-scenes power struggle that turned Justin Bieber's UK tour into a fiasco', *The Mail Online*, 11 March. Available online: http://www.dailymail.co.uk/tvshowbiz/article-2290885/Justin-Bieber-London-The-scenes-power-struggle-turned-tour-fiasco.html (accessed 2 February 2017).

Gramsci, A. (1977), *Antonio Gramsci: Selections from political writings (1910–1920)*, Q. Hoare (Ed.) and J. Matthews (Trans.), New York: International Publishers

Greening, J. (2016), 'Full text: Education secretary Justine Greening's conference speech', *The Spectator*, 4 October. Available online: http://blogs.spectator.co.uk/2016/10/full-text-education-secretary-justine-greenings-conference-speech/ (accessed 2 February 2017).

Greenwald, G. (2016), 'Democrats, Trump, and the ongoing, dangerous refusal to learn the lesson of Brexit', *The Intercept*, 9 November. Available online: https://theintercept.com/2016/11/09/democrats-trump-and-the-ongoing-dangerous-refusal-to-learn-the-lesson-of-brexit/ (accessed 23 February 2017).

Greg, P. and Gardiner, L. (2015), *A steady job? The UK's record on labour market security and stability since the millennium*. London: Resolution Foundation.

Gunter, A. (2010), *Growing up bad: Black youth, road culture & badness in an East London neighbourhood*, London: Tuffnell Press.

Gurney-Read, J. (2016), 'Nicky Morgan: Children misled by "instant success" of X Factor,' *The Telegraph*, 14 January. Available online: http://www.telegraph.co.uk/education/educationnews/12100281/Nicky-Morgan-Children-misled-by-instant-success-of-X-Factor.html (accessed 29 January 2017).

Halberstam, J. (2011), *The queer art of failure*, Durham, NC: Duke University Press.

Hall, S. (1997), 'Introduction', in S. Hall (ed.), *Representation: Cultural representations and signifying practices*, 1–11, London: Sage.

Hall, S. (1988), *The hard road to renewal. Thatcherism and the crisis of the left*, London: Lawrence & Wishart.

Hall, S. (1987), *Minimal selves, ICA documents 6: Identity*, London: Institute of Contemporary Arts.

Hall, S. and Jacques, M. (1983), *The politics of Thatcherism*, London: Lawrence & Wishart.

Hall, S. and Jefferson, T. (eds), (1976), *Resistance through rituals*, London: Hutchinson.

Hall, S. and O'Shea, A. (2013), 'Common sense neoliberalism' *Soundings*, 55 (Winter): 8–25.

Hall, S., Massey, D. and Rustin, M. (2013), 'After neoliberalism? The Kilburn manifesto', Soundings. Available online: https://www.lwbooks.co.uk/sites/default/files/00_manifestoframingstatement.pdf (accessed 26 July 2016).

Hamad, H. (2014), *Postfeminism and paternity in contemporary US film: Framing fatherhood*, London: Routledge.

Hardie, B. (2013), 'Tabloid tales from LA LA Land: 3am's round-up of this week's US celeb mags', *The Mirror*, 16 May. Available online: http://www.mirror.co.uk/3am/us-gossip/kim-kardashian-kanye-west-kourtney-1893362 (accessed 2 February 2017).

Harless, K. (2013), '"She would have been a Belieber": Justin Bieber causes outrage after writing "tasteless" message in guest book at Anne Frank museum', *The Mail Online*, 15 April. Available online: http://www.dailymail.co.uk/news/article-2308938/Justin-Bieber-causes-outrage-Anne-Frank-hopefully-Belieber-message.html (accessed 2 February 2017).

Harding, R. (2017), 'A backlash against austerity?', *British Social Attitudes*. Available online: http://www.bsa.natcen.ac.uk/latest-report/british-social-attitudes-34/key-findings/a-backlash-against-austerity.aspx (accessed 31 July 2017).

Harvey, D. (2014), *Seventeen contradictions and the end of capitalism*, London: Profile Books.

Harvey, D. (2005), *A brief history of neoliberalism*, Oxford, UK: Oxford University Press.

Harvey, L. (2014), Performing 'ordinary': Prince Harry, charity and military masculinity, *Celeb Youth*, 30 January. Available online: http://www.celebyouth.org/performing-ordinary-prince-harry-charity-and-military-masculinity/ (accessed 27 January 2017).

Harvey, L., Allen, K. and Mendick, H. (2015), 'Extraordinary acts and ordinary pleasures: Rhetorics of inequality in young people's talk about celebrity', *Discourse & Society*, 26 (4): 428–444.

Harvey, L., Ringrose, J. and Gill, R. (2013), 'Swagger, ratings and masculinity: Theorising the circulation of social and cultural value in teenage boys' digital peer networks', *Sociological Research Online*, 18 (4): online: http://www.socresonline.org.uk/18/4/9.html (accessed 28 July 2017).

Harris, A. (2004), *Future girl: Young women in the twenty-first century*, London: Routledge.

Helliwell, J., Layard, R. and Sachs, J. (2016), *World happiness report 2016, update (vol. I)*, New York: Sustainable Development Solutions Network.

Hello Magazine (2013), 'Kate Middleton and Prince William planning modest nursery', *Hello*, May 26. Available online: http://www.hellomagazine.com/royalty/2013052612758/kate-middleton-prince-william-modest-nursery/ (accessed 27 January 2017).

Hermes, J. (1995), *Reading women's magazines: An analysis of everyday media use*, Cambridge, UK: Polity.

Hill Collins, P. (2012), 'Just another American story? The first black first family', *Qualitative Sociology*, 35 (2): 123–141.

Hill Collins, P. (2005), *Black sexual politics: African Americans, gender, and the new racism*, New York: Routledge.

Hitchen, E. (2016), 'Living and feeling austerity', *New Formations: A Journal of Culture/Theory/Politics*, 87 (1): 112–118.

HM Treasury (2010), *Spending review 2010*, London: The Stationery Office.

Hochschild, A. R. (1979), *The managed heart: Commercialization of human feeling*, Berkeley: University of California Press.

Hodkinson, P. (2008), *Understanding career decision-making and progression: Careership revisited*, London: John Killeen Memorial Lecture.

Hoffman, C. (2013), 'Mr. and Mr. Smith: Will and Jaden psych up for After Earth',
    Vulture, 26 May. Available online: http://www.vulture.com/2013/05/will-and-
    jaden-smith-on-working-together.html (accessed 27 January 2017).
Hollander, J. A. and Einwohner, R. L. (2004), 'Conceptualizing resistance',
    Sociological Forum, 19 (4): 533–554.
Hollingworth, S. (2015), Performances of social class, race and gender through
    youth subculture: Putting structure back in to youth subcultural studies, *Journal
    of Youth Studies*, 18 (10): 1237–1256.
Holmes, S. (2004), '"All you've got to worry about is the task, having a cup of
    tea, and what you're going to eat for dinner": Approaching *Celebrity in Big
    Brother*', in S. Holmes and D. Jermyn (eds), *Understanding reality television*,
    111–135, London: Routledge.
hooks, b. (1994), *Teaching to transgress: Education as the practice of freedom*,
    London: Routledge
Horton, D. and Wohl, R. (1956), 'Mass communication and para-social
    interaction: Observations on intimacy at a distance', *Psychiatry*, 19 (3): 215–229.
Huffpost Celebrity (2013), 'Kim Kardashian was voted "most likely to lie about
    her ethnicity" in high school', *Huffington Post*, 10 July. Available online: http://
    www.huffingtonpost.com/2013/07/10/kim-kardashian-high-school-most-likely_
    n_3572893.html (accessed 25 July 2014).
Huppatz, K. (2012), *Gender capital at work: Intersections of femininity,
    masculinity, class and occupation*, Basingstoke, UK: Palgrave Macmillan.
Iannucci, L. M. (2010), *Will Smith: A biography*, Santa Barbara, CA: Greenwood
    Publishing.
Ingram, N. and Allen, K. (2016), '"Talent-spotting" or "social magic"? Inequality,
    cultural sorting and constructions of the ideal graduate in elite professions',
    paper given at Constructions of the Higher Education student – A one-day
    conference, September 2016, University of Surrey, UK.
ImanifestWealth (2010), 'Will Smith power of your subconscious mind –
    alchemist', YouTube, 14 June. Available online: https://www.youtube.com/
    watch?v=2EIBFNsenF4 (accessed 27 July 2016).
Jackson, C. (2006), *Lads and ladettes in school: Gender and a fear of failure*,
    Maidenhead, UK: Open University Press.
Jenkins, H. (2006), *Fans, bloggers, and gamers: Exploring participatory culture*,
    New York: New York University Press.
Jensen, J. (1992), 'Fandom as pathology', in L. Lewis (ed.), *The adoring
    audience: Fan culture and popular media*, 9–29, New York: Routledge.
Jensen, T. (2014), 'Welfare commonsense, poverty porn and doxosophy',
    Sociological Research Online, 19 (3). Available online: http://www.socresonline.
    org.uk/19/3/3.html (accessed 28 July 2017).
Jensen, T. (2013), 'Riots, Restraint and the New Cultural Politics of Wanting',
    Sociological Research Online, 18 (4). Available online: http://www.socresonline.
    org.uk/18/4/7.html (accessed 28 July 2017).
Jenson, T. and Ringrose, J. (2014), 'Sluts that choose vs doormat gypsies', *Feminist
    Media Studies*, 14 (3): 369–387.
Jensen, T. and Tyler, I. (2015), '"Benefits broods": The cultural and political
    crafting of anti-welfare commonsense', *Critical Social Policy, 35*
    (4): 470–491.

Jensen, T. and Tyler, I. (2012), 'Austerity parenting: New economies of parent-citizenship', *Studies in the Maternal*, 4 (2). Available online: https://www.mamsie.bbk.ac.uk/articles/10.16995/sim.34/ (accessed 28 July 2017).

Keay, D. (1987), 'Margaret Thatcher: Interview for Woman's Own', *Woman's Own*, 23 September. Available online: http://www.margaretthatcher.org/document/106689 (accessed 10 December 2016).

Kehily, M. J. and Nayak, A. (2008), 'Global femininities: Consumption, culture and the significance of place', *Discourse: Studies in the Cultural Politics of Education*, 29 (3): 325–342.

Kelly, P. and Pike, J. (eds) (2016), *Neo-liberalism and austerity: The moral economies of young people's health and well-being,* London: Palgrave.

Kenway, J. and Hickey Moody, A. (2011), 'Life chances, lifestyle and everyday aspirational strategies and tactics', *Critical Studies in Education*, 52 (2): 151–163.

King, B. (2008), 'Stardom, celebrity and the para-confession', *Social Semiotics*, 18 (2): 115–132.

Kirby, P. (2016), *Leading People 2016: The educational backgrounds of the UK professional elite*. A report for the Sutton Trust. Available at: http://www.suttontrust.com/researcharchive/leading-people-2016/ (accessed 15 July 2016).

Lawler, S. (2005), 'Introduction: Class, culture and identity', *Sociology*, 39 (5): 797–806.

Lawler, S. (1999), '"Getting out and getting away": Women's narratives of class mobility', *Feminist Review* 63 (1): 3–24.

Lawler, S. (2008), *Identity: Sociological perspectives*, 1st edition. Cambridge, UK: Polity.

Legacy Education Resources (undated), 'Actor Will Smith's work ethic', Available online: http://www.character-education.info/resources/Will_Smith's_Character.htm (accessed 28 July 2016).

Lesko, N. (2001), *Act your age! A cultural construction of adolescence,* Hove, UK: Psychology Press.

Life is but a dream (2013), [TV programme], BBC1, March 28, 10.35.

Levitas, R. (2012), 'The just umbrella: Austerity and the big society in coalition policy and beyond', *Critical Social Policy*, 32 (3): 320–343.

Littler, J. (2013), 'Meritocracy as plutocracy: The marketing of "equality" under neoliberalism', *New Formations*, 80 (8): 52–72.

Littler, J. (2004), 'Celebrity and "meritocracy"', *Soundings*, 26: 118–130.

Littler, J. (2003), 'Making fame ordinary: Intimacy, reflexivity and keeping it real', in J. Rutherford (ed.), *Mediactive: Ideas, knowledge, culture*, 8–25, London: Lawrence & Wishart.

Livingstone, S. and Sefton-Green, J. (2016), *The class: Living and learning in the digital age*, New York: New York University Press.

Loveday, V. (2015), 'Working-class participation, middle-class aspiration? Value, upward mobility and symbolic indebtedness in higher education', *The Sociological Review*, 63 (3), 570–588.

Lucey, H. and Reay, D. (2002), 'Carrying the beacon of excellence: Social class differentiation and anxiety at a time of transition,' *Journal of Education Policy*, 17 (3): 321–336.

Lupton, R., Burchardt, T., Hills, J., Stewart, K. and Vizard, P. (eds) (2016). *Social policy in a cold climate: Policies and their consequences since the crisis*. Bristol, UK: Policy Press.

Mac an Ghaill, M. (1994), *The making of men: Masculinities, sexualities and schooling*, Buckingham, UK: Open University Press.

MacDonald, R. (2016), 'Precarious work: The growing precarité of youth', in A. Furlong (ed.), *The international handbook of youth and young adulthood*, 156–163, London: Routledge.

MacDonald, R. (2011), 'Youth transitions, unemployment and underemployment: Plus ça change, plus c'est la même chose?', *Journal of Sociology*, 47 (4): 427–444.

MacDonald, R. and Marsh, J. (2005), *Disconnected youth? Growing up in Britain's poor neighbourhoods*, Basingstoke, UK: Palgrave Macmillan.

Malik, S. (2014), 'The dependent generation: Half young European adults live with their parents', *The Guardian*, 24 March. Available online: https://www.theguardian.com/society/2014/mar/24/dependent-generation-half-young-european-adults-live-parents (accessed 26 July 2016).

Marsh, J., Brooks, G., Hughes, J., Ritchie, L., Roberts, S. and Wright, K. (2005), *Digital beginnings: Young children's use of popular culture, media and new technologies*, Sheffield, UK: University of Sheffield.

Marshall, P. D. (1997), *Celebrity and power: Fame in contemporary culture*, Minneapolis: University of Minnesota Press.

Marwick, A. (2015), 'You may know me from YouTube: (Micro)-celebrity in social media', in P. D. Marshall and S. Redmond (eds), *A Companion to Celebrity*, Hoboken, NJ: John Wiley.

Marwick, A. and boyd, d. (2011), 'To see and to be seen: Celebrity practice on Twitter', *Convergence: The International Journal of Research into New Media Technologies*, 17 (2): 139–158.

Marx, K. (1976/1867), *Capital: A critique of political economy (volume one)*, London: Penguin.

Matthews, L. (2017), 'Here's the full transcript of Angela Davis's women's march speech', Elle, 21 January. Available online: http://www.elle.com/culture/career-politics/a42337/angela-davis-womens-march-speech-full-transcript/ (accessed 23 February 2017).

May, T. (2016), 'Britain, the great meritocracy: Prime minister's speech', The British Academy, London, 9 September. Available online: https://www.gov.uk/government/speeches/britain-the-great-meritocracy-prime-ministers-speech (accessed 10 December 2016).

McCarthy, T. and Jacobs, B. (2016), 'Melania Trump convention speech seems to plagiarise Michelle Obama', *The Guardian*, 19 July. Available online: https://www.theguardian.com/us-news/2016/jul/19/melania-trump-republican-convention-plagiarism-michelle-obama (accessed 21 February 2017).

McCormack, K. (2014), 'She's a workaholic! Emma Watson spends her 24th birthday on a film set in Canada', *Express*, 16 April. Available online: http://www.express.co.uk/celebrity-news/470709/ Emma-Watson-spends-her-24th-birthday-filming-new-movie-Regression-in-Canada (accessed 24 February 2017).

McDonald, C. (2016), 'Have more famous people died in 2016?', BBC News, 30 December. Available online: http://www.bbc.co.uk/news/magazine-38329740 (accessed 23 February 2017).

McDowell, L. (2012), 'Post-crisis, post-Ford and post-gender? Youth identities in an era of austerity', *Journal of Youth Studies*, 15 (5): 573–590.

McRobbie, A. (2013), 'Feminism, the family and the new "mediated" maternalism', *New Formations,* 80 (1): 119–137.

McRobbie, A. (2008), *The aftermath of feminism: Gender, culture and social change*, London: Sage.

McRobbie, A. and Garber, J. (1977), 'Girls and subcultures: An exploration', in S. Hall and T. Jefferson (eds), *Resistance through rituals: Youth subcultures in postwar Britain*, 177–188, London: Hutchinson.

Meacham, J. (2012), 'The American dream: A biography', *Time*, 21 June. Available online: http://content.time.com/time/specials/packages/article/0,28804,2117662_2117682_2117680-1,00.html (accessed 10 December 2016).

Mendick, H. (2015), 'The best Jeremy Corbyn fandom and why it matters', *CelebYouth*, 19 August. Available online: http://www.celebyouth.org/corbyn-fandom/ (accessed 23 February 2017).

Mendick, H. (2006), *Masculinities in mathematics*, Maidenhead, UK: Open University Press.

Mendick, H., Allen, K. and Harvey, L. (2016), 'Gender and the emergence of the "geek celebrity" in young people's celebrity talk in England', *International Journal of Gender, Science and Technology*, 8 (2): 202–220.

Mendick, H., Allen, K. and Harvey, L. (2015), '"We can get everything we want if we try hard": Young people, celebrity, hard work', *British Journal of Educational Studies*, 63 (2): 161–178.

Meyers, E. (2009), '"Can you handle my truth?" Authenticity and the celebrity star image', *Journal of Popular Culture*, 42 (5): 890–908.

Meyers, S. (2016), 'The Republican Convention's rough start: A closer look', Late Night with Seth Meyers, 19 July. Available online: https://www.youtube.com/watch?v=2Z51Qer8h1I (accessed 26 July 2016).

Mirza, H. (2015), 'Respecting difference: Widening participation in post-race times', in C. Alexander and A. Arday (eds), *Aiming higher: Race, inequality and diversity in the academy*, 27–30, London: Runnymede.

Muiznieks, N. (2014), 'Youth human rights at risk during the crisis', Council of Europe, 3 July. Available online: www.coe.int (accessed 10 December 2016).

Murray, S. and Oullette, L. (2009), 'Introduction', in S. Murray and L. Oullette (eds), *Reality TV: Remaking television cultures*, 1–20, New York: New York University Press.

Nayak, A. (2006), 'Displaced masculinities: Chavs, youth and class in the post-industrial city', *Sociology*, 40 (5): 813–831.

Negra, D. and Holmes, S. (2008), 'Introduction: Going cheap? Female celebrity in reality, tabloid and scandal genres', *Genders Online*, 48 (Fall). Available online: http://www.colorado.edu/gendersarchive1998-2013/2008/12/01/introduction-special-issue-going-cheap-female-celebrity-reality-tabloid-and-scandal (accessed 28 July 2017).

Negra, D. and Tasker, Y. (2014), *Gendering the recession: Media and culture in an age of austerity*, Durham, NC: Duke University Press.

Nixon, T. (2013), 'Em-brace Watson: Star flies into the arms of male pal', *The Sun*, 11 June. Available online: https://www.thesun.co.uk/archives/news/794807/em-brace-watson-star-flies-into-the-arms-of-male-pal/ (accessed 23 February 2017).

Nolan, D. (2011), *Emma Watson: The biography*, London: John Blake.

Novara Media (2016), 'Reports', YouTube, various dates. Available online: https://www.youtube.com/watch?v=4GtFPGtsAr4&list=PL9f7WaXxDSUoEdtJaVvHlJzaLmJvJZzqj (accessed 23 February 2017).

Nunns, A. (2016), *The candidate*, London: Verso.

Office for National Statistics (2016), 'Families and households in the UK: 2016, Office for National Statistics, 4 November. Available online: https://www.ons.gov.uk/peoplepopulationandcommunity/birthsdeathsandmarriages/families/bulletins/familiesandhouseholds/2016 (accessed 2 December 2016).

Office for National Statistics (2015), 'Analysis of employee contracts that do not guarantee a minimum number of hours', Office for National Statistics, 25 February. Available online: http://www.ons.gov.uk/ons/dcp171776_396885.pdf (accessed 2 December 2016).

Office for National Statistics (2013), 'Full report: Graduates in the UK labour market 2013', Office for National Statistics, 19 November. Available online: http://www.ons.gov.uk/ons/dcp171776_337841.pdf (accessed 2 December 2016).

Osborne, G. (2012), 'George Osborne speech to the Conservative conference', *The New Statesman*, 8 October. Available online: http://www.newstatesman.com/blogs/politics/2012/10/george-osbornes-speech-conservative-conference-full-text (accessed 1 December 2014).

Osgerby, B. (2004), *Youth media,* New York: Routledge.

Pantazis, C. (2016), Policies and discourses of poverty during a time of recession and austerity, *Critical Social Policy*, 36 (1): 3–20.

Parpart, J. L. (2010), 'Choosing silence', in R. Ryan-Flood and R. Gill (eds), *Secrecy and silence in the research process: Feminist reflections*, 15–29, London: Routledge.

Parsons, T. (2013), 'Justine Bieber's Anne Frank comments were clumsy but he did good', *The Mirror,* 20 April. Available online: http://www.mirror.co.uk/3am/celebrity-news/tony-parsons-justin-biebers-anne-1842705 (accessed 2 February 2017).

Paule, M. (2013), *smartgirls.tv: Discourses of achieving girlhood in schools, on screen, and online*, PhD Thesis, Oxford Brookes University, UK.

Perryman, J., Ball, S., Maguire, M. and Braun, A. (2011), 'Life in the pressure cooker – school league tables and English and mathematics teachers' responses to accountability in a results-driven era', *British Journal of Educational Studies*, 59 (2): 179–195.

Peterson, A. H. (2014), *Scandals of classic Hollywood*, New York: Plume.

Philo, G. And Miller, D. (2014), 'Cultural compliance: Media/ cultural studies and social science', in G. Philo and D. Miller (eds), *Market killing: What the free market does and what social scientists can do about it*, 3–86, New York: Routledge.

Phipps, A. (2008), *Women in science, engineering and technology: Three decades of UK initiatives*, Stoke-on-Trent, UK: Trentham.

Plummer, K. (1995), *Telling sexual stories*, London: Routledge.

Pomerantz, A. (1986), 'Extreme case formulations: A way of legitimizing claims', *Human Studies*, 9 (2): 219–229.

Positive Money (2016), 'UK citizens could have received £6384 each', *Positive Money*, 2 November. Available online: http://positivemoney.org/2016/11/uk-citizens-could-have-received-6834/ (accessed 23 February 2017).

Potter, J. (1996), *Representing reality discourse, rhetoric and social construction*. London and Thousand Oaks, CA: Sage.

Powell, A. (2017), 'Youth unemployment statistics. Briefing paper. Number 5871', House of Commons Library, 12 July. Available online: http://researchbriefings.parliament.uk/ResearchBriefing/Summary/SN05871#fullreport (accessed 26 July 2017).

Pramaggiore, M. and Negra, D. (2014), 'Keeping up with the aspirations: Commercial family values and the Kardashian brand', in B. Weber (ed.), *Reality gendervision: Sexuality & gender on transatlantic reality television*, Durham, NC: Duke University Press.

Projansky, S. (2014), *Spectacular girls: Media fascination and celebrity culture*, New York: New York University Press.

The pursuit of happyness (2006), [Film] Dir. Gabriele Muccino, USA: Sony Pictures.

Purtill, J. (2016), 'How one million young people staying home elected Donald Trump', ABC, 10 November. Available online: http://www.abc.net.au/triplej/programs/hack/one-million-young-people-staying-home-elected-donald-trump/8014712 (accessed 23 February 2017).

Puwar, N. (2004), *Space invaders: Race, gender and bodies out of place*, London: Berg.

Quinn, B. (2016), 'Young Britons living in "suspended adulthood", research finds', *The Guardian*, 22 September. Available online: https://www.theguardian.com/society/2016/sep/22/young-people-living-in-a-suspended-adulthood-finds-research (accessed 12 December 2016).

Raco, M. (1999), 'From expectation to aspirations: State modernisation, urban policy, and the existential politics of welfare in the UK', *Political Geography*, 28 (7): 436–444.

Radway, J. (1984), *Reading the romance: Women, patriarchy and popular culture*, London: Verso.

Reay, D. (2013), 'Social mobility, a panacea for austere times: Tales of emperors, frogs, and tadpoles', *British Journal of Sociology of Education*, 34 (5–6): 660–766.

Reay, D. (1998), *Class work: Mothers' involvement in their children's primary schooling*, London: UCL Press.

Reay, D., David, M. E. and Ball, S. J. (2005), *Degrees of choice: social class, race and gender in higher education*, Stoke-on-Trent, UK: Trentham.

Reay, D., Davies, J., David, M. and Ball, S. J. (2001), 'Choices of degree or degrees of choice? Class, "race" and the higher education choice process', *Sociology*, 35 (4): 855–874.

Reid, S. (2013), 'Mythbusters: Strivers versus skivers', *New Economics Foundation*, 11 April. Available online: http://www.neweconomics.org/blog/entry/mythbusters-strivers-versus-skivers (accessed 26 July 2016).

Reife, J. (2013), 'Emma Watson wants girls to run the world – in Hollywood, at least', *Refinery 29*, 24 May. Available online: http://www.refinery29.com/2013/05/47423/emma-watson-bling-ring-interview (accessed 12 June 2015).

Ringrose, J. and Walkerdine, V. (2008), 'Regulating the abject: The TV make-over as site of neoliberal reinvention toward bourgeois femininity', *Feminist Media Studies*, 8 (3): 227–246.

Roberts, K. (2009), 'Opportunity structures then and now', *Journal of Education and Work*, 22 (5): 355–368.

Roberts, K. (2003), 'Problems and priorities for the sociology of youth', in A. Bennett, M. Cieslik and S. Miles (eds), *Researching Youth*, 13–28, Basingstoke, UK: Palgrave Macmillan.

Roberts, S. (2014), 'Introduction: Masculinities in crisis? Opening the debate', in S. Roberts (ed.), *Debating modern masculinities: Change, continuity, crisis?*, 1–16, Basingstoke, UK: Palgrave Macmillan.

Roberts, S. and Allen, K. (2016), 'Millennials v baby boomers: A battle we could have done without', *The Conversation*, 6 April. Available online: https://theconversation.com/millennials-v-baby-boomers-a-battle-we-could-have-done-without-57305 (accessed 21 February 2017).

Roberts, S. and Evans, S. (2012), '"Aspirations" and imagined futures: The im/possibilities for Britain's young working class', in W. Atkinson, S. Roberts and M. Savage (eds), *Class inequality in austerity Britain*, 70–89, Basingstoke, UK: Palgrave Macmillan.

Roberts, S. and MacDonald, R. (2013), 'Marginalising the mainstream? Making sense of the missing middle of youth studies', *Sociological Research Online*, 18 (1). Available online: http://www.socresonline.org.uk/18/1/21.html (accessed 28 July 2017).

Robertson, J. (2013), 'Justin Bieber falls down stairs and shows off injuries moments before a photoshoot – video', *The Mirror*, 24 June. Available online: http://www.mirror.co.uk/3am/celebrity-news/justin-bieber-falls-down-stairs-1986762 (accessed 2 February 2017).

Rojek, C. (2001), *Celebrity*, London: Reaktion.

Rose, N. (1999), *Governing the soul: The shaping of the private self* (2nd edition), London: Free Association Books

Rose, N. (1996), *Inventing our selves: Psychology, power, and personhood*, Cambridge, UK: Cambridge University Press.

Ross, E. (2013), 'Kardashian flaunts her lovely lady lumps', *The Sun*, 12 March. Available online: https://www.thesun.co.uk/archives/news/579318/kim-kardashian-flaunts-her-lovely-lady-lumps/ (accessed 2 February 2017).

Rose, T. (1994), *Black noise: Rap music and black culture in contemporary America*, Hanover, NH: University Press of New England.

Said, E. (1995), *Orientalism*, Harmondsworth, UK: Penguin.

Sastre, A. (2013), 'Hottentot in the age of reality TV: Sexuality, race, and Kim Kardashian's visible body', *Celebrity Studies*, 5 (1-2), 123–137.

Saturday Night Live (2016), 'The day Beyoncé turned black', SNL, 14 February. Available online: https://www.youtube.com/watch?v=ociMBfkDG1w (accessed 10 December 2016).

Sayer, A. (2014), *Why we can't afford the rich*, Bristol, UK: Policy Press.

Schwartz, T. (2013), 'Emma Watson: "Ignoring fame was my rebellion"', *Screener*, 17 May. Available online: http://screenertv.com/news-features/emma-watson-ignoring-fame-was-my-rebellion/ (accessed 23 February 2017).

Sellar, S. (2015), '"Unleashing aspiration": The concept of potential in education policy', *Australian Educational Researcher*, 42 (2): 201–215.

Senft, T. (2013), 'Microcelebrity and the branded self', in J. E. Burgess and A. Bruns (eds), *A companion to new media dynamics*, 346–354, Malden, MA: Blackwell.

Shildrick, T. and MacDonald, R. (2006), 'In defense of subculture: Young people, leisure and social divisions', *Journal of Youth Studies*, 9 (2): 125–140.

Shildrick, T., MacDonald, R., Webster, C. and Garthwaite, K. (2012), *Poverty and insecurity: Life in low-pay, no pay, Britain*, Bristol, UK: Policy Press.

Sieczkowski, C. (2014), 'Feminist activist says Beyonce is partly "anti-feminist" and "terrorist"', *Huffington Post*, 9 May. Available online: http://www. huffingtonpost.com/2014/05/09/beyonce-anti-feminist_n_5295891.html (accessed 24 November 2016).

Skeggs, B. (2005), 'The making of class and gender through visualizing moral subject formation', *Sociology*, 39 (5): 965–982.

Skeggs, B. (2004), *Class, self, culture*, London: Routledge.

Skeggs, B. (1997), *Formations of class and gender*, London: Sage.

Skeggs, B. and Wood, H. (2012), *Reacting to reality television: Performance, audience and value*, London: Routledge.

Skeggs, B., Tornhill, S. and Tollin, K. (2008), 'On the economy of moralism and working-class properness: An interview with Beverley Skeggs', *Eurozine*, 28 April. Available online: http://www.eurozine.com/articles/2008-04-28-skeggs-en.html (accessed 10 December 2016).

Smart, G. (2013), 'Queen B', *The Sun*, 1 April. Available online: https:// www.thesun.co.uk/archives/bizarre/471624/queen-b/ (accessed 10 December 2016).

Smart, G. (2013), 'Justin Bieber's in need of a babysitter', *The Sun*, 4 May. Available online: https://www.thesun.co.uk/archives/bizarre/710187/justin-biebers-in-need-of-a-babysitter/ (accessed 2 February 2017).

SMCP (Social Mobility and Child Poverty Commission) (2015), *State of the nation 2015: Social mobility and child poverty in Great Britain*, London: SMCP.

Smith, D. (2014), 'Charlie-is-so-"English"-like: nationality and the branded-celebrity person in the age of YouTube', *Celebrity Studies*, 5 (3): 256–274.

Splash! (2013), [TV programme] ITV1, January–February, various times.

Sportsbeat (2012), 'Daley's coach compares diver to tennis underachiever Kournikova', *The Sports Review*, 25 February. Available online: http://www. thesportreview.com/tsr/2012/02/tom-daley-coach-anna-knournikova/ (accessed 24 November 2016).

Stacey, J. (1994), *Stargazing: Hollywood cinema and female spectatorship*, London: Routledge.

Stahl, G. (2016), *Identity, Neoliberalism and aspiration: Educating white working-class boys*, London: Routledge.

Standing, G. (2014), *A precariat charter: From denizens to citizens*, London: Bloomsbury.

St Clair, R., Kintrea, K. and Houston, M. (2013), 'Silver bullet or red herring? New evidence on the place of aspirations in education', *Oxford Review of Education*, 39 (6): 719–738.

St Croix, T. (2016), *Grassroots youth work: Policy, passion and resistance in practice*, Bristol, UK: Policy Press.

Steedman, C. (1986) *Landscape for a good woman*, London: Virago.

Stuhr-Rommereim, H. (undated), 'The Comfort of Cruel Images: On Representation, Happiness, and Violence', Academia.edu. Available online: https://www.academia.edu/5994464/The_Comfort_of_Cruel_Images_On_Representation_Happiness_and_Violence (accessed 10 December 2016).

Sukarieh, M. and Tannock, S. (2015), *Youth rising? The politics of youth in the global economy,* Abingdon, UK: Routledge.

Tarrant, A. and Terry, G., Ward, M., Ruxton, S., Martin, R. and Featherstone, B. (2015), 'Are male role models really the solution? Interrogating the "war on boys" through the lens of the "male role model" discourse', *Boyhood Studies*, 8 (1): 60–83.

Taylor-Gooby, P. F. (2013), *The double crisis of the welfare state and what we can do about it,* Basingstoke, UK: Palgrave Macmillan.

Thatcher, M. (1979) 'Speech to Conservative rally in Cardiff', The Margaret Thatcher Foundation, 16 April. Available online: http://www.margaretthatcher.org/document/104011 (accessed 27 January 2017).

This is Money (2010), 'YouTube "geek" one day, millionaire celeb the next', *This is Money*, 10 December. Available online: http://www.thisismoney.co.uk/money/article-1709238/YouTube-geek-one-day-millionaire-celeb-the-next.html (accessed 26 July 2017).

Thomson, R., Bell, R., Holland, S., Henderson, S., McGrellis, S. and Sharpe, S. (2002), 'Critical moments: Choice, chance and opportunity in young people's narratives of transition', *Sociology*, 36 (2): 335–354.

Thornton, M. (2013), 'A very middle class baby who will secure the future of the royal family', *The Mail Online,* 23 July. Available online: http://www.dailymail.co.uk/news/article-2374279/Kate-Middleton-gives-birth-middle-class-Royal-baby-boy-secure-monarchys-future.html#ixzz4WzYuqyhB (accessed 27 January 2017).

Tinson, A., Ayrton, C., Barker, K., Born, T. B., Aldridge, H. and Kenway, P. (2016), *Monitoring poverty and social exclusion*, York, UK: The Joseph Rowntree Foundation.

Tomlinson, S. (2005), *Education in a post-welfare society,* Maidenhead, UK: Open University Press.

Turner, G. (2010), 'Approaching celebrity studies', *Celebrity Studies*, 1 (1): 11–20.

Turner, G. (2006), 'The mass production of celebrity: '"Celetoids", reality TV and the "demotic turn"', *International Journal of Cultural Studies*, 9 (2): 153–165.

Turner, G. (2004), *Understanding celebrity*, London: Sage.

Twomey, R. (2013), '"Kate Middleton isn't interested in a lavish life" says Royal source', *Marie Claire*, 3 April. Available online: http://www.marieclaire.co.uk/news/celebrity-news/kate-middleton-isn-t-interested-in-a-lavish-life-says-royal-source-125975 (accessed 27 January 2017).

Tyler, I. (2013), *Revolting subjects: Social abjection and resistance in neoliberal Britain*, London: Zed Books.

Tyler, I. (2008), 'Chav mum chav scum', *Feminist Media Studies*, 8 (1): 17–34.

Tyler, I. and Bennett, B. (2015), 'Against aspiration', in The Centre for Labour and Social Studies (ed.), *What is aspiration? And how should progressives respond*, 6-8, London: Class.

Tyler, I. and Bennett, B. (2010), 'Celebrity chav: Fame, femininity and social class', *European Journal of Cultural Studies*, 13 (3): 375–393.

Unison (2016), *A future at risk: Cuts in youth services*. London: Unison.

Valentine, G., Skelton, T. and Cambers, D. (1998), 'An introduction to youth and youth cultures', in T. Skelton and G. Valentine (eds), *Cool places: Geographies of youth cultures,* 1–33, London: Routledge.

Vaughn, A. (2012), *Beyoncé*, New York: Sterling.

Varoufakis, Y. (2015), 'Austerity used as narrative to conduct a class war', Question Time, BBC, 24 September. Available online: https://www.youtube.com/watch?v=B0_iiQKESAs (accessed 2 February 2017).

Veblen, T. (1994), *The theory of the leisure class: An economic study of institutions* (reprint), Mineola, NY: Dover Publications.

Walkerdine, V. (1990), *Schoolgirl fictions*, London: Verso.

Walkerdine, V. and Lucey, H. (1989), *Democracy in the kitchen: Regulating mothers and socialising daughters*, London: Virago.

Walkerdine, V., Lucey, H. and Melody, J. (2001), *Growing up girl: Psychosocial explorations of gender and class*, Basingstoke, UK: Palgrave Macmillan.

Ward, M. (2015), *From Labouring to learning: Working-class masculinities, education and de-industrialization*, Basingstoke, UK: Palgrave Macmillan.

Waters, J. L. and Leung, M. W. H. (2016), 'Domesticating transnational education: Discourses of social value, self-worth and the institutionalisation of failure in "meritocratic" Hong Kong', *Transactions of the Institute of British Geographers*. [Online First]

Watts, B., Fitzpatrick, S., Bramley, G. and Watkins, D. (2014), *Welfare sanctions and conditionality in the UK*, York, UK: The Joseph Rowntree Foundation.

Watts, N. (2011), 'David Cameron flies back to UK for emergency meeting on riots', *The Guardian*, 9 August. Available online: https://www.theguardian.com/politics/2011/aug/09/david-cameron-london-riots-cobra (accessed 14 July 2016).

Weekes, D. (2002), 'Get your freak on: How black girls sexualise identity', *Sex education*, 2 (3): 251–262.

When Kate met William: A tale of two lives (2011) [TV Programme], ITV, 26 April 21.00.

Williams, A. and Srnicek, N. (2016), *Inventing the future: Postcapitalism and a world without work*, London: Verso.

Williams-Grut, O. (2015), 'Britain is in the middle of a privatisation boom bigger than Margaret Thatcher's – but no one seems to notice', *Business Insider*, 9 July. Available online: http://uk.businessinsider.com/george-osborne-plans-to-raise-31-billion-through-public-sector-sell-offs-in-2015-2015-7 (accessed 27 December 2015).

Williamson, M. (2010), 'Female celebrities and the media: The gendered denigration of the "ordinary" celebrity', *Celebrity Studies*, 1 (1): 118–120.

Willis, P. (1977), *Learning to labour: How working class kids get working class jobs*, London: Gower Publishing.

Wintour, P. and Lewis, P. (2011), 'X-Factor culture fuelled the UK riots, says Iain Duncan Smith', *The Guardian*, 9 December. Available online at: https://www.theguardian.com/uk/2011/dec/09/x-factor-culture-fuelled-riots (accessed 10 September 2013).

Wood, H. (2016), 'The politics of hyperbole on Geordie Shore: Class, gender, youth and excess', *European Journal of Cultural Studies*. [Online First]

Wood, H. and Skeggs, B. (eds) (2011), *Reality television and class,* London: Palgrave Macmillan.

Yelin, H. (2016) '"White trash" celebrity: Shame and display', in N. Rooks, V. Pass and A. Weekley (eds), *Women's magazines in print and new media,* 176–191, New York: Routledge.

YouGov UK (2014), 'Celebrity culture "a threat to today's youth"', *YouGov,* 14 July. Available online: https://yougov.co.uk/news/2014/07/14/celebrity-culture-threat-todays-youth/ (accessed 29 January 2017).

INDEX